The concise

<SGML>

companion

Ian Stevens

FIDELITY INVESTMENTS

The concise

companion

Neil Bradley

ADDISON-WESLEY

Harlow, England • Reading, Massachusetts
Menlo Park, California • New York • Don Mills, Ontario
Amsterdam • Bonn • Sydney • Singapore • Tokyo • Madrid
San Juan • Milan • Mexico City • Seoul • Taipei

Addison Wesley Longman Limited
Edinburgh Gate
Harlow
Essex CM20 2JE
England

and Associated Companies throughout the World.

Published in the United States of America by Addison Wesley Longman Inc., New York.

The programs in this book have been included for their instructional value. They have been tested with care but are not guaranteed for any particular purpose. The publisher does not offer any warranties or representations nor does it accept any liabilities with respect to the programs.

Many of the designations used by manufacturers and sellers to distinguish their products are claimed as trademarks. Addison-Wesley has made every attempt to supply trademark information about manufacturers and their products mentioned in this book. A list of the trademark designations and their owners appears on page xii.

Cover designed by odB Design & Communication, Reading
Illustrations by Margaret Macknelly Design, Tadley
Typeset by the author
Printed and bound in the United States of America

First printed 1996

ISBN 0-201-41999-8

British Library Cataloguing-in-Publication Data
A catalogue record for this book is available from the British Library.

Library of Congress Cataloging-in-Publication Data is available.

'Entities should not be multiplied unnecessarily. No more things should be presumed to exist than are absolutely necessary.'

William of Ockham – Ockham's Razor

'A child of five would understand this – send somebody to fetch a child of five.'

Groucho Marx – Duck Soup

Preface

SGML (the ***Standard Generalized Markup Language***) is an increasingly popular ISO standard concerned with document markup. Employed to reveal the underlying structure of a document, it establishes a neutral, information-rich environment from which material can be selected, extracted and manipulated for information exchange, or for delivery in a form tailored to the specific requirements of any target audience and publishing medium.

The Concise SGML Companion serves the ***programmer, analyst*** or ***consultant*** involved in the management, processing, transfer or publication of SGML documents – by first exploring the theory of SGML, then detailing its practical realization in popular applications such as **HTML** and **CALS tables**. Detailed study of the language is supported by the inclusion of a cross-referenced 'road map' of the building blocks that comprise the standard, and an extensive glossary of SGML terms and related topics.

Essentially, this book is biased toward 'hands-on' people, with a real application in mind and limited time in which to research the application of SGML. Specifically (and in order to help justify its 'concise' tag) this book does not:

- include lengthy philosophical discussions on the merits of each SGML feature
- include various, possibly inappropriate, case studies of SGML in use
- give tutorial descriptions of little used features of SGML (such as link, rank and datatag)
- include exercises and tests of the reader's understanding (motivation to learn is assumed)
- describe techniques or structure models not currently supported by a wide range of authoring or publishing software

As an example of SGML in use, this book was prepared and published using the standard.

Acknowledgments

A special thanks to Andrew Dorward for encouraging me to persevere with this book, and to Andrew Clark for much generous help. Thanks also to Richard Lowe, Bob Wilkinson and Sue Edwards, to Pindar Plc for material support, and to Adobe for FrameMaker+SGML (which was used both in the preparation and publication of this book). A large debt is owed to the authors of previous works on the subject – the *SGML Handbook*, in particular, is recommended to all serious students of the language. Thanks to all those involved at Addison-Wesley; also to Les and Mark (of Viking Software), for establishing me on this rocky road; but most of all to my mother, for patiently steering a distracted child toward reading.

Feedback

Comments and suggestions for a possible future edition are welcome. They should be sent to the author, who can be found at '*neil@bradley.co.uk*' and '*n.bradley@pindar.co.uk*'.

Updates, additions and corrections can be obtained from the author's Web page at '*http://www.bradley.co.uk*', which also contains a hypertext version of the Glossary and links to various SGML related sites.

Neil Bradley

October 1996

Contents

Trademark notice

Adobe™ and Postscript™ are trademarks of Adobe Systems Inc.

Aldus® is a registered trademark of the Aldus Corporation.

Apple® and Macintosh® are registered trademarks of Apple Computer, Inc.

IBM™ is a trademark of International Business Machines Corporation.

Microsoft® and MS-DOS® are registered trademarks and Windows™ is a trademark of the Microsoft Corporation.

Sun™ is a trademark of Sun Microsystems, Inc.

T_EX™ is a trademark of the American Mathematical Society.

UNIX® is a registered trademark in the US and other countries, licensed exclusively through X/Open Company Ltd.

1. Using this book

Conventions used

Names or terms that appear **in this style** have specific meaning within SGML, or typesetting and publishing in general, and are explained in the *Glossary*. A significant term appears in bold typeface (and also appears in the *Index*) on its first occurrence, and thereafter whenever its use is significant or its role is further defined.

Text appearing 'in this style' represents example data, usually an SGML fragment. Larger examples are separated from the text:

    and indented like this.

Though bold typeface may be used to emphasize part of an example, such as 'look at **this** word,' it does not have the significance described above.

Examples of printed or displayed output appear:

    indented and in this style.

Words displayed *in this style* are either quotations or simply 'attention grabbers.'

Words that appear in THIS style are SGML keywords. First and significant occurrences of a keyword appear like **THIS**.

A name that is followed by a superscript number, such as 'element[(013)],' is an SGML construct that is described by a chart in the *Road Map* section (see the introduction to that section for a full explanation).

Introductory chapters

It is recommended that the following chapters be read in the order provided.

Overview	SGML in context, why a standard for structured information is important
Electronic markup	The concepts that led to SGML
SGML markup	Document tagging using SGML

Document compo-nents	How system rules, document structure rules and documents are distinguished and linked
Entities	The division of documents into separate objects
DTD	The document structure rules in detail
SGML declaration	The system dependent rules in detail

Special topics

The following chapters explore discrete topics, so may be read in any order, though all previously described chapters should be read first:

Cross-references	The theory and practice of hypertext linking
CALS tables	The popular coding scheme for tabular material
ISO 9573 math	The popular coding scheme for mathematical formulae
HTML	The HyperText Markup Language, as used by the World Wide Web
SGMLS and NSGMLS parsers	The popular and related entity manager/parser utilities

Reference material

The final chapter and following sections provide condensed reference material:

Charts and tables	Various reference tables
Road Map	The SGML standard described using structure charts
Glossary	A dictionary of SGML related terms

To aid navigation, the *Road Map* section is marked at the page corners. The *Index* is similarly marked, so the *Glossary* is found between these marked blocks.

2.   Overview

This chapter introduces the concepts behind SGML, describes the historical background and highlights the benefits of using this standard.

S.G.M.L.?

The name SGML is an acronym for Standard Generalized Markup Language. Each part of the name depicts a key aspect of the SGML concept.

The nature and purpose of this format can be revealed through analysis of the name *Standard Generalized Markup Language*, but in order to gain the historical perspective it is necessary to take the initials out of sequence, and to start with the letters 'M' and 'L.'

'M' stands for **Markup**. The term 'mark up' (using two words) refers to marks added to an author's manuscript by an editor. As well as corrections to the text, these editorial marks include instructions regarding the required layout and style of the text. For example, a mark up instruction may identify a title, and explain that it should appear centered, in 18pt Helvetica typeface. SGML concerns itself with electronic 'markup' (a single word), where the instructions take the form of special character sequences actually embedded in the text data stream. These character sequences are termed 'markup codes', or **tags**.

```
<tag>text surrounded by tags</tag>
```

'L' stands for **Language**. A typesetting language usually comprises a list of pre-defined formatting tags. The SGML language, in contrast, provides a mechanism for defining such lists for specific purposes.

'G' stands for **Generalized**. Because this language has no pre-defined set of markup instructions, it has almost limitless application. In practice, however, it is used mostly for the electronic delivery and publication of structured and semi-structured documents, such as technical manuals, reference books and academic journals. The term '**generic**' is also used to suggest identification of objects rather than specification of output formats. Documents contain more useful information about their content if each component is identified by name, not by a series of style changes.

Finally, 'S' stands for **Standard**. Released as **ISO 8879:1986**, SGML is just one of a number of related standards grouped under the heading of *Information processing – Text and office systems*. The **WG8** working group at the **ISO** is responsible for the continued development of SGML, along with other related standards.

A brief history

SGML is a long-standing and robust format derived from earlier languages. It showed early promise as an exchange format for technical manuals in the defense industry.

SGML is derived from **GML** (*Generalized Markup Language*) which was developed in 1969 by IBM, and used extensively on IBM mainframe systems. This language helped to introduce the concept of generic coding (the separation of content from style).

SGML became a standard in 1986, and remained unchanged in its first 10 years (except for some minor re-definitions and clarifications in 1988). It is a measure of how robust the SGML standard was from the beginning that after more than 10 years of use, employed in a variety of industries and applications, it has not needed to move beyond what is still effectively 'version 1.' Indeed, the specification for SGML was perhaps too advanced, with several of its features to this day under-utilized.

Until the late 1980s, use of the standard remained largely in the government arena, and focused particularly on technical documentation controlled by the US Department of Defense. By the early 1990s, however, it had branched out into many other domains, and is now an increasingly popular solution to general publishing needs.

Why use SGML?

There are many markup languages in existence, but SGML embodies a unique combination of features.

Moving to SGML is no trivial matter, and is rarely a quick or cheap option. Its strengths must be understood and compared with the requirement before deciding whether it is the most effective solution to a problem. The combination of benefits listed below is unique to SGML.

SGML:

- is system independent
- is non-proprietary
- separates content from format
- facilitates strict control over information content
- provides an information-rich environment for creation of free-text databases

The SGML format is designed to operate on any computer platform, and all popular platforms are now well supported by SGML-aware software products.

SGML is an international standard, and is not dominated by a single commercial interest. Users of this standard do not fear the demise of their supplier, or an enforced move to an updated standard. In addition, SGML has no direct competition. Existing and forthcoming standards either complement SGML or overlap its functionality in a limited respect.

SGML promotes the view that *the message is more important than the messenger*. The *message* is the raw information – the words, tables, pictures etc. The *messenger* is the organization and visual appearance of that information, designed to be suitable for a specific medium (usually paper), along with the hardware and software required to deliver that representation. By making a clean break between the two, information is freed from specific software packages and output formats.

SGML enables a high degree of control over information content. It ensures that documents conform to agreed structural standards by providing a mechanism that allows a document to be compared with rules defined for a specific class of documents. This is vital if information is to be re-used at a later date. Software 'filters' (translating from one format to another) can then be developed with *complete confidence* that the markup used during document preparation was both consistent and appropriate.

SGML structures are in some respects analogous to records and fields in a structured database. A query can be targeted, for example, at text held in titles. Information can also be extracted and manipulated into new forms for new publications.

The benefits described above ultimately combine to provide the single, and most important, benefit of *efficiency*. The move to SGML can result in a long-term cost benefit, because of the high level of automation achievable once the core data is held in a controlled and structured format – in some cases allowing fully automated publication (in appropriate formats) to paper, CD-ROM and online media, and at the same time facilitating targeted database searches and data manipulation.

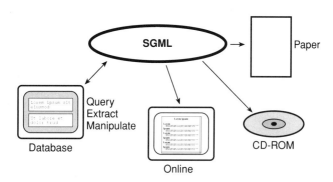

Consider as an example the use of SGML in the preparation and publication of a multi-volume dictionary of music. Tight rules are enforced on structure during the authoring and editing of all articles in the dictionary. When the material is ready for publication, batch pagination software is used to produce the set of books, including automatic generation of the table of contents, the index and page-numbered cross-references. At the same time, a software filter is used to transform the data into the import format of a CD-ROM database application, providing keyword, free-text search and **hypertext** links between entries. Another filter transforms the data into single entry files (or 'pages') in **HTML** format for delivery (with regular updates) over the **World Wide Web**, including links between each article-based file, and out to external sources of information. Specialized products, such as 'American 20th Century Composers' or 'The History of String Instruments,' are extracted and published automatically in all the forms described above. Finally, the data is stored in a text retrieval system and database, for future research by contributors and to control updates intended for the next issue.

The future

Minor enhancements to SGML are under way, and improved function-ality through the use of additional standards will add to the power of SGML.

Further refinements to SGML are in progress, and will be released under the designation '**ISO/IEC 8879**.' Apart from some adjustments to some preset limits, which are to be increased, no part of this book is likely to be invalidated by the minor additions and re-definitions expected.

Of much greater impact will be the integration of SGML with other standards either recently or soon to be released. Complementary and overlaying standards such as HTML, HyTime, DSSSL and SPDL will enhance its range and efficiency.

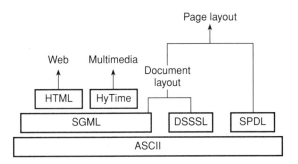

ASCII is a long-established existing standard for the storage and transfer of textual information between systems. It serves as a base layer for SGML and all the other formats described below, and is described in detail in the next chapter (although, strictly speaking, SGML usually rests upon **ISO/IEC 646**, this standard is almost identical to ASCII, which is more widely known). The next revision of SGML is expected to support the multi-byte **ISO 10646** character set, an extension of ASCII that supports many more characters.

HTML is an existing and improving standard for delivering information over the **Web**. It is described in Chapter 12.

HyTime simply uses existing SGML concepts to define a standard method for describing the integration of time-based information such as music and video. It also improves on the SGML method of maintaining hypertext links (see Chapter 9 for details).

DSSSL (*Document Style and Semantics Specification Language*) is a standard for defining style-sheets that describe how SGML data should be **composed** for a particular application. It also includes text formatting instructions that enable the information to be presented in a different order to that in which it is stored. Vendors of DTP packages may one day add DSSSL import filters. The complex task of mapping logical structures to formatted output should then only need to be performed once. A change of system or receipt of documents from another source should not require the work to be re-done.

SPDL (*Standard Page Description Language*) is a standard for describing exactly how information is to be placed on a page. It is therefore a neutral equivalent to **PostScript**. SPDL takes the output of DSSSL, along with font information and page area details, to create a description of the content of each page.

Together, these standards offer an independent and powerful approach to sharing and disseminating information.

3. Electronic markup

SGML does not stand in isolation; there is a historical perspective that still influences the scope and behavior of this standard. In preparation for later descriptions of the language, this chapter provides an overview of text-based data formats and typesetting languages.

ASCII

ASCII provides a standard scheme for electronic storage and exchange of text data. Extensions exist to represent extra characters.

SGML owes its strength and flexibility in part to its use of **ASCII** (the *American Standard Code for Information Interchange*). An understanding of the intentions and limitations of ASCII is fundamental to appreciation of the history, purpose and scope of SGML. ASCII is itself a very important standard, utilized by a wide range of system and application software.

From the start, computers were designed to understand and manipulate numbers (and were originally termed 'number crunchers'). In order to store text in a computer, a numeric value must be used to represent each **character** (such as a letter 'a,' digit '3,' or symbol '%'). A group of such number-to-character representations, including at least the characters typically found on typewriters and computer keyboards, is termed a **character set**.

When information is transferred between two computers that use incompatible character sets, the numeric values are preserved but the mappings differ, and the text becomes unintelligible:

```
System A           System B
A = 23    --->     23 = C
B = 24    --->     24 = D
C = 25    --->     25 = E
```

Assuming the incompatible representation schemes shown above, the term 'SGML' would be corrupted to 'UION' on transfer to System B. Moves to avoid this problem resulted in the ASCII standard, which assigns an agreed value to each character. With very slight modification, ASCII was also adopted as an ISO standard (**ISO/IEC 646**).

A data file that conforms to the ASCII format is termed a **text file**, though this term also applies to platform specific alternatives such as **EBCDIC**. The text file format is often used as a base format for transfer of information between systems and application software. Many word processors, for instance, have an option such as 'Save as Text.'

As SGML employs ASCII as a base layer, an SGML document may be created, viewed and edited using existing text editors and word processors (though this is no longer strictly necessary, due to the widespread use of SGML-aware word processors).

Extended ASCII

ASCII defines values for only 128 characters (a **7-bit** representation), which means that it can only represent the Roman alphabet (a–z, A–Z), arabic numerals (0–9), the symbols that appear on typewriters and computer keyboards, and a few invisible control characters required to format the text for viewing or printing. There are no spare values to represent accented characters, such as 'é,' Greek letters or scientific symbols.

Visible ASCII characters (ordered by ascending value):

```
!"#$%&'()*+,-./0123456789:;<=>?@ABCDEFGHIJKL
MNOPQRSTUVWXYZ[\]^_`abcdefghijklmnopqrstuvwx
yz{|}~
```

Modern computers allow access to an extra 128 characters (using **8-bit** character sets), but have assigned non-standard values for these characters. For example, an Apple Macintosh text file should not be copied to an MS-DOS based system without passing it through a filter that moves the extra characters to their correct positions in the latter's character set. This problem is addressed by **ISO 8859/1**, which defines a standard 256-value character set. This standard is used by **HTML** on the **Web**, by Microsoft Windows and Sun OS UNIX (but not by MS-DOS or by the Apple Macintosh). A chart of this character set is shown in Chapter 14.

There are forthcoming standards that use two or more **bytes** to represent each character, increasing the range of values available for representing characters. The **ISO/IEC 10646** standard uses two bytes or four bytes (a **16-bit** or **32-bit** representation), so can potentially represent over 4 billion unique characters. SGML will be able to utilize this standard, but awaits support from operating systems and applications.

In the meantime, SGML rests upon the 128 character ISO 646 base, and has its own mechanism for representing a wider range of characters. A sequence of normal ASCII characters represents a single extended character. For example, the sequence 'é' represents the letter 'é' (this mechanism is described in Chapter 6). Groups of such representations are defined by the ISO, and some of the most common groups are shown in Chapter 14.

Formatting limitations

Formatting can be crudely applied using spaces or tabs, and there are special non-printing characters that are used to specify line endings (usually the carriage return (**CR**) character and line feed (**LF**) character). Note that MS-DOS systems use CR and LF in sequence, whereas the Apple Macintosh uses only CR and UNIX uses only LF. The issue of line ending codes is relevant to SGML, and their interpretation in an SGML document is discussed later.

An IBM PC ASCII example (the control characters [CR] and [LF] are not usually visible):

```
[spaces]   Centered Title [CR][LF]
Simple formatting uses spaces to[CR][LF]
center the title above. Also note[CR][LF]
MS-DOS line ending codes[CR][LF]
(not usually visible).[CR][LF]
```

ASCII cannot represent stylistic information such as bold, underline or italic. In order for the data file to specify stylistic information (and improved formatting options) an implied significance must be given to certain character sequences. Many typesetting systems and word processors take this approach.

Typesetting languages

Typesetting languages employ special character sequences to specify style and format commands which may be grouped into macros with generic names.

In traditional **typesetting** systems, **markup** instructions are used to specify how the text is to be formatted. The file is treated as a **data stream**, a sequential series of characters which are read and processed by software in strict order. The **composition** software prints normal characters that it reads from the data file, but detects markup characters and avoids printing them. The markup characters are recognized as an instruction, or **tag**, which must be interpreted and obeyed. The tag may switch fonts, for example, or signify a line break. Any following characters then appear in the new style or at the new position on the page. In the example below there are two markup tags, '*ITA' and '*ROM':

```
Are you going to *ITA Scarborough *ROM fair?
```

In this fictional markup language, the first instruction switches-on an **italic** font, and the second instruction switches-on a **roman** (normal) font. In this example, the place name *Scarborough* appears in italic typeface when the data is printed:

Are you going to *Scarborough* fair?

The process of converting tagged data into output formats is often termed **composing**. When composing for paper output, the physical limitations of the page require the document to be split into page-sized units, in a further step called **pagination** (making pages).

Some markup tags may have **parameters**, which modify or add meaning to the tag. The tag '*FONT [name] [point size]' has two parameters that specify a font family and a point size. For example, '*FONT Times 18'.

Although modern word processors and DTP systems hide markup codes from the author by employing a **WYSIWYG** (*What You See Is What You Get*) interface, the markup still exists in one form or another (though it may be stored using a less intelligible, more efficient machine-readable scheme).

As stated above, the composing software must detect the difference between data to be printed and instructions to be obeyed. In the fictional markup language described, this would be achieved by assigning significance to the asterisk character, '*', and to the next space in the data stream, so that '*ITA ' is identified as a tag to be obeyed, not text to be printed. The asterisk and space are assigned the role of **markup delimiter** characters.

Most typesetting languages define an allowed list of tags, each one having a pre-defined purpose. Of particular interest, in comparing this approach with SGML, is that these systems tend to focus on the appearance of the information. In the example above, the location name 'Scarborough' was not identified as an object within the surrounding text, except by inference (through careful analysis of the surrounding style tags).

Macros

Some typesetting languages allow a commonly used sequence of formatting instructions to be grouped and stored, for reference by a single tag whenever they are needed. The **macro** concept involves the use of named groups, or **macro definitions**, and references, or **macro calls**, to these groups.

This technique introduces the concept of **generic** coding because the macro name is likely to reflect its intended use, not the style of the following text. A macro called '*TITLE' has an obvious meaning. It is only necessary to identify a title in the document, and apply this macro to it, not remember and apply a series of style tags. The document author need not be concerned with either specifying or understanding the formatting codes held in the macro definition. In addition, the author need not be concerned with the final appearance of the title.

Most modern word processors and DTP packages have 'style-sheet' definition facilities, which are analogous to macro definitions.

The use of macros makes the markup process inherently less error-prone and more efficient, and leads naturally to the aims of the SGML standard.

4. SGML markup

SGML markup builds on the concept of macro-based typesetting languages covered in the previous chapter. This chapter concentrates on the SGML scheme for marking-up text.

Element tags

SGML tags enclose identified objects, build hierarchies and may be abbreviated in various ways to improve keying efficiency.

SGML tags usually surround an identified object in the data stream. A **start-tag**[(014)] and an **end-tag**[(019)], together with the data enclosed by them, represent an **element**[(013)]. By default, a tag is delimited using the '<' and '>' characters. An end-tag is delimited by '</' and '>':

```
Are you going to <name>Scarborough</name>
fair?
```

In this way, an SGML document identifies discrete objects, much as a data-base contains records with named fields.

Viewing an SGML tagged document will *not* reveal a hidden layer – a set of rules that ensure the markup used is valid according to a pre-defined specification. Tag names, legal tag locations and parameter value restrictions are controlled by a Document Type Definition, or **DTD** for short. The process of comparing the DTD rules against the tags found in a particular document is accomplished by a **parser**. The format and scope of the DTD, and a more detailed study of the role of the parser, are covered in later chapters. As the DTD is stored separately from the text (either before it, or in another file), it will not appear in any of the examples in this chapter, though its role is referred to in several places.

The elements available for use in a particular document are determined by the author of the DTD that is applicable to that document. For the example above, the relevant DTD must contain an **element declaration**[(116)] that defines an element called 'Name'.

Note: Within this book, a reference to an example or DTD specific element name appears with an initial capital letter, for example 'Name', though these items are not usually case sensitive, and are generally keyed in a single case for convenience within a document.

The data is prepared for publishing by mapping element tags to conventional typesetting tags:

This approach allows the choice of output style to be changed at any time:

Element structures

SGML elements may enclose other elements in order to build a **hierarchy** of objects. A hierarchical structure may be visualized in various ways – as boxes within boxes, for example, or as **tree** branches.

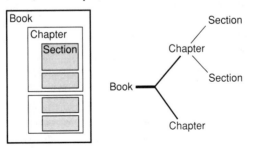

In a typical example, a Book may contain a number of Chapters, and each Chapter in turn may contain a number of Sections. The DTD controls this structure, and may not, for instance, allow a Book to directly contain a Section (or a Section to contain a Book!).

Each element must be completely enclosed by another element. For example, a Section may not straddle two Chapters.

An element that cannot directly contain text, but can contain other elements, is said to have **element content**[026]. In the example above, the Book element has element content because it can only contain Chapter elements. Similarly, a Section element may be defined to contain only Paragraph and List elements:

```
<section>
    <p>...</p>
    <p>...</p>
    <list>...</list>
</section>
```

However, at some point in the hierarchy the actual document content must appear. An element may be defined to contain only text, a mixture of text and further elements, or to have no content at all.

An element that may contain only text is said to have **data content**. For example, an Emphasis element may be defined to contain only text:

```
<em>emphasized phrase</em>
```

An element that may contain a mixture of elements and text is said to have **mixed content**[025]. For example, a Paragraph element may contain both text and Emphasis elements:

```
<p>This paragraph contains an <em>empha-
sized phrase</em> in the middle.</p>
```

Finally, an element may have no content, for example it may be a marker for a Figure. Such an element is termed an **empty element**:

```
<p>This paragraph contains a figure <fig>
here.</p>
```

Empty elements may also be used to describe a block of text that spans proper structures. To avoid breaking the true document hierarchy, two empty elements are used to indicate the start and the end of the block, as shown below. However, this mechanism is normally only of use for extracting such material for non-SGML processing, as the embedded structures will be invalid. **Composition** software designed for SGML structures is also unlikely to be able to switch-on and switch-off a specific style for the enclosed text, and a parser is not able to validate these blocks for missing block end-tags.

```
<chapter>.........
....<rev>.............</chapter>
<chapter>........
..........<revend>.....</chapter>
```

When describing the relationship between element structures, the terminology of the family tree is often adopted (an analogy that clearly fits a tree-like view of structures). From the perspective of a specific Chapter element, in a typical example structure, adjacent Chapter elements are **siblings** (like brothers or sisters), the Book is its **parent**, and any contained Sections are its **children**. The Book element is an **ancestor** to all other elements, including Section elements and all their children.

The largest element in the tree is the one at its base (the trunk of the tree). It is the ultimate ancestor of all other elements, and may be known as the 'outermost element,' or officially as the **document element**[012]. The Book element in the example above is a typical example of a document element.

The degree to which an element's content is organized into child elements is often termed its **granularity**. A coarse granularity denotes few or no children. A fine granularity denotes many children (and also possibly grand-children). For example, a Name may be tagged with a coarse granularity or with a fine granularity:

```
<name>J. Smith</name>

<name>
    <initial>J</initial>
    <surname>Smith</surname>
</name>
```

Note: The cost of **up-converting** legacy data to SGML format is affected by the choice of granularity. A fine granularity is likely to involve more manual intervention. A difficult and costly process of this kind may be termed a **high energy** process. The reward for this effort, however, is **low energy**, totally automated **down-conversion** to various output formats. The choice of granularity is therefore dictated by future requirements. Taking the example above, future creation of a list of names sorted by surname would be aided by the finer granularity version, as the surname is specifically and therefore unambiguously identified for software extraction.

Some hierarchical structures may be recursive. An element may directly or indirectly contain instances of itself, in which case it may be termed a

nested element. In a typical example, a list consists of a number of items, and each item may contain a further complete list. The List element is nested, and consequently so is the Item element. When published, the third Item in the outer list may be automatically numbered '3', and the first embedded Item '3.1':

```
<list>
    <item>
        <list>
            <item>
                <p>Nested Item</p>
```

Nested structures may cause difficulties to programmers or to composing software, as there is no theoretical limit to the level of nesting, yet each level requires consideration of output style. Note, however, that there is a practical limit to nesting that is defined by the language (a value setting that may be changed).

The use of hierarchical and recursive structures not only provides a powerful means to logically identify document components, but also facilitates more extensive formatting of output than is possible using macros or stylesheets. It allows formatting to be applied on a context-sensitive basis. The content of a Title element may be formatted differently, depending on whether it occurs directly within a Book, Chapter or Section, and the indentation of a List can be increased if it resides within another List.

Omitted and minimized tags

Markup tags may be shortened or omitted without disrupting the document structure, but only where the context permits, where the DTD rules allow, and when some optional features of SGML are enabled on the local system. This is termed **minimization**, and is intended to aid the process of manually keying tags (a process no longer necessary, and now rarely applied). So long as the following techniques are applied legally, it is possible to convert the document into a non-minimized form at any time. This process is called **normalization**. The fragment shown below is a fully normalized structure identifying a personal name:

```
<name>
    <initial>J</initial>
    <surname>Smith</surname>
</name>
```

Though it may seem a confusing contradiction, an element that is officially required may in fact be omitted from the document. This is possible simply because its presence can be implied. For the sake of following examples, it will be assumed that all the elements shown above are required by the DTD.

In some cases, the start-tag may be omitted. This is an option where it is obvious by context that the element must have started:

```
<name>
    J</initial>
    Smith</surname>
</name>
```

In this case, the Name start-tag is enough to signify the start of a required Initial element, and the Initial end-tag similarly signifies the start of the Surname element. This is a widely used technique, as it is intuitive to apply.

In some cases, the end-tag may be omitted. This is an option where it is obvious by context that the element has ended:

```
<name>
    <initial>J
    <surname>Smith
</name>
```

In this case, the Surname start-tag is enough to signify the end of the Initial element, and the Name end-tag similarly signifies the end of the Surname element. This is also a widely used technique.

Alternatively, the end-tags may be present but may omit the element names. These are known as **empty end-tag**[021] elements:

```
<name>
    <initial>J</>
    <surname>Smith</>
</name>
```

Another technique abbreviates both the start-tag and end-tag. The end-tag is a **null end-tag**[023], '/', and the start-tag is a **net-enabling start-tag**[018] (net = null end-tag), which ends with the same character, '/':

```
<name>
    <initial/J/
    <surname/Smith/
</name>
```

This is not a widely used feature, but can be convenient when the element content is restricted to text and is likely to be brief. For example:

```
Water is H<sub/2/O
```

Water is H_2O

The start-tag may be empty if it is the same as the previous start-tag. This is known as an **empty start-tag**[(016)]:

```
<initial>J</initial><>M</initial>
```

Here, the '`<>`' tag has an implied meaning of '`<initial>`', duplicating the previous element. This is also not a widely used feature, but may be seen, for example, in tabular material (along with omitted end-tags) to represent Entry tags:

```
<row><entry>Red<>1<>urgent<>immediate action
<row><entry>Yellow<>2<>important<>attention
required
<row><entry>Green<>3<>normal<>no action
```

Short references

Markup can be implied from the contextual use of normal text characters using **short reference** mappings. This is not strictly a tag minimization technique, as it avoids the need for tags – of any size. However, it can be considered as the ultimate minimization technique, as it may involve the insertion of *no* extra characters. For example, the use of the quotation mark character to surround quoted text could be interpreted as markup, in which case the following fragments would be considered equivalent:

```
<p>Alice in Wonderland thought "What is the
use of a book without pictures or conversa-
tions?".</p>

<p>Alice in Wonderland thought <quote>What
is the use of a book without pictures or
conversations?</quote>.</p>
```

The mapping of strings or individual characters to element tags can be made context-sensitive. Taking the example above, a quotation mark found within a Paragraph element is mapped to the start-tag '`<quote>`', whereas a quotation mark found within a Quote element is mapped to the end-tag '`</quote>`'.

This technique could be used to help convert legacy data to SGML, and is especially suitable for tabular material, where the line-ending codes are mapped to Row elements and tab or comma characters are mapped to Entry elements:

```
Red [TAB] 1 [TAB] Danger [CR][LF]
Yellow [TAB] 2 [TAB] Alert [CR][LF]
Green [TAB] 3 [TAB] Normal [CR][LF]
```

Attributes

An attribute is used to refine the meaning of an SGML element. It is embedded in the start-tag, consists of a name and a value, and belongs to a type category that may restrict its range of values. Various minimization techniques may be used.

An attribute provides refined information about an element. If an element can be compared to a noun, then an attribute can be compared to an adjective. An element representing a vehicle may have an attribute that declares the number of doors, possibly '4', and another giving its color, possibly 'yellow'.

Attributes are embedded in the element **start-tag**[014], and generally take the form '`name="value"`'. The **attribute name**[144] identifies the attribute in question, because a single element may contain several different attributes, such as Doors and Color. The **attribute value**[035] provides the *current* setting for the named attribute, such as '4' or 'yellow'.

The attribute name is defined by the author of the **DTD**, who may also give it a default value. The DTD also specifies which elements may contain the named attribute. An attribute called Doors may be defined, and given a default value of '4', which the document author may change to '2' or '3' (or any other value):

```
Purchased <vehicle doors="3" color="blue">
bus</vehicle>.
```

Attribute values may be translated into output text. The example above may be converted to:

Purchased *a 3 door, blue* bus.

In many cases the attribute value does not itself appear in formatted output. Instead, an attribute may be used to provide administrative information, or control the appearance of an object.

For example:

```
<book draft="3.4">
<list offset="5mm">
```

Each attribute must have a declared **attribute type**. The attribute type is defined within the **DTD**. For now, consideration will be given to two of the most commonly used types, CDATA and NUMBER. An attribute defined to be of type CDATA (character data) may have a value that consists of general characters. An attribute defined to be of type NUMBER, however, may contain only digits, so could not even be used to hold the value '3.4' or '9mm'. The Vehicle element described above illustrates a use of both these types. Assuming that the Doors attribute was defined to be of type NUMBER, the document author would not be able to enter 'four' as the attribute value.

When an attribute value is restricted to a single word or number the quotes are not necessary. This is because the next space or chevron unambiguously ends the value (though this feature may be disabled in some systems):

```
<list offset=yes indent=15>
```

An attribute value may be further restricted to one word from a group of words, termed a **name group**[069]. In the following example, the Offset attribute value is restricted to a value of either 'yes' or 'no'. Any other value would be illegal (though this is not obvious from the example – the limitation is defined in and controlled by the DTD). In this situation, the attribute name and the **value indicator** ('='), may also be absent:

```
<list yes>
```

However, where an element contains more than one attribute it may appear that this approach involves some ambiguity:

```
<list offset=no emphasis=yes>
<list no yes>
```

In the second example above it would not be possible to determine which value applied to which attribute (the order of appearance is not significant). The standard avoids this problem by disallowing shared name group values. One attribute in the example above must therefore be re-defined, possibly to allow values of 'true' and 'false' instead. The three examples below are equivalent, and the latter examples are unambiguous and therefore legal:

```
<list offset="no" emphasis="true">
<list true no>
<list no true>
```

There may also be a default value. This is the assumed value to be applied when no attribute value is given by the document author. If 'no' were declared as the default value, then the following two examples would be equivalent:

```
<list offset="no">

<list>
```

When an attribute value is used simply to switch-on an optional feature, a single value may be declared. The presence of the attribute value indicates one state, its absence indicates the alternative. The attribute name need not appear. The example above could be re-defined to make the Offset attribute take a single value of 'offset'. The first example below specifies an offset list, whereas the second specifies a normal list:

```
<list offset>

<list>
```

Note: With a short list of options to consider, the DTD designer may choose to avoid the use of attributes. The previous example could be re-defined using two elements called, for example, '`<list>`' and '`<offlist>`,' with neither element requiring an attribute to modify its purpose.

Comments and marked sections

Comments and marked sections are optional segments of the SGML document that are identified for special treatment. They do not form part of the document hierarchy, and both are embedded in markup declarations. Comments are ignored. The content of marked sections can be ignored, or just the embedded markup can be ignored.

This section describes two methods by which some of the document content can be set aside, or treated in a special manner. The affected text may be ignored, or may contain significant .markup characters which are to be treated as normal text. These techniques allow comments to be added, for example, without fear of them appearing in a published version of the document.

Note: A comment or marked section may be included in a document, but may also be used in a DTD. In fact, both are more commonly found in the DTD, where they help to organize and document the rules that it contains.

Markup declarations

Before describing comments and marked sections it is necessary to introduce the markup construct on which they depend. Both comments and marked sections are embedded within **markup declaration** tags (other uses of this tag are explored in Chapters 6 and 7).

A markup declaration is delimited by the characters '<!' and '>'. These are known as the **MDO** (Markup Declaration Open) and **MDC** (Markup Declaration Close) delimiters. Declarations do not form part of the document structure, so may be employed almost anywhere. They may be inserted, for example, between two element tags that the DTD states must be consecutive:

```
<initial>J</initial>
<! ..... >
<surname>Smith</surname>
```

Markup declarations are sometimes used to group a number of other declarations. The embedded declarations are held in a subset structure, by default identified using square bracket characters '[' and ']'. These are known as the **DSO** (Declaration Subset Open) and **DSC** (Declaration Subset Close) delimiters:

```
<! ... [
    <! ..... >
    <! ..... >
]>
```

Comments

A **comment**[092] is used to hold annotations that are not intended for publication. It is delimited by the characters '--'. For example, '--this is a comment--'. A comment is embedded in a markup declaration. When it is the sole content of a markup declaration, it forms a **comment declaration**[091], and there must be no spaces between the comment delimiters and the MDO:

```
<!-- This is a comment -->
```

When a markup declaration is used for another purpose, such as to define an element (see Chapter 7), a comment may be included to explain the declaration. This is considered good practice:

```
<!definition -- explanation -- >
```

Marked sections

A **marked section declaration**[093] is a portion of the document that is to be treated in a special manner. It is contained within square brackets, '[' and ']', and includes a keyword that specifies how the document fragment is to be treated. This is followed by the document fragment itself, which is further enclosed by embedded square brackets:

```
<![ keyword [ document fragment ]]>
```

The document fragment is processed by a **parser** according to the restrictions set by the keyword, which may be one of the following:

- IGNORE
- INCLUDE
- TEMP
- CDATA
- RCDATA

For example:

```
<![ IGNORE [ Here is some text. ]]>
```

The IGNORE keyword indicates that the enclosed data (possibly including both text and markup tags) is to be ignored by the parser, and therefore not passed to the application. For instance, the text will *not* appear in a published document.

In contrast, the INCLUDE keyword indicates that the enclosed text is to be treated normally. This may appear superfluous, as a marked section has no effect at all when it contains the INCLUDE keyword, so need not be present. However, by this means it is possible to 'remove' the enclosed data at any time, simply by changing its status to IGNORE, and to retrieve it by changing its status back again.

The TEMP keyword simply indicates that the embedded information is temporary. The parser may, for example, warn that it should be removed. Its status may later be changed to IGNORE, for instance.

The CDATA and RCDATA keywords specify that the enclosed data is to be treated as pure text (the distinction being that the latter allows entity references to be recognized and replaced, as described in Chapter 6). If a block of text contains characters that are normally interpreted as SGML markup, a marked section may be used to tell the parser to treat these characters as normal text:

```
<para>This is not<![ CDATA [ a <para> element. ]]></para>
```

In the example above, the second Paragraph start-tag is not parsed, so it does not begin a new paragraph in the text:

This is not a <para> element.

The keywords may also be used together:

```
<![ IGNORE CDATA [ a <para> element. ]]>
```

Processing instructions

Application specific information is held in a processing instruction.

The intention of SGML is to be independent of specific composing or pagination requirements. However, dependence cannot always be avoided, so application specific instructions may be required.

Unlike comments and marked sections, a **processing instruction**[044] contains information required for a specific application. It is not therefore specified by a markup declaration, the contents of which must be obeyed by all applications. Instead, it is bounded by the characters '<?' and '>'. The content may be any valid SGML characters (apart from '>', which will be interpreted as the end of the processing instruction), and the format of the content is assumed to be significant only to the target application, and not checkable by the parser:

```
<p>It would be nice to end the page
<?*NEW_PAGE>
<?:page break>
here</p>
```

In the example above, a Paragraph contains two processing instructions, each forcing a new page in the required syntax of differing pagination applications. It is the task of the application to decide which of the processing instructions it understands, if any.

Line endings

ASCII line ending codes are either ignored or treated as spaces, depending on context.

SGML markup requires the presence of an underlying text-based data format such as ASCII. Text format data files usually contain line ending codes to make the content legible, and SGML must take these codes into consideration.

ASCII defines two control characters that may be used as line ending indicators, Carriage Return (CR) and Line Feed (LF). An ASCII-based system will employ one or both of these to end a line of text.

SGML also defines two special characters, Record Start (RS) and Record End (RE). By default, the RS is mapped to the LF control code, and the RE is mapped to the CR control code. Each line of text is assumed to be a 'record' that is bounded by these two characters. The following are equivalent:

```
My first line[CR][LF]
My second line[CR][LF]

[RS]My first line[RE]
[RS]My second line[RE]
```

Depending on the context, these codes are either ignored, treated as markup delimiters or converted into spaces when the document is composed.

Both characters are ignored if occurring between declarations and markup tags when normal text is not allowed (when it is in **element content**[(026)]). The two examples below are equivalent:

```
[RS]<MyBook>[RE]
[RS]<MyChap>[RE]
[RS]<!-- Comment -->[RE]
[RS]<ttl> ....

[RS]<MyBook><MyChap><!-- Comment --><ttl>
```

The Record Start character is treated as a separator within markup, like a space character, and is ignored within text data. The two examples below are equivalent:

```
[RS]<MyElem
[RS]MyAttr="1">Unbro
[RS]ken word

<MyElem MyAttr="1">Unbroken word
```

In the example above, a space is assumed between the element and attribute names, so 'MyElem' is distinct from 'MyAttr', but no space is placed between 'Unbro' and 'ken', giving the word 'Unbroken'.

The Record End character is treated in the same manner within markup, but its role is more complex within text. Between text characters it is treated as a space. It is ignored if it immediately follows a start-tag, or immediately precedes an end-tag. The fragments below are equivalent:

```
<P>[RE]               <-- (ignore)
No line ends[RE]      <-- (convert to space)
here.[RE]             <-- (ignore)
</P>

<P>No line ends here.</P>
```

The Record End is also ignored if the record in which it occurs contains *only* markup declarations and/or processing instructions:

```
Normal line[RE]       <-- (convert to space)
<?Process>[RE]        <-- (ignore)
<!--Comment-->[RE] <-- (ignore)
of text

Normal line <?process><!--Comment-->of text
```

Normal line of text

It is clear that the scheme outlined above assumes an operating system that uses two line ending characters, such as MS-DOS, and this is not too surprising when it is recognized than SGML originated within IBM. It does not easily fit with single character line ending systems such as UNIX and the Apple Macintosh. The next revision of SGML is expected to simplify the scheme.

5. Document components

The purpose of this chapter is to introduce the three components of an SGML compliant document, and to describe how they interact with each other. Each component is described more fully elsewhere. The content of one of these components may be loosely described as the 'real' document, and was covered in the previous chapter.

The three components of an **SGML document entity**[(002)] form the backbone of a complete **SGML document**[(001)], and may even form the entirety of the SGML document. They provide the system dependent rules, the document structure rules (the DTD) and at least some of the document content.

The **SGML declaration**[(171)] specifies system and software constraints. The **prolog**[(007)] defines the document structure, and the **document instance set**[(010)] contains the 'real' document.

Perhaps the most significant quality of a document that comprises these components is that it carries its own rules, enabling it to be validated using an SGML **parser**, without reference to any other explicit rules. The parser reads the SGML document and detects errors of various kinds – whether resulting from file corruption, missing information or incorrect use of the standard. The parser 'learns' about the format and structure of the document as it actually reads it, with each component providing information to the parser about the legal content of the remaining components. The order in which the three components appear is therefore important.

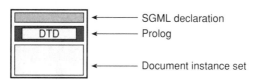

One way to approach this topic is to consider the need to deliver an SGML document to another party. The recipient will make no assumptions about the hardware or software used in its preparation, or the nature of its content. For now it will be assumed that the three components are contained within a single data file, though this need not be the case (later it will be shown how they are typically split into separate data files).

SGML declaration

The system dependent part of an SGML document is introduced. A full technical description appears in a later chapter.

The **SGML declaration**[171] segment of an SGML document prepares the parser for the remaining data by specifying character sets in use (usually based on ASCII or ISO 646), setting system variable space limits and selecting optional parts of the SGML standard.

This component is the only part of the SGML document that has a fixed syntax, thus allowing it to be processed by a parser on any system without further preparation.

The start of an SGML declaration is defined by the characters '<!SGML', followed by the version of the standard. It is completed by the close chevron, '>':

```
<!SGML ISO 8879:1986 .....
.....>
```

The SGML standard defines the rules that apply to an SGML document, but does not specify exactly how to apply them. Implied rules are defined by an **abstract syntax**, and include, for example, a rule stating that a special character will be used to begin an element start-tag, but without specifying which character to use.

A mechanism is provided for defining a **concrete syntax** from the abstract syntax. The concrete syntax specifies the actual keywords and special characters that separate markup from data. For example, it includes a physical value for the character to be used to begin an element start-tag, such as '<'.

The SGML declaration has a default concrete syntax, which is known as the **reference concrete syntax**. The defaults include specifying the use of the '<' character to begin a start-tag, and '>' to end one. For example, a start-tag for an element called Name would by default appear as '<name>'.

As the values and settings of the reference concrete syntax are already known to the parser, they need not be physically included in the SGML declaration.

A change to any part of the concrete syntax must be declared in the SGML declaration, and creates a **variant concrete syntax**. For example, a variant may re-define the start-tag open character to '!', giving '!name>' (though this is rare, and should only be considered for applications where the default special character is both significant within many documents, and is also heavily used within each document).

There is also a **reference quantity set** that sets limits on the number or size of various objects, which works in a similar manner. For example, it states that a start-tag name consists of at most eight characters. This too can be changed.

Whenever the phrase 'by default...' is used in this book, this refers to an initial value or setting specified explicitly within the default SGML declaration, or implicitly from the reference concrete syntax or reference quantity set.

Every SGML application could have its own unique SGML declaration (including a variant concrete syntax and/or a variant quantity set), but due to the desirability of maintaining standards only one variant is in common use. Devised by the US Department of Defense, it is sometimes referred to as the **CALS declaration**. The **CALS** (*Continuous Acquisition and Life Cycle Support*) variant differs mainly in respect of the legal scope of some constraints. For example, the reference quantity set restricts tag names to a maximum length of eight characters, but the CALS variant allows up to 32 characters. The default declaration would enforce a brief element name to identify a 'Company President,' such as '<compres>', whereas the CALS variant would allow the code to be named '<company-president>' (if so desired). Note that in the next revision of SGML, the standard declaration is expected to be upgraded to provide similar extensions.

Prolog

The prolog defines a document type, containing DTD declarations.

The **prolog**[007] structure is defined by the inherent rules of the SGML language, and its syntax is fixed by the SGML declaration. It consists of at least one **document type declaration**[110]. Although more than one is allowed (along with other structures not covered in this book), typically the prolog consists of a single document type declaration.

The document type declaration may directly contain a **Document Type Definition**, or **DTD** (note the similarity of names – the terms 'declaration' and 'definition' are not quite interchangeable). The DTD defines legal element names, and any restrictions on their location and quantity. It also defines allowed and required attributes, and their legal and default values. The DTD appears before the document instance so that the parser can be informed of the legal document structure (including elements that are required or permissible) prior to reading the actual document text.

A document type declaration is contained within a **markup declaration**, and is identified by the keyword **DOCTYPE**. The next word is the name of the **document element**[012] used in the document instance that follows it.

A document type declaration containing a DTD:

```
<!DOCTYPE Book [
......
<!ELEMENT chapter    - - (title?, (para|table)*>
<!ATTLIST chapter    Ident  ID  #REQUIRED>
.....
]>
```

This example, as stated above, may comprise the entire prolog.

The DTD is contained within a declaration subset (the square brackets, '[' and ']'). Later it will be shown that all or part of the DTD may be stored elsewhere.

The example DTD fragment defines an element called Chapter, which contains an optional Title and any number of Paragraphs and Tables. In the second line of the DTD, an attribute called Ident is defined for the Chapter element.

```
<chapter ident="c3">
```

The syntax of a DTD is fully explained in Chapter 7.

Document instance

The document instance may be considered the 'real document.' It consists of raw data and markup tags.

A **document instance set**[010] is an electronic representation of a single document (despite the word 'set' appearing in the name) that is structured according to the same rules as other documents in a *real* set of documents. An example would be the second volume of an encyclopedia of music (*Bach to Bolivia*), or the third issue of a journal (*Issue 3 – March 96*). In each case, all the documents in the set have common structures and formats.

Essentially, the document instance is a combination of raw data and markup tags. Both the tags and the information they enclose obey character usage and quantity limits defined in the SGML declaration, and conform to the rules defined in the prolog.

A fragment of a document instance:

```
<chapter ident="c3">
<title>Extract</title>
<para>An extract from a Document
Instance</para>
</chapter>
```

This fragment follows the DTD rules partly shown in the previous section.

The complete document instance is enclosed by a single element, which is known as the **document element**[012]. This element must be defined in the DTD, but need not be the outermost element defined there. If the fragment shown above were an entire document instance, then the document element would be the Chapter element, even though the DTD may define Chapter to be a child of Book. However, the prolog must reflect this choice:

```
<!DOCTYPE chapter ......>
<chapter>
.....
</chapter>
```

Splitting the components

The SGML declaration may be stored in one file, the DTD in another, and the prolog and document instance in a third, so avoiding duplication of information. The concept of entities is introduced, as they are used to link the components.

In previous sections the three components have been described separately, but they have been considered subunits of the same file:

```
<!SGML ........>
<!DOCTYPE book .........>
<book>.....</book>
```

It is now time to consider a more realistic organization of this information within a working environment. The three components of an SGML document are often split among several data files on the system.

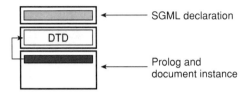

Typically, the SGML declaration is contained in its own file. The prolog and document instance are combined in one file, although the prolog contains a reference (within the document type declaration) to a separate file containing the DTD.

The reason for this arrangement is that the same DTD and SGML declaration are generally used to specify the rules for many documents. This approach avoids unnecessary duplication.

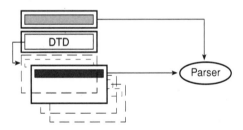

A separately stored DTD is an example of an **SGML text entity**[004]. The parser relies upon an **entity manager** to access and insert the DTD into the document type declaration.

```
<!DOCTYPE Book SYSTEM "MYBOOK.DTD"[]>
```

In this example, the keyword SYSTEM identifies an **entity reference** to an entity contained within the system file called 'MYBOOK.DTD.'

Part of the DTD may physically remain within the document type declaration:

```
<!DOCTYPE Book SYSTEM "MYBOOK.DTD"[
<!ENTITY % MyEnt  "INCLUDE" >
]>
```

Any declarations appearing in the **document type declaration subset**[112] (the square brackets) precede the content of the entity, despite the fact that the entity reference appears first. Although referenced before the open square bracket, '[', the entity content is placed after the close square bracket, ']'. This fact is important because it allows the document author to prefix the main DTD with entity declarations that override those within the DTD (see Chapter 6 for details).

The keyword PUBLIC may appear instead of SYSTEM, in which case the identity of a file is referenced from an entry in a **catalog** file. This topic is covered in more detail in the next chapter.

The parser

The parser both uses and validates the DTD and document instance, but cannot check for all possible errors.

The parser compares a DTD against a document to which it applies, and also obeys marked section constraints. It may be an application in its own right, where its only role is to check the document, or it may be part of a larger application, such as an SGML-aware word processor, where it can also control and aid the authoring process by intelligently guiding the document author.

In order to check a document, the **parser** is provided with the three components described above. First, the parser reads the **SGML declaration**[171], checks its format and reads the system dependent rules that it holds. The parser then reads the **prolog**[007] and embedded **DTD**. The DTD is checked against the inherent rules of SGML and the limits set in the SGML declaration, and is also checked for logical consistency. Finally, the **document instance set**[010] is read and compared with the rules provided in the DTD and SGML declaration.

If no errors are generated by the parser, then the various components form a legal **SGML document**[001].

In practice, the parsing process is often activated by selection of a data file containing just the document instance. The SGML declaration need not be present (if the default settings can be assumed). Though not strictly legal, the document type declaration may also be absent, and some applications will accept the file and prompt the user for another file containing the relevant DTD.

A note of caution: A document may be valid according to the rules of SGML, but still contain errors. For example, the parser cannot detect a missing chapter, or the inadvertent use of a bulleted list instead of a numbered list. Likewise, an Author element may incorrectly contain a document title, and a Title element may incorrectly contain an author's name. The use of a parser does not replace careful visual checking of the document content.

6. Entities

An 'entity' is a named object of a specified classification ('John' is the name of an entity of type 'Person'). An SGML **entity** is a named collection of characters which form a distinct unit.

Overview

Entities and entity references are introduced and typical uses are explored.

An entity comprises at least a name and some content. An entity may be named 'SGML', for example, and have a content of 'Standard Generalized Markup Language'. The content may be stored in the **prolog**[(007)], or in a separate data file.

For each entity, there may be any number of **entity references** (including none). Each reference effectively 'points to' a specific entity, indicating that the entity content is required at this point in the data stream.

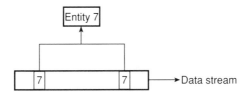

An SGML entity may be created to hold a unit of information in one or more of the following circumstances:

- the same information is used in several places, and duplication would be both error-prone and time-consuming
- the information may be represented differently by incompatible systems
- the information is part of a large document that requires splitting into manageable units
- the information involves non-SGML characters

In order to illustrate these uses with examples, the form that an entity reference takes will be introduced here, although it is described more fully in a later section. An entity reference appears in the text data stream, and in general begins with an ampersand character, '&', and ends with a semicolon character, ';'. An entity reference to an entity called 'SGML' would appear as '&SGML;'.

The first point listed above can be illustrated with the example of a brief phrase that is repeated many times in the document. In a book on SGML, the name 'Standard Generalized Markup Language' may appear often. To avoid keying the whole name, and also avoid the misspellings that may result from this tedious task, an entity may be created to hold the text, and this entity may be named 'SGML'. A reference would appear as:

```
The &SGML; format includes entities.
```

The second point listed above can be illustrated with the example of an 'extended character' (a character not defined within ASCII) such as 'é' (e acute). This character is represented in an entity by a system specific character value or control character sequence. Representation by an entity reference allows it to be transferred between systems unambiguously:

```
The caf&eacute; is open.
```

A large document, such as a text book, may be split into chapter-sized units for simultaneous editing by several authors, or to overcome system limitations:

```
<book>
&chap1;
&chap2;
&chap3;
</book>
```

The final point can be illustrated using the example of a compressed image. Many image formats involve the use of non-SGML characters, including all the character values normally reserved for control functions. Such formats cannot be included within the text data stream, so the image will never be physically included. However, an entity reference can indicate where the image should appear when the document is published:

```
Here is a photograph &MyPhoto; of J. Smith.
```

At some point, most entity references are replaced by the entity itself. Entity replacement could take place prior to publishing or delivering information. This action is performed by the **entity manager** (which may be just part of a larger application, such as a parser or word processor).

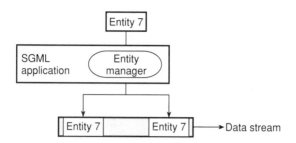

After entity replacement has taken place, the first example above becomes:

```
The Standard Generalized Markup Language format includes
entities.
```

The Standard Generalized Markup Language format includes entities.

The second example becomes:

```
The caf/'/e is open.
```

The café is open.

The third example becomes:

```
<book>
<chapter>........</chapter>
<chapter>...........</chapter>
<chapter>....</chapter>
</book>
```

The fundamental structure of an **SGML document**[001] depends on the use of entities. An SGML document directly contains one or more entities, starting with the **SGML document entity**[002]. This entity contains the three components described in the previous chapter.

Following the required entity described above, the SGML document may also contain any number of further entities, of various types. These entities (called **external entities**) may be stored in separate data files, and referenced from the DTD and document instance, but during transfer to another system they may be combined into a single unit (possibly using **SDIF** (*SGML Document Interchange Format*)).

Entity declarations

An entity is acknowledged to exist via a declaration. The declaration includes a unique name for the entity. A default can be declared to cope with invalid references.

A declaration is required to announce the existence of an entity. It may physically contain the entity, or may only contain a reference to it. An entity is declared in the **prolog**[(007)] component, defined using a **markup declaration**, and recognized as an **entity declaration**[(101)] by the keyword ENTITY:

```
<!ENTITY .. ... ........>
```

A later reference to an entity may only be made if the entity can be identified by name.

By default, the length of the name is restricted to only eight characters and must consist of characters defined by the NAME keyword. It must contain only alphabetic characters and the symbols '.' and '-', and it also must begin with an alphabetic character. Legal names include 'MyEnt' and 'my.ent'. An entity name is by default case-sensitive. An entity named 'MyEntity' is not the same as an entity named 'myentity' or 'MYENTITY'.

The entity name may appear directly after the ENTITY keyword within the declaration:

```
<!ENTITY myentity .......>
```

The name is often followed by the content of the entity or a reference to the content, enclosed in literal delimiters:

```
<!ENTITY myentity "content of 'myentity'">
```

Only the first declaration for a particular named entity is acknowledged. Redefinitions are ignored:

```
<!ENTITY myentity "content of 'myentity'">
<!ENTITY myentity "THIS CONTENT IS IGNORED">
```

This rule is important because it allows a document author to include entity declarations in the prolog that override declarations in the file containing the DTD (recall that the DTD entity is merged-in at the *end* of the document type declaration).

Default entity

It is possible to declare one entity to be the **default entity**. This entity will be used as a substitute whenever an entity reference is made to any non-existent entity. One use of this feature is to place a warning message in the text:

```
<!ENTITY #DEFAULT "** Missing Entity **">
```

Note that the example above is a little misleading. The parser should be used to detect missing entities (or mis-named entity references). A default entity should not be used where error detection is a priority. Instead, this mechanism may be used to temporarily avoid error messages or replace known errors with a standard symbol or phrase.

General and parameter entities

The problem of DTD authors and document authors creating conflicting entities is resolved by defining two types of entity – the general entity and the parameter entity.

A potential problem may seem to arise in the declaring of entities. It is quite common for the DTD designer to declare some entities to aid construction of the DTD, and for the author of a particular document instance to declare more entities (in the prolog) to aid the authoring process. The potential conflict occurs if both parties use the same entity name, as the document author cannot be expected to read the DTD to see if a particular entity name is already in use.

This problem is avoided by the use of two kinds of entity, the general entity and the parameter entity. A **general entity** is an entity that may be referred to within the document instance, and is available to authors of documents. All previous examples were of this type. A **parameter entity** is an entity that may only be referenced within markup declarations, and is therefore generally the province of DTD designers (although the author of a document instance may use them in marked sections).

A parameter entity declaration is specified by including a percent sign, '%', after the ENTITY keyword. This character is known as the **parameter entity reference open delimiter** (and defined by the PERO keyword):

```
<!ENTITY % myentity ........>
```

A general entity of the same name may be declared (simply by omitting the PERO character), and the two will be considered separate entities. The means by which they are distinguished in references is discussed later.

Internal entities

An internal entity has content that is stored within the declaration.

When the entity content is brief and consists of legal SGML characters, it may be stored within the entity declaration, and therefore be labeled as an **internal entity**.

Typical examples are standard phrases, such as 'Standard Generalized Markup Language', and characters not included in the standard ASCII character set, such as 'é.'

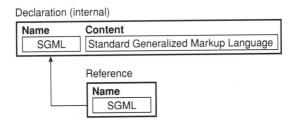

Internal entity content is delimited by double or single quotes (the choice is left to the author, except when the text contains one or other of these characters – in which case the alternative character must be used):

```
<!ENTITY myEntity 'this text contains "double" quotes'>

<!ENTITY eacute "[eacute]">

<!ENTITY SGML "Standard Generalized Markup Language">
```

The examples above show the simplest form of declaration, with content held in a **parameter literal**[(066)], which may contain normal characters, character references, parameter entity references and element tags.

External entities

An external entity has content which is stored remotely. The entity content is located using a system identifier or using a public identifier, which has a complex and rigid format.

When the entity content is extensive, is available to more than one document type or contains non-SGML characters, it will be defined as an **external entity**.

In an external entity, the **entity declaration**[(101)] does not contain the entity, but instead contains an identifier that *locates* the entity.

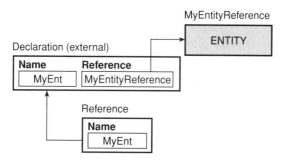

The identifier is either a system identifier or public identifier, either directly or indirectly indicating a data file on the system.

A **system identifier**[(075)] has no rigid format, but typically takes the form of a file path and file name, using the syntax required by the local operating system. This information follows the keyword SYSTEM. For example:

```
<!ENTITY myent SYSTEM "C:\ENTS\MYENT.SGM" >
```

This method of identifying remote information is system dependent and inflexible. It also offers little information on the content of the data file.

Where an entity is likely to be used on various systems and possibly by various organizations, a **public identifier**[(074)] may be used instead. A public identifier is system independent, location independent, provides more information on its purpose and may be officially registered (and therefore guaranteed unique). The keyword **PUBLIC** is used to indicate a public identifier:

```
<!ENTITY myent PUBLIC
"-//MyCorp//ENTITIES Superscript Chars//EN">
```

A **formal public identifier**[079] has a rigid structure composed of several parts – the identifier type, the **owner identifier**[080], the **public text class**[086], the **public text description**[087] and the **public text language**[088].

Identifier type

The identifier type is required, and must be one of the following:

- registered
- non-registered
- ISO

For a public identifier to be guaranteed unique, it must be **registered**. The **ISO** standard **ISO 9070** covers the generating of a unique public identifier. A **registered owner identifier**[082] has the symbol '+' for the identifier type. An **unregistered owner identifier**[083] has the symbol '-' (minus/hyphen). An **ISO owner identifier**[081] contains the text 'ISO 8879:1986'. The identifier type is separated from the rest of the name by a double solidus, '//':

```
<!ENTITY ..... PUBLIC "+//.....">
<!ENTITY ..... PUBLIC "-//.....">
<!ENTITY ..... PUBLIC "ISO 8879:1986//..">
```

Note: There has been a change of character separating the ISO numbers from the dates. Originally a hyphen, '-', it has changed to a colon, ':'. For example, 'ISO 8879-1986' has become 'ISO 8879:1986'.

The owner identifier is the name of the person or organization that owns the entity content. The owner identifier is not applicable in the case of ISO entities, as the identifier type has already established that ISO is the owner. Another double solidus separates the owner identifier from following details:

```
"+//MyCorp//....."
"-//MyCorp//....."
"ISO 8879:1986//....."
```

Public text class

The **public text class**[(086)] comprises a keyword that specifies the type of information contained by the entity, and must be one of the types listed below.

The CAPACITY class indicates that the entity content is a file that contains **capacity set** values that override the default values defined in the **SGML declaration**[(171)] (see the next chapter).

The CHARSET class indicates that the remote data file contains a character set definition.

The DOCUMENT class indicates that the remote data file contains a valid **SGML document**[(001)], with all the structures described throughout this book.

The DTD class indicates that the remote data file contains a **Document Type Definition**, including declarations for elements, entities and short references.

The ELEMENTS class indicates that the remote data file contains an **element set**[(114)], containing declarations only for elements.

The ENTITIES class indicates that the remote data file contains an **entity set**[(113)], containing declarations only for entities (commonly for character entities, such as the ISO sets).

The LPD class indicates that the remote data file contains a **link type declaration subset**, which is beyond the scope of this book to describe.

The NONSGML class indicates that the remote data file contains a **non-SGML data entity**[(006)], which is composed of uncontrolled characters (a parser would not check the content of such an entity).

The NOTATION class indicates that the remote data file contains **character data** that documents the format of a notation. The public identifier may be accompanied by a system identifier that locates software to process an entity conforming to the given notation.

The SHORTREF class indicates that the remote data file contains a **short reference set**[(115)] (entity declarations and short reference declarations).

The SUBDOC class indicates that the remote data file contains an **SGML subdocument entity**[(003)], a complete subdocument, including prolog and document instance (but sharing the current SGML declaration).

The SYNTAX class indicates that the remote data file contains a **concrete syntax**, possibly including quantity sets, naming rules and delimiters, etc. (see the next chapter).

The TEXT class indicates that the remote data file contains an **SGML text entity**[(004)], a document fragment that conforms to the rules of the current SGML declaration and DTD.

An example of an ENTITIES class public entity:

```
"-//MyCorp//ENTITIES ....."
```

Public text description

The **public text description**[(087)] is free text that provides additional information about the content of the external data:

```
"-//MyCorp//ENTITIES Superscript Chars .."
```

Language

The final component of the public text owner identifier is the **language**, which is a keyword from the list provided in **ISO 639** (see Chapter 14). It is separated from the public text description by a double solidus '//'. The keyword for English language, for example, is 'EN':

```
"-//MyCorp//ENTITIES Superscript Chars//EN"
```

Entity types

An entity may contain data to be treated in a special manner or to be ignored by the parser.

The **entity type**[(109)] specifies what kind of data the entity may contain.

If no entity type is provided for an internal entity, then the literal text may contain normal characters, character references (described later), parameter entity references and element tags:

```
<!ENTITY MyEnt "My &OtherEnt; text">
```

Likewise, if no entity type is provided for an external entity, then the entity is considered to be a fragment of an SGML document. It may contain data and markup:

```
<!ENTITY MyEnt SYSTEM "MYDOC.SGM">
```

```
<para>A remote
paragraph</para>
```

Keywords are used to declare an entity to be one of the following types:

- CDATA (character data)
- SDATA (specific character data)
- PI (processing instruction)
- STARTTAG (start-tag name)
- ENDTAG (end-tag name)
- MS (marked section start)
- ME (marked section end)
- NDATA (non-SGML data)
- SUBDOC (subdocument)

These types of entity are grouped into the following categories:

- Data text (internal)
- Bracketed text (internal)
- External

A **data text**[106] entity is used with internal entities, and includes the types:

- CDATA (character data)
- SDATA (specific character data)
- PI (processing instruction)

A **bracketed text**[107] entity is also used with internal entities, and includes the types:

- STARTTAG (start-tag name)
- ENDTAG (end-tag name)
- MS (marked section start)
- ME (marked section end)

An external entity type includes the types:

- CDATA (character data)
- SDATA (specific character data)
- NDATA (non-SGML data)
- SUBDOC (subdocument)

Data text

A data text entity contains legal SGML characters, but is not expected to contain markup tags or entity references. The parser will simply check its content for valid characters. It is used when the referenced text may contain data which would normally be considered significant to the parser. There are three types of data text entity: CDATA, SDATA and PI.

The **CDATA** type represents character data. The content will be assumed to be system independent. For example:

```
<!ENTITY MyEnt CDATA "Ignore '&this;' entity">
```

An **SDATA** entity contains legal SGML characters, and is very similar to a CDATA entity. The distinction is that SDATA entities are expected to be system specific, and may require modification if the document is moved to another system. The SDATA keyword acts as a warning of this fact. For example, the character 'é' (e acute) may be generated by different means on two imaginary systems:

System (A):

```
<!ENTITY eacute SDATA ":123^B:876">
```

System (B):

```
<!ENTITY eacute SDATA "!243">
```

A document transferred between these systems would contain the neutral reference 'é', which would be replaced by either ':123^B:876' or '!243' prior to composing the text, depending on which system it resides on at the time.

A **PI** entity contains literal processing instruction data. An entity of this type should be used in preference to a **processing instruction**[044] as it offers several advantages. It is always easy to find as it appears in the prolog, one change to the content affects all references, and the character '>' may appear in the data. It is distinguished from a CDATA entity in that a Record End (RE) character at the end of the entity is ignored, not converted to a space.

Bracketed text

A **bracketed text**[107] entity contains an element start-tag, **STARTTAG**, element end-tag, **ENDTAG**, marked section, **MS**, or markup declaration, **MD**. The delimiting characters are inferred, and to be inserted by the entity manager. The example below replaces the entity reference '&MyTag;' with the element start-tag '<chapter>':

```
<!ENTITY MyTag STARTTAG "chapter">
<book>
&MyTag;
<title>The Chapter title</title>
```

External types

External entities may be defined as one of the following types: CDATA, SDATA, NDATA or SUBDOC. In each case it is followed by a notation name, which is used to identify software that can process the data.

The CDATA and SDATA types have the same significance and distinctions as described previously.

An external character data entity (with NOTATION):

```
<!NOTATION TeX SYSTEM "SHOWTEX.EXE">
<!ENTITY MyEnt "C:\ENTS\MYENT.ENT" CDATA TeX>
```

An external **NDATA** entity is not restricted to SGML valid characters. The parser will validate its existence, but not validate its content. A typical example of an NDATA entity would be an image, perhaps stored in a compressed format. The keyword is followed by a data type name, as previously defined in a notation declaration:

```
<!NOTATION CGM SYSTEM  "">
<!-- CGM = Image Format -->
<!ENTITY Logo "C:\ENTS\LOGO.CGM" NDATA CGM>
```

A **SUBDOC** entity contains a prolog and document instance (SGML data that conforms to a different DTD, but the same SGML declaration).

External entity management

An entity manager uses system and public identifiers to locate external entities. Entries in catalog files simplify the management of entities.

The various means by which the entity manager can provide access to an external entity can be illustrated using the example of an external DTD, as specified in the document type declaration introduced in the previous chapter. However, the following explanations apply equally to all external entity declarations.

The keyword **SYSTEM** indicates that the quoted information following provides the location of the entity on the computer system using a **system identifier**[075]:

```
<!DOCTYPE book SYSTEM "C:\SGML\MYBOOK.DTD">
```

The example above specifies a DTD that is held in a data file called 'MYBOOK.DTD', which is located in the 'SGML' directory on drive 'C:' according to MS-DOS conventions.

There are two problems with this approach. Because the file location information is present in every document prolog, relocation of the DTD file from the given directory would involve editing every declaration, and a similar problem arises if the document were moved to another operating system, such as UNIX (which has no concept of a drive letter, and uses the solidus '/' character instead of the reverse solidus '\' character to denote directory structures). The situation is improved if the location information is stored elsewhere. The entity manager may use a **catalog** file which maps file names to given locations:

```
SYSTEM      "MYBOOK.DTD"       C:\SGML
```

The document type declaration may then be simplified:

```
<!DOCTYPE book SYSTEM "MYBOOK.DTD">
```

In this case, a change of DTD location requires only an edit to the catalog, and not to many document prologs. Each system can also locate DTD files in a different place. The same DTD residing on a UNIX system may be referred to in a local catalog file as follows:

```
SYSTEM      "MYBOOK.DTD"       /usr/neil/sgml/dtds
```

It may be possible to identify an external entity file using only the name of the entity. A catalog file is used to locate the DTD, as described above. SGML encourages this approach by allowing the parameter to be omitted:

```
<!DOCTYPE book SYSTEM>
```

However, file names and entity names suffer from character length constraints, so are not very informative. A **public identifier**[074] is intended to overcome this problem. A public identifier always assumes use of a catalog file, as described above, but descriptive text replaces the file name in the document type declaration:

```
<!DOCTYPE mybook
          PUBLIC "-//MyCorp//DTD My Book//EN">
```

The keyword **PUBLIC** identifies this example as a public identifier. The catalog file simply matches the text between quotes to a specific data file on the local system.

```
PUBLIC "-//MyCorp//DTD My Book//EN" C:\SGM\MYBOOK.DTD
```

The result is effectively the same as for the system identifier – the DTD file is located and merged-in to the document type declaration.

An entity declaration may contain both a public identifier and a system identifier. The system identifier follows the public identifier, and the keyword SYSTEM is omitted because the purpose of the second literal string is unambiguous:

```
<!DOCTYPE MYBOOK
          PUBLIC "-//MyCorp//DTD My Book//EN"
          "MYBOOK.DTD">
```

This approach gives the entity manager two means of identifying the required entity.

Although the use of catalog files simplifies the maintaining of SGML document storage, each SGML-aware software application may use its own syntax for the catalog filing system, in which case the information must be repeated for each application. In an attempt to avoid this unnecessary duplication, the **SGML Open** group has produced a standard format (see the last section of this chapter).

Entity references

A reference to an entity is made wherever the entity is required. Parameter references are distinguished from general references. The use of designated markup characters as normal data characters can be achieved using a character reference, function character or entity reference.

An entity reference appears at each location in the document where the content of the specified entity is required. The content replaces the reference (usually at the time of parsing or composing). The reference is composed of the name of the entity, surrounded by appropriate delimiter characters.

Note: A reference to a DTD is a special case. The declaration is not named, so cannot be referred to using a name. The reference is implied, and takes effect at the end of the declaration subset, where the close square bracket appears (or would appear if not present). There are similar exceptions within the SGML declaration.

General and parameter references

If the reference is to a general entity it is identified by the entity reference open delimiter, **ERO**, by default '&'. If the reference is to a parameter entity it is identified by the parameter entity reference open delimiter, **PERO**, by default '%'. In both cases the end of the reference is indicated by the entity reference close delimiter, **ERC**, usually ';'. In this way, the same entity name may be used for both a parameter entity and a general entity without confusion. The entity reference '`%myentity;`' is distinguished from '`&myentity;`'.

The ERC is only required when the next real character could be confused with part of the entity name. Suppose that there were two entities, one called 'abc' and another called 'abcd'. The parser would not be able to determine which entity was intended when encountering the text '`&abcdefg`'. The ERC therefore avoids such confusion, and the example '`&abc;defg`' unambiguously refers to the 'abc' entity. The ERC is not required (but is usually still included) when the entity name is followed by a space character, or other separator. For example, '`&abcd efg`' refers to the entity named 'abcd'.

Special characters

When the character used as the ERO delimiter is also required as a real character in the text, it may itself need to be represented by an entity. For example, the text '`abc&def`' would cause the parser to look for an entity called 'def'. Changing this to '`abc&amp;def`' avoids this error. However, the entity reference is not required if the ampersand character is followed by a space. For example, '`Smith & Son`'.

The entity set **ISOnum** contains, among others, entities that may be used to include special characters in the document. For example, if the left chevron, '<', is required, then to avoid any confusion with markup tags it should be represented by the entity '<' (less than). Other useful entities are '&' (ampersand) and '>' (greater than).

```
<para>The example &lt;para&gt; is not
interpreted.
```

The example <para> is not interpreted.

Letters and symbols not covered by ASCII, such as accented European letters, Greek letters and mathematical symbols, have standard ISO entity declarations, and are grouped into entity files. The most commonly required are:

- **ISOnum** (symbols, including '<', '>' and '&')
- **ISOlat1** (accented Western European letters)
- **ISOgrk1** (Greek letters)
- **ISOpub** (publishing characters)
- **ISOtech** (technical symbols)

Some of these entity sets are described in Chapter 14.

Character references

The value of any character can be represented by a **character reference**[062]. A character reference is identified by the character reference open delimiter, CRO, by default '&#'. This is followed by a decimal value that represents an ASCII character. As the ASCII value for the letter 'A' is decimal 65, it can be represented by the character reference 'A'. Care is advised, because the values of some characters are different depending on the character set used. The character replacement may change, for example, if the document is transmitted in this form to another system.

The same mechanism is used to specify the use of a function character defined in the reference concrete syntax, such as '&#RE;' or '&#TAB;'.

Standard catalog format

A standard syntax for catalog entries, developed by the SGML Open committee, allows many applications to share one source of information.

Two problems were identified by the **SGML Open** committee relating to the locating of entities on a system. First, when each application that accesses SGML entities uses its own catalog format, entity location details must be duplicated. Second, the recipient of an SGML document consisting of several files (not merged using **SDIF**) needs a simple method to identify the base document and all of its components.

Both problems are solved by defining a common catalog format. The 'SGML Open Technical Resolution 9401:1995 (Amendment 1 to TR9401)' paper on entity management defines such a format.

This simple format comprises a number of identifier mappings consisting of a keyword, followed by a public identifier or entity name and an equivalent system identifier:

```
DOCUMENT   "MYBOOK.SGM"
PUBLIC   "-//myCorp//DTD My DTD//EN"   MYDTD.SGM
ENTITY   "chap1"   CHAPTER1.SGM
```

In the example above, the file 'MYBOOK.SGM' is identified as the base document (the starting point). The DTD is located in the system file 'MYDTD.SGM', and the first chapter of the document is referred to by an entity called '&chap1', which is associated with a file called 'CHAPTER1.SGM'.

An SGML declaration file can be specified, or matched to specific DTD identifiers where more than one declaration is used on the system. However, there is no system identifier.

Note that the **NSGMLS** parser described in Chapter 13 uses an extended version of this format for its catalog files.

7. DTD

The **DTD** (*Document Type Definition*) is the mechanism by which document structure rules are defined. A DTD exists within the document type declaration, and itself comprises a number of declarations. It specifies the legal element tags and attribute modifiers for a specific type of document, thereby defining the document **hierarchy** and **granularity**. It may also declare various **entities**.

There are products that simplify the writing, amending and viewing of DTDs by translating the declarations described below into graphical representations. However, the principles must still be understood, and it is sometimes not possible to make use of such tools. For example, it may be necessary to study a printout of a DTD.

The DTD used to create this book is included in Chapter 14 as an example.

DTD components

Document Type Definition is the collective name for various declarations that together describe a document structure. This includes element, attribute, entity and notation declarations.

As indicated in the previous two chapters, the DTD appears in the document type declaration, either directly within the subset (the square brackets, '[' and ']'), or more conveniently in a separate data file, referred to by a system or public identifier. A combination of both is possible, in which case the external declarations are inserted (by the **entity manager**) at the end of the subset. This is convenient because subsequent declarations of the same entity are ignored, so an entity declared in the subset overrides one with the same name in the external DTD, giving more control to the document author. This mechanism may be used in conjunction with marked sections (described later), to switch parts of the DTD on or off:

```
<!DOCTYPE MYBOOK SYSTEM "C:\DTDS\MYBOOK.DTD" [
<!ENTITY ISOmath "INCLUDE">
<!ENTITY EUROmath "IGNORE">
<-- The MYBOOK.DTD entity content is inserted
    below this comment, using the ISOMath model -->
]>
```

In the example above, local entity declarations are used to enable or disable parts of the remote DTD that define alternative models for describing mathematical formulae (see Chapter 11 for a description of one of these models).

The DTD is composed of declarations. Each declaration conforms to the markup declaration format, '<! . . . . . . >', and is classified using one of the following keywords:

- ELEMENT (tag definition)
- ATTLIST (attribute definitions)
- ENTITY (entity definition)
- NOTATION (data type notation definition)
- SHORTREF (short reference definition)
- USEMAP (short reference context use mappings definitions)

The most common of these are **ELEMENT**, **ATTLIST** and **ENTITY**, as they are used to construct the tag structures that all documents contain. **NOTATION** is also widely used (generally for graphic formats). Although ENTITY declarations were covered in the previous chapter, the use of entities to aid construction of the DTD requires further discussion.

Partly for the purposes of readability it is advised that notation declarations appear first, followed by entity declarations, then by paired element/attribute declarations. However, this ordering is not simply cosmetic. Notation declarations must precede any references from entities, and entity declarations must precede any references to them.

Element declarations

Element declarations are used to create elements and define their content, and model groups build document hierarchies.

An **element declaration**[116] is used to create a new element and define its content. The keyword **ELEMENT** identifies an element declaration, and this is generally followed by the name of the new element:

```
<!ELEMENT title ..... >
```

If the SGML declaration allows element minimization, then the element declarations must include minimization options for the element being defined. Two tokens are used, called **start-tag minimization**[123] and **end-tag minimization**[124], both of which have a value of '-' (required) or 'O' (may be omitted), separated by spaces. In the following example, the Title end-tag is optional:

```
<!ELEMENT title - O ..... >
```

Care must be taken when employing this feature, however, as a start-tag may not be omitted in any of the following circumstances:

- when another element could be used at the same point
- when it is not required to appear at this position
- when its content type is CDATA or RCDATA
- when it contains a **required attribute** or **current attribute**

An end-tag *can* be omitted when its presence is implied by the document ending, or when it is immediately followed by:

- the end-tag of its parent element
- the start-tag of an element it does not contain (a sibling element)
- a data character, when characters are not allowed in the element

The legal content of an element is the final required part of the declaration. If no child elements exist, the element may have a simple **declared content**[125], using the keyword CDATA, RCDATA or EMPTY:

```
<!ELEMENT title - o CDATA>
<!ELEMENT para - o RCDATA>
<!ELEMENT image - o EMPTY>
```

In the example above, the Title element may contain character data and the Paragraph element may contain replaceable character data (that is, may include entity references):

```
<title>This is a CDATA title</title>.
<para>This is an &SGML; format RCDATA element</para>
```

The Image element is EMPTY, indicating that it has no end-tag, and is used purely to indicate the position of the external image:

```
There is an image at this point<image...> in the text.
```

When child elements are allowed, the declaration contains the keyword ANY, or it contains a **model group**[127]. An element declared to have a content of ANY may contain all of the other elements declared in the DTD.

```
<!ELEMENT book - o ANY>
```

A model group is used to describe enclosed elements and text. The structure of a model group can be complex, and is explained fully in the next section:

```
<!ELEMENT book - o (para+, chapter+)>
```

Finally, the declaration may include a comment, which may help to maintain the DTD, and which some authoring software may display within element selection menus as an aid to document authors:

```
<!ELEMENT slttl   - - CDATA -- Section 1 Title -->

<!ELEMENT srcty1 - - CDATA -- Security Level 1 -- >
```

Elements	
s1ttl	Section 1 Title
srcty1	Security Level 1

Model and name groups

The definition of document structures in element declarations involves the use of model groups that are arranged using sequence connectors and occurrence indicators. Ambiguous structures are also described.

A **model group**[(127)] or **name group**[(069)] is used within element declarations, and within other declaration types, for a variety of purposes. Perhaps the most important use of a model group is to define the legal placement of element tags within the document structure, and the following descriptions will concentrate on this usage before explaining alternative uses.

A **model group**[(127)] is used to define an element that has mixed content or element content. An element defined to have **element content**[(026)] will contain only **child** elements. An element defined to have **mixed content**[(025)] will contain a mixture of elements and free text. Although it is possible to specify only text in a mixed content model, a more efficient method to do this was described in the previous section.

A model group is bounded by brackets, and contains at least one **content token**[(128)] that may be the name of an included element. In this way document hierarchies are built. For example, a model group used in the declaration for a Book element may refer to embedded Front Matter and Body elements, '(fmatter, body)'. The declarations for these elements may in turn specify the inclusion of further elements, such as Title and Chapter.

Sequence control

When a model group contains more than one content token, the child elements must be organized according to the requirement. The organization of elements is controlled using three logical connector operators; ','
(**sequence connector**), '|' (**or connector**) and '&' (**and connector**).

The sequence rule '(a, b, c)' indicates that element A is followed by element B, which in turn is followed by element C:

```
<a>...</a><b>...</b><c>...</c>
```

The rule '(a | b | c)' indicates a choice between the elements A, B and C (only one can be selected):

```
<b>...</b>
```

The rule '(a & b & c)' indicates that all three elements are expected, but in any sequence. They may be reversed, for example, or B may appear first:

```
<b>...</b><c>...</c><a>...</a>
```

It is not legal to mix these operators because this would introduce ambiguity. The rule '(a, b, c | d)' is invalid, for example, because it may indicate that 'D' is an alternative to *all* the other elements, or that 'D' is an alternative only to element C (A and B still being required). The solution to this problem is to use enclosed model groups. Further brackets are placed according to the meaning required – '((a, b, c) | d)' indicates the first meaning, whereas '(a, b, (c | d))' indicates the latter. In the last example, the outer model group made use of the SEQ connector and the inner model group made use of the OR connector.

Quantity control

Wherever a particular element may be legally used it may also be allowed to repeat, or to be absent. Occurrence rules are governed using **quantity indicators**.

If the element is required and may not repeat, no further information is required. All of the previous examples indicated a required presence (except where the '|' connector allowed a choice of elements).

If the element is optional, and cannot repeat, it is followed by a question mark, '?'. For example, '(a, b?)' indicates that element B is optional, so the legal sequences are 'a' and 'a, b'.

If the element is required and may repeat, the element name is followed by a plus, '+'. For example, '(a, b+)' indicates that element B must appear, but may also repeat. Legal sequences include 'a, b', 'a, b, b', 'a, b, b, b ...'.

If the element is optional and also repeatable, the element name is followed by an asterisk, '*'. For example, '(a, b*)' indicates that element B may occur any number of times, and may also be absent. Legal sequences include 'a', 'a, b', 'a, b, b', 'a, b, b, b ...'. The '*' may be seen as equivalent to the (illegal) combination of '?+'.

The special characters can all be re-defined within the SGML declaration, using the keywords **OPT** (for optional), **PLUS** (for required and repeatable) and **REP** (for optional and repeatable.)

In some circumstances, an element may be required to appear at least twice. For example, a list structure may be obliged to hold more than one item. This can be achieved using the following technique: '(item, item+)' (but ensure that the second Item repeats, not the first, as this would lead to ambiguities, which are described later).

A model group may itself have an occurrence indicator. The entire group may be optional, required or repeatable. The example '(a, b)?' indicates that the elements A and B must either occur in sequence, or both be absent. The example '(a, b)*' indicates that the sequence A then B may be absent, but if present may also repeat any number of times, allowing 'a, b, a, b, a, b'. The example '(a, b)+' indicates that elements A and B must exist, but may also then repeat.

Note: When creating a DTD, there may be several ways to achieve a required effect. The briefest representation possible should always be used for clarity. For example, the rule '(a+)?' is more simply defined as '(a*)'

A commonly used structure is '(a | b)*', indicating that any number of elements A and B may appear in any order:

```
<b>...</b><b>...</b><a>...</a><b>...</b>
```

This scheme allows elements to be mixed with text characters, which are represented by the keyword '**PCDATA**' (parsed character data), preceded by the **reserved name indicator** '#' to avoid confusing this with a defined element with the same name. A Paragraph may, for example, contain both normal text and Subscript and Superscript elements:

```
(#PCDATA | sub | super)*
```

This is an example of a **mixed content**[025] model. A single parsed character data token represents any number of individual characters, entity references and included elements (explained later), though they can all be absent (it has an implied occurrence indicator of '*'). The legal sequence '#pcdata, sub, #pcdata' is applied in the example below (note that the Sub element also contains #pcdata):

```
Water is H<sub>2</sub>O.
```

Ambiguities

Some care should be taken when creating model groups as it is possible to confuse the parser. There are several ways of creating an ambiguous content model.

Ambiguities arise when the element encountered by the parser in the data stream matches more than one token in the model. The example below illustrates such a case:

```
(item?, item)
```

On encountering an Item element, the parser cannot tell whether it corresponds to the first token in the group (the optional Item) or to the second (the required Item). If the parser assumes the first case then discovers no more Item elements in the data, an error will result (because the second Item is required). If the parser assumes the second case, then encounters another Item, an error will also result (because no more Items were allowed). The parser is not designed to look ahead to see which situation is relevant, because some examples of this problem would require the parser to search a long way (possibly to the end of the document), complicating the process and hindering efficiency. Although theoretically possible, this was deemed impractical. The example above could be made valid simply by switching the '?' to the second token.

If optional model groups contain the same initial element, the parser cannot determine which model group is being followed. For example:

```
((surname, employee) | (surname, customer ))
```

On encountering a Surname element, the parser is unsure which model group is active and, as before, will not look ahead to determine which is in use. Such problems can be resolved by re-defining the model groups as follows:

```
(surname, (employee | customer ))
```

A **mixed content**[025] model group involving anything other than the OR connector is an **ambiguous mixed content** model. For example, use of the sequence connector is ambiguous:

```
<!ELEMENT item - - (surname, #PCDATA)>
```

The reason for this is that Record End (**RE**) characters are significant in character data (they are treated as spaces). The following example illustrates the potential problem:

```
<item>[RE]          <-- ignore
[RE]                <-- make a space (in text data!)
<surname>Smith</surname>Some text
</item>
```

The second RE is interpreted as data (recall that the first RE is ignored in any circumstance), and the parser therefore assumes that the Surname element is missing. This is reported as an error. Even if the Surname element had been optional, an error would still have resulted. The second RE would indicate the start of character data and an illegally positioned Surname element would then be encountered.

Element declaration groups

Groups are utilized in various parts of a declaration, to create the document hierarchy, to avoid unnecessary duplication, and to specify elements that may be used anywhere within the specified element, or nowhere within the specified element.

The legal content of an element may be defined within a **model group**[127], as described above:

```
<!ELEMENT seqlist - o (item+)>
```

In other parts of the declaration a **name group**[069] is used. The main difference between a name group and a model group is that a name group does not allow further embedded groups. However, the techniques described above are used to specify which elements may be included.

A single element declaration may be used to define several elements that have the same content, using a name group to specify the names of the elements. The examples below are equivalent:

```
<!ELEMENT (title|para) - - (#PCDATA | sub | sup)*>
<!ELEMENT title - - (#PCDATA | sub | sup)* >
<!ELEMENT para  - - (#PCDATA | sub | sup)* >
```

In this case, the OR connector is used, but any legal sequence connector has the same effect because in this context the name group is only being used to provide a list of element names, not to describe their relationship to each other.

Name groups are also used to specify inclusions and exclusions. **Inclusions**[139] specify the elements that may appear anywhere within the declared element, and within all child elements. They appear at the end of the declaration and begin with the PLUS character, '+':

```
<!ELEMENT book    (chapter+) +(image | table)>
<!ELEMENT chapter (section+)>
<!ELEMENT section (para+)>
```

In this example, a Book must directly contain some Chapter elements, but may also contain Image and Table elements. They may appear directly within a Chapter, Section or Paragraph, and within any other subelement. The choice of connector is irrelevant in this context, though the convention is to use the OR connector, '|'.

Exclusions[140] have the opposite effect. They exclude elements from appearing within the defined element and its children. They appear at the end of the declaration, and begin with a MINUS character, '-'. They are often used to override an inclusion made at a higher point in the hierarchy. For example, if a Section and its children may not contain an Image, the previous declarations may be amended to:

```
<!ELEMENT book    (chapter+) +(image | table)>
<!ELEMENT chapter (section+)>
<!ELEMENT section (para+) -(image)>
```

```
Book ──┬── Chapter ──┬── Section ──┬── Para
       ├── Table      ├── Table      └── Table
       └── Image      └── Image
```

They may also be used to prevent unwanted element nesting. For example, if a Warning may contain a List, and a List may contain a Warning, it is therefore possible for a Warning to indirectly contain another Warning. This meaningless and confusing possibility could be avoided by making the Warning explicitly exclude itself. This exclusion takes precedence over the embedded List definition.

When a single declaration contains both inclusions and exclusions, the exclusions must appear first:

```
<!ELEMENT section (para+) -(image) +(xref)>
```

Attribute declarations

The meaning or behavior of an element is modified by the use of attributes. Each attribute has a name, a value type and a default value or requirement option.

The DTD specifies the name, value type, default value or requirement options for an attribute.

An **attribute definition list declaration**[141] assigns an **attribute definition list**[142] to one or more elements. Within this list, each **attribute definition**[143] defines a specific attribute.

An attribute declaration is identified by the keyword ATTLIST (attribute list):

```
<!ATTLIST  ... ... .....
           ... .....>
```

The attribute list first contains a reference to the element or elements (using a model group) that will contain the declared attributes:

```
<!ATTLIST  chapter ... .....
           ... .....>
<!ATTLIST  (seqlist | randlist) ... .....
           ... .....>
```

The rest of the declaration consists of a list of parameters that define for each attribute the **attribute name**[143.1], its **declared value**[145] and its **default value**[147].

Attribute name

The first parameter is the attribute name, which is of type NAME and therefore follows the same restrictions on length and character usage as element names:

```
<!ATTLIST  seqlist first .....
           offset .....
           type ..... >
```

In this example, three attributes are defined for use in the Sequence List element.

Declared value

The second parameter describes the type of the attribute, which can restrict the range of possible values it may hold. An attribute is declared to be one of the following types:

- CDATA
- ENTITY
- ENTITIES
- ID
- IDREF
- IDREFS
- NAME
- NAMES
- NMTOKEN
- NMTOKENS
- NUMBER
- NUMBERS
- NUTOKEN
- NUTOKENS
- notation
- name token group

For example:

```
<!ATTLIST  seqlist first   CDATA
                   offset  NUMBER
                   type    ( alpha | number )>
```

Default restrictions on character usage for each of these attribute types are provided in the *Attribute Types* table in Chapter 14.

Many of these types are divided into singular and plural forms, for example NUMBER and NUMBERS. The plural form simply indicates a series of values that conform to the same restrictions as the singular form. As a NUMBER attribute may contain '123', a NUMBERS attribute may therefore contain '123 987 454':

```
<picture boundary="5 12 35 55">
```

The **ENTITY** type is a special case, indicating that the attribute value is actually an entity reference. For example, an element containing an attribute of type ENTITY may be used as a place-holder for images:

```
<!ENTITY MyLogo ..... >
<!ELEMENT myelem - O EMPTY>
<!ATTLIST myelem      myentity ENTITY ...>
...
<myelem myentity="MyLogo">
```

The ID and IDREF types are special cases that are used to create hypertext
links. They are covered in detail in Chapter 9.

The **NOTATION** option specifies that the element content conforms to a non-
SGML syntax, such as T_EX, which the attribute of type NOTATION identifies. The parser ignores all markup characters, apart from end-tag start
delimiters, '</' (which end the element). In the example below, the Format
attribute has been defined to be of type NOTATION:

```
<image format="TeX">
-$${ \Gamma (J^psi ......
</image>
```

The **name token group**[068] option restricts values to one of a finite set. For
example, the definition '(left | right | center)' specifies that the
value must be one of these tokens. When used in a start-tag, the value need
not be delimited by quotes (because no space can appear within a token), or
be identified by the attribute name (because duplicate token values are not
allowed):

```
<title center>
```

In some cases, it is practical for a group to contain a single option:

```
<!ATTLIST list  dummy  (indented)  .....>
```

In this example, the List element has an attribute called Dummy, which can
take only one value, 'indented'. This technique discourages entry of the
attribute name, as the value alone specifies the alternative form. An application should assume that a missing value indicates the normal form:

```
<list>                < -- normal list

<list indented>       < -- indented list
```

Default value

The final parameter is the **default value**[147], which specifies either the
requirement options or the implied value of the attribute.

A token, or a string enclosed in literal delimiters, is an **attribute value specification**[033]. For example, '*"center"*' would set the default value to Center if no value is provided by the document author.

If preceded by the keyword **FIXED**, then the provided value is the only value the attribute can take. This may seem odd, though the **SDA** and **HyTime** DTD fragments both employ this feature to map user-defined elements to pre-defined structures. In the SDA scheme, for example, the DTD carries details of required mappings to another DTD. In the example below, the Coden element will be mapped to the Para element in the SDA DTD, and this mapping is never changed:

```
<!ELEMENT coden - - (#PCDATA)>
<!ATTLIST coden SDAFORM  CDATA  #FIXED "para">
```

As an alternative, four keywords are available:

- REQUIRED
- IMPLIED
- CONREF
- CURRENT

Of these, the two most commonly used are REQUIRED and IMPLIED. A **REQUIRED** attribute value simply indicates that a value must be provided by the document author. An SGML-aware word processor will, for example, display an entry screen for input of required attributes when the element is created by the document author. An **IMPLIED** attribute value indicates that the attribute may be absent from the element, in which case the application software assumes a default value.

The **CONREF** keyword indicates that the attribute value is a **content reference attribute**. A content reference attribute value explicitly entered in an element renders the element content empty, to be replaced by the application.

The **CURRENT** keyword allows an attribute to inherit a previous value when it is not stated by the document author. In the example below, the second Paragraph also has a security rating of 'high' (assuming that the Security attribute is of type CURRENT):

```
<para security="high">.......</para>
<para>......</para>
```

An attribute list example:

```
<!ATTLIST seqlist sepchar    CDATA      #IMPLIED
                  offset     NUMBER     #REQUIRED
                  type       ("alpha"|"num")  "num">
```

The example Sequence List element has three attributes. The Sepchar attribute is not essential, but if used specifies the character that separates the items. It is therefore declared to be of type CDATA (allowing any legal SGML character). The Offset attribute holds a numeric value that determines the level of indent for the list, and must be specified. The Type attribute is implied, and specifies whether the list is a numeric list or an alphabetic list. If neither value is specified by the document author, 'num' is assumed (and may be inserted automatically by an authoring or composition package). An example of usage:

```
<seqlist sepchar="d" offset="3" type="alpha">
```

Entities and marked sections

Entities simplify the building of the DTD by avoiding the need for repetition. Marked sections can define alternative DTD components.

Just as a document author may use a general entity to avoid unnecessary repetition, so a DTD author may use a **parameter entity** in a similar fashion to aid construction of the DTD. The use of entities can reduce the workload, make authoring errors less likely and clarify the DTD structure (although they can also, if used too frequently, render the DTD unintelligible). For example, a model group that is in common use may be represented by an entity:

```
<!ENTITY % common  "(para | list | table)">
```

Within element declarations a reference is made to the parameter entity:

```
<!ELEMENT chapter - - ((%common;)*, section*) >
<!ELEMENT section - -  (%common;)*>
```

Note than an entity reference must not be qualified by an occurrence indicator. In the example above, a model group was used to hold the '%common;' reference. It would not be legal to use '%common;*' instead.

Entities may also be used to facilitate use of marked sections. A marked section requires a defining keyword; typically either **INCLUDE** or **IGNORE**. If marked sections are used to define optional parts to the DTD, or to create two variants of the same DTD within one file, then the active group of marked sections at any one time can be defined using an entity:

```
<!ENTITY % MyStandard "INCLUDE">
<!ENTITY % MyVariant "IGNORE">
...
<![ %MyStandard; [
       <!ENTITY % Text "#PCDATA | sup | sup | temp">
]]>
<![ %MyVariant; [
       <!ENTITY % Text "#PCDATA | sup | sup">
]]>
```

In this example, all the marked sections containing parameter entity reference 'MyStandard' are to be included (along with all their embedded element and attribute list declarations), and the other marked sections are to be ignored. The effect is to include the first Text entity declaration, which includes the Temp element. Note that, although this mechanism is available to document instance authors, it is more typically used by DTD authors.

When alternative marked sections contain only entity re-definition, as in the example above, the coding can be simplified by taking advantage of the fact that entity re-declarations are ignored. The example below achieves the same effect:

```
<!ENTITY % MyStandard "INCLUDE">
...
<![ %MyStandard; [
       <!ENTITY % Text "#PCDATA | sup | sup | temp">
]]>
<!ENTITY % Text "#PCDATA | sup | sup">
```

In this example, the second Text entity declaration is ignored if the first is included by setting the MyStandard entity value to 'INCLUDE', but is enacted if the first declaration is ignored by setting MyStandard to 'IGNORE'.

Notation declarations

A notation declaration identifies, names and provides access to non-SGML data formats.

A **notation declaration**[148] informs the parser of non-SGML formats used in the document instance. This includes formats that contain characters that are not legal within SGML documents (for example, an image format may have no concept of characters, and may use all the available byte values), and formats that do conform to SGML character usage, but not to the SGML syntax (such as PostScript).

Notation name and definition

The keyword **NOTATION** identifies a notation declaration, and is followed by the notation name, which is at the discretion of the DTD author but should be an obvious name for the format:

```
<!NOTATION TeX ..... >
```

Note: T_EX is a typesetting language.

The notation name is followed by an external notation identifier, possibly involving both a public and a system identifier:

```
<!NOTATION TeX PUBLIC "-//MyCorp//NOTATION TeX
 Help File//EN" "SHOW_TEX.EXE">
```

The public identifier may locate a file that contains information on the data format. The system identifier may specify the name of an application suitable for processing data that conforms to the named format. Typically, the format information and application details are not available, though a notation identifier must still be present if a later reference is made to the non-SGML format:

```
<!NOTATION TeX SYSTEM "">
```

Usage

The declared notation may be referred to in entity declarations, following the **NDATA** (notational data) keyword:

```
<!ENTITY Logo SYSTEM "LOGO.TEX" NDATA TeX>
```

The declared notation may also be referred to in attribute declarations, for elements that contain formats other than SGML (but conforming to legal SGML character usage):

```
<!ELEMENT IMAGE   - - CDATA>
<!ATTLIST IMAGE   format NOTATION (TeX | CGM) "CGM">
.....
<IMAGE format="TeX">
$${ \Gamma (J^psi .......
</IMAGE>
```

Note that the parser can make no use of this information, but passes it to the application (which hopefully can).

Short reference declarations

Short references enable normal data characters to represent element tags, and are created using entity declarations, short reference mapping declarations and short reference use declarations.

Short references are data characters that may double as markup. For example, a quotation mark may represent the start and end of a Quote element. Using short references, the following examples may be equivalent:

```
<p>As Alice wondered: "What is the use
of a book without pictures or conversations?".</p>

<p>As Alice wondered: <quote>What is
the use of a book without pictures or
conversations?</quote>.</p>
```

The character or string to be assigned a markup role must be pre-defined in **short reference delimiters**[192]. The short reference delimiter characters are specified in the SGML declaration. One of the default delimiters is the quotation mark character. The complete default list is provided in Chapter 14.

A **short reference mapping declaration**[150] is employed to map the short reference delimiter to an entity. An **entity declaration**[101] specifies which start-tag or end-tag that the delimiter represents. A **short reference use declaration**[152] specifies a context within which a particular mapping is active.

The format of an entity declaration has been covered previously. In this context, the bracketed text STARTTAG and ENDTAG options may be used to define start-tag and end-tag replacements for the delimiter.

```
<!ENTITY OpenQ STARTTAG "quote">
<!ENTITY CloseQ ENDTAG "quote">
```

In this example, a reference to the entity OpenQ signifies that the Quote element start-tag, '<quote>', is required. A reference to the entity CloseQ signifies that the Quote element end-tag, '</quote>', is required.

```
... &OpenQ;What is the use of a book without pictures or
conversations?&CloseQ; ...
```

The **short reference mapping declaration**[150] assigns a name to one or more delimiter-to-entity mappings. It begins with the keyword **SHORTREF**, which is followed by the name of the mapping definition and one or more of the following components – a delimiter, followed by the name of an entity containing the markup replacement:

```
<!SHORTREF Pmap '"' OpenQ
               '*' FootRef>
<!SHORTREF Qmap '"' CloseQ>
```

In this example, the first declaration defines a map called Pmap, which has two substitutions, the first substituting the quotation mark delimiter with the content of the OpenQ entity, and the second substituting the asterisk delimiter with the content of the FootRef entity. The second declaration defines a map called Qmap, which contains a single substitution of the quotation character with the CloseQ entity.

The example above illustrates the need for context-sensitive mappings. The quotation mark character must sometimes be mapped to the Quote start-tag, and sometimes to the Quote end-tag, using the Pmap and Qmap mappings, respectively. The first quotation mark in the example must map to the start-tag. The second quotation mark in the example must map to the end-tag. Context-sensitive mappings are provided by the **short reference use declaration**[152]. Following the keyword **USEMAP**, the declaration contains the name of the short reference map, for example 'Pmap,' and the names of elements that need to be open for the map to be active:

```
<!USEMAP Pmap p>
<!USEMAP Qmap quote>
```

In this example, the Pmap mapping is only active when the short reference delimiter appears within a Paragraph element, and the Qmap mapping is only active when the short reference delimiter appears within a Quote element. Model groups may be used to extend the options:

```
<!USEMAP Pmap (p | item | phrase)>
```

Only the innermost element in the hierarchy is considered in deciding which map to use. In the example fragment above, the Paragraph element is still open when the second quotation mark character is encountered, but the previous mapping has also opened the Quote element, so this is now the current element, and Qmap is therefore active instead of Pmap.

8. SGML declaration

The **SGML declaration**[171] is the first part of an SGML document entity[002], preceding the prolog[007] and document instance set[010]. It is identified by the delimiters '<!SGML' and '>'. The version of SGML follows the open delimiters. At this point there is only one version, which consists of the ISO number for the standard, including the year of publication, delimited by quotes '<!SGML "ISO 8879:1986" ......>'. The next revision of SGML is expected to add a new variant called 'ISO 8879:1986 (ENR)', with 'ENR' standing for Extended Naming Rules.

The SGML declaration defines system specific configurations of the standard, including the character set used, optional features used, and limits on the number or size of various objects. Some of these settings allow the local system to re-define the physical representation of the SGML markup language. However, the SGML declaration itself uses the default settings, so ensuring that a parser requires no preparation in order to read and understand it. Theoretically, if a document does not contain an SGML declaration, the 'system default' declaration is assumed by a parser. In practice, this default configuration usually follows various suggested settings that are described below.

The SGML declaration is divided into six clauses:

- the Document Character Set
- the Capacity Set
- the Concrete Syntax Scope
- the Concrete Syntax
- the Feature Use settings
- the Application Specific Information

Document character set

The document character set is the character set used by the local system and is included for human reference only.

The **document character set**[172] is a human readable reminder of the legal character set used by the local system, and is ignored by a parser. The keyword **CHARSET** introduces this clause.

A **base character set**[(174)] defines the character set to be used. A standard character set is referenced, usually using a public identifier. The keyword **BASESET** is used to introduce the standard character set:

```
CHARSET
      BASESET "ISO 646-1984//CHARSET....."
```

Changes to this standard set are then defined in a **described character set portion**[(175)]. The keyword **DESCSET** is used to introduce the changes to this set. The DESCSET parameters fall into groups of three. First, there is a character value to start the range. Second, there is a quantity value to specify how many characters are affected. Third, there is a new character value that specifies the target range start:

```
CHARSET
      BASESET "ISO 646-1984//CHARSET..."
      DESCSET 0 9 UNUSED
              9 2 9
              . . .
```

In the example above, from character zero there are nine characters that are unused (characters 0 to 8). From character nine, two characters are mapped to character nine onward (so there is no change to characters 9 and 10).

It is possible to have further paired BASESET and DESCSET definitions. The **ISO/IEC 646** character set only defines 128 characters, whereas most modern systems allow 256 characters. A further definition for the remaining 128 characters is typical.

Capacity set

The capacity set clause defines the maximum quantities for various objects that appear in the prolog and document instance.

An SGML application may use the **capacity set**[(180)] to discover how much memory it needs to reserve for storage of objects. A declaration received from another system may be tested for possible problems processing documents on the local system.

The keyword **CAPACITY** introduces this clause.

The capacity set may contain either a public identifier to an external entity that contains a list of definitions, or may directly contain a list of capacity definitions:

```
CAPACITY
     SGMLREF
     ELEMCAP 7000
```

The keyword **SGMLREF** states that the **reference capacity set** defaults are in effect, except for any override settings that follow. In this case the number of elements allowed in a document is re-defined to just 7000 (from an implied default of 32000).

Capacities should not be confused with quantities (described later), which are used to define the lengths of various objects, not the total number of objects to expect. The difference is subtle, and reflects likely programming techniques. Capacities may dictate the size of memory-based structures such as stacks and heaps. Quantities are more likely to determine the size of memory buffers.

Concrete syntax scope

The concrete syntax scope clause specifies which components of an SGML document use the concrete syntax.

The **concrete syntax scope**[181] clause dictates whether the concrete syntax defined in the next clause applies to the prolog as well as to the document instance. Note that the **SGML declaration**[171] itself uses the reference concrete syntax, so is unaffected by this clause.

The keyword **SCOPE** introduces this clause, and is followed by another keyword that indicates the actual scope. A scope setting of **DOCUMENT** states that the declared syntax applies to both the prolog and the document instance. A scope setting of **INSTANCE** states that the declared syntax applies only to the document instance, and that the prolog conforms to the reference concrete syntax:

```
SCOPE
     INSTANCE
```

When INSTANCE is specified, the character set declared for the document instance must be the same as that defined in the reference concrete syntax, and the quantity set values must at least equal those set in the reference concrete syntax. It must also be possible to recognize the characters that end the prolog and start the document instance set (so that the parser can detect it).

Concrete syntax

The concrete syntax clause specifies characters that should not appear in documents, the character set used in documents, the characters assigned to common functions, the characters that may appear in names and tokens, the characters that are significant in markup and markup declarations, the physical names assigned to abstract concepts and the maximum size of various objects.

The standard SGML declaration contains a public entity reference to the **reference concrete syntax**. Any change made to these defaults creates a **variant concrete syntax**. Also note that the term 'by default,' used in this and preceding chapters, refers to values defined in the reference concrete syntax (or reference quantity set).

Following the **SYNTAX** keyword there is either a reference to a public concrete syntax, or a list of definitions. The default declaration refers to the public reference concrete syntax, as shown below:

```
SYNTAX
    PUBLIC "ISO 8879-1986//SYNTAX Reference//EN"
```

Any change to the public reference requires all of the following definitions to be completed, either directly within the declaration or within a replacement external entity:

- the shunned character number identification
- the syntax-reference character set
- the function character identification
- the naming rules
- the delimiter set
- the reserved name use
- the quantity set

Shunned character number identification

The **shunned character number identification**[184] definition identifies characters that have some special role on the local system, and may cause problems if appearing in a document. For example, an end-of-file character should be shunned, as its presence would prematurely end the reading and processing of a document file.

The keyword **SHUNCHAR** introduces this section, and if no characters are shunned the keyword **NONE** is all that follows:

```
SHUNCHAR
        NONE
```

If the document character set includes control characters, these can all be shunned using the keyword **CONTROLS**. Other shunned characters are specified using decimal character values:

```
SHUNCHAR
        CONTROLS   127   255
```

The parser may detect any shunned characters appearing in a document instance and generate an error accordingly.

Syntax-reference character set

The **syntax-reference character set**[185] definition has an identical purpose and syntax to the document character set[172] defined in the first clause, except that it identifies the character set used by the **SGML declaration**[171] (not the prolog and document instance).

Function character identification

Function characters are special characters, of which there are at least three, the record-end (**RE**), the record-start (**RS**) and the word-space (**SPACE**), to which others may be added. The keyword **FUNCTION** introduces this section:

```
FUNCTION
        RE       13
        RS       10
        SPACE    32
        TAB      SEPCHAR   9
```

The default settings are as shown above. Each standard function has a name, for example 'RS,' and a decimal character value, for example '10.' Such a character can be represented in data using a **character reference**[062], either a **numeric character reference**, '
', or a **named character reference**, '&RS;'. The character values are determined by the syntax-reference character set, described above.

Additional function characters may be defined after the fixed ones. Each one consists of an **added function**[187] name, a **function class**[188] and also a character number. In the default example, the only additional function is the TAB function, of class type SEPCHAR, with a value of '9'.

The class must be one of the following:

- **FUNCHAR** (inert function)
- **SEPCHAR** (separator character)
- **MSOCHAR** (markup-scan-out character)
- **MSICHAR** (markup-scan-in character)
- **MSSCHAR** (markup-scan-suppress character)

An **inert function** is a function that has no meaning to SGML, so performs no role in the parsing process. Such a function will be defined purely for local use.

A **separator character function**, such as the Tab character, is added to the space character in that the parser views it as white space, to be used as markup parameter separators.

A **markup-scan-out character** and a **markup-scan-in character** are used in combination. These functions switch-off and switch-on parser checking for SGML markup. A **markup-scan-suppress character** performs both these roles, but for only the next real character in the data stream (it performs the role of an 'escape code'). The effect of these mechanisms is similar to the use of a marked section of type CDATA. None of these are applied by default, but are used in multi-character set applications for character set switching.

Naming rules

Naming rules dictate the characters allowed in a **name**[(055)] and a **name token**[(057)] (which is the same as a name, except that it has no name start character definitions), and within a **number token**[(058)], which is the same as a name token except that it must begin with a digit.

The standard specifies that names can begin with an upper case or lower case letter, and consist of further letters, as well as digits; for example 'MyElem9'. The naming rules section of the Concrete Syntax identifies additional characters to be allowed in names, and specifies whether lower case letters are distinguished from upper case letters.

A number of definitions follow the **NAMING** keyword. These are Lower Case Name Start (**LCNMSTRT**), Upper Case Name Start (**UCNMSTRT**), Lower Case Name Character (**LCNMCHAR**), Upper Case Name Character

(**UCNMCHAR**) and Name Case (**NAMECASE**). All must be present, even if some are not required as part of the re-definition.

The first two definitions add to the characters allowed at the start of names, and by default they add no characters:

```
NAMING
        LCNMSTRT    " "
        UCNMSTRT    " "
```

If used, these definitions must each contain the same number of additional characters, and they may also define the same characters:

```
        LCNMSTRT    ":#,"
        UCNMSTRT    "^##"
```

Character positions within the strings are significant. In the example above, the '^' symbol is the upper case equivalent of the ':' symbol, because both characters are in the same position (character one in the string).

The distinction between upper case and lower case echoes the same distinction in normal letters (such as 'a' and 'A'), and becomes important if letter case is deemed insignificant to the name, in which case characters are standardized to upper case. In the example above, ':' would become '^', and ',' would become '#', but '#' would remain unchanged. The name ':myname' would be considered the same as '^MYNAME', and '#myname' would be the same as '#MYNAME'.

The next two definitions are similar, but affect all characters in the name except for the first character. The definitions cannot re-use any of the characters used in the name-start definitions (because they inherit those definition values anyway). By default, both definitions add the same two characters, the hyphen '-' and the full-point '.':

```
        LCNMCHAR    "-."
        UCNMCHAR    "-."
```

The parser is able to ignore any case differences (by translating all to upper case), or to observe differences, so that 'My.Elem' is not the same name as 'MY.ELEM'. The keyword **NAMECASE** precedes information regarding case-sensitive rules for general objects (such as element names and delimiter strings), and for entities specifically:

```
        NAMECASE
            GENERAL    YES
            ENTITY     NO
```

The keyword **YES** specifies replacement of lower case with upper case (ignore case in comparison). The keyword **NO** specifies no replacement (case is significant). The example above shows the default situation, where only entity names are distinguished by case, so the entity 'MyEnt' is not the same as 'myent', but the element 'MyElem' is the same as 'myelem'.

Delimiter set

The **delimiter set**[(190)] section specifies the characters that may be used as delimiters and abbreviations for entity references (short references). The keyword **DELIM** precedes information on both general delimiters and short references:

```
DELIM
      GENERAL SGMLREF
      SHORTREF SGMLREF
```

The example above shows the default case. In both cases the reference concrete syntax defaults are used without modification (see the first page of the *Glossary*).

The keyword **GENERAL** precedes the required keyword **SGMLREF**, which is simply there as a reminder that defaults exist. Replacement definitions are added using names and literal pairs. The name must be one of the abstract syntax keywords:

```
GENERAL SGMLREF
        STAGO   "*"
        TAGC    "-"
```

In the example above, markup tag delimiters are re-defined. A start-tag would appear as '*mytag-' instead of the default '<mytag>'.

The **short reference delimiters**[(192)] keyword **SHORTREF** precedes a list of delimited strings, each one adding a character or characters that may be mapped to entity names, and be accepted as a reference to the entity:

```
SHORTREF
    SGMLREF
    "**" -- note open --
```

The example above adds the string '**' to the default set. A **short reference mapping declaration**[(150)] may be used to map this string to an entity name, and an **entity declaration**[(101)] may replace the entity reference with an element start-tag:

```
<!ENTITY mynote STARTTAG "note">
<!SHORTREF general "**" mynote
                .... ......>
```

The data fragment below includes the '**' short reference:

```
<p>This is a **special NOTE.
```

The parser translates this to:

```
<p>This is a <note>special NOTE.
```

Reserved name use

The **reserved name use**[193] section allows reserved names to be changed. The most likely use for this feature is to create foreign language variants of the SGML language for DTD authors not conversant with English. The keyword **NAMES** introduces this feature, and it is always followed by another keyword, **SGMLREF**, to indicate that defaults exist. All default values are implied, so the reference concrete syntax contains only:

```
NAMES
      SGMLREF
```

Replacement values are entered as pairs of names and literal values. The name is the default name, and the literal contains the replacement for it:

```
NAMES
      SGMLREF
      ELEMENT "MYELEM"
      ENTITY  "MYENTITY"
```

The example above re-defines the reserved name keyword ELEMENT to 'MYELEM'. An element declaration appearing in a conformant DTD would appear as:

```
<!MYELEM book -- (chapter+)>
```

Reserved names that are utilized within the SGML declaration itself cannot be changed. The SGML declaration always uses the reference concrete syntax (if this were not the case, a further preparation stage would be required). For example, the keyword SGMLREF may not be altered.

Quantity set

The **quantity set**[194] section allows re-definition of maximum values for the quantities of various objects, such as the number of characters in a name (default eight characters), or the number of levels of element nesting allowed (default 24 levels). The default or re-defined values are intended to be used by SGML application software, including parsers, to reserve enough memory for current state information. For example, to store the name of the current element by default requires eight bytes of memory to be reserved. Note that this definition is distinct from capacity set definitions, such as the total number of elements allowed in a document (default 35000), where buffers are not relevant but other kinds of storage (such as stacks or heaps) are relevant.

The keyword **QUANTITY** introduces this section, and is always followed by the keyword **SGMLREF** as a reminder that default values exist. Changes to default values are defined using name and number pairs (the full list of reserved names for the quantity definitions are provided in the *Reference Quantity Set* table in Chapter 14):

```
QUANTITY
     SGMLREF
  NAMELEN 32
```

In the example above, the length of the NAME type is re-defined to a maximum of 32 characters (as it is in the **CALS declaration**). Taking advantage of this re-definition, an element can be named 'thisismyelement' and an entity may be named 'ThisIsMyLongEntity'. It is almost certain that the forthcoming revision to SGML will also increase these and other limits, as the existing values were set when computer memory was relatively meager compared with today's systems.

Feature use

The feature use clause of the SGML declaration determines the types of markup minimization allowed and the possibility of linking to style-sheets, and also controls the use of other, miscellaneous features of the language.

Following the **FEATURES** keyword, a number of other keywords introduce areas of control, and fall into three general categories:

- markup minimization
- link type features
- other features

Markup minimization

Markup minimization is used to reduce the number of keystrokes required to add markup to a document during the authoring process. The size of a document in terms of storage requirements is also affected (perhaps significantly in the case of large and heavily coded documents).

Markup minimization features have no effect on markup structures, and a document instance created using one or more of the minimization techniques described below may be converted into the fully expanded form at any time. This can be done without affecting the document structure (and is termed **normalizing** the document).

The keyword **MINIMIZE** identifies the section of the SGML declaration concerned with markup minimization. Following this keyword there are a number of declarations, each comprising at least a relevantly named keyword and a declared setting (**YES** or **NO**) in the following order:

```
MINIMIZE
     DATATAG   NO
     OMITTAG   YES
     RANK      NO
     SHORTTAG  YES
```

All of these features tend to be ignored by software that generates SGML markup, such as most modern SGML-aware word processors, which automatically produce fully **normalized** markup.

The **DATATAG** keyword is used to indicate the possibility of using normal data characters simultaneously as markup characters. It is a precursor to the facilities offered by the short reference feature. By default, this feature is inactive, and is rarely activated, and is not further explored in this book.

The **OMITTAG** keyword is used to indicate the possibility of omitting markup tags. It is used in conjunction with element declarations in the DTD:

```
<!ELEMENT init - O .....>
```

By default this feature is active, so the '-' or 'O' characters are required in element declarations. When de-activated these characters would be omitted.

The **RANK** keyword allows element rank values to be omitted from markup tags. For example, the element Head3 is represented as just 'head', and context supplies the information that this is a third level header. The rank concept is not popular, is not well supported by software, and by default this minimization technique is inactive. It is probably best to avoid it.

The **SHORTTAG** keyword allows various parts of markup tags to be omitted by allowing the **minimized start-tag**[015] and **minimized end-tag**[020] options to be used.

This includes the **empty start-tag**[016] and **empty end-tag**[021]:

```
<para>First para</para><>Second para</> ...
```

This also includes the **unclosed start-tag**[017] and **unclosed end-tag**[022]:

```
<para<emphasis>Bold paragraph.</emphasis</para>
```

And finally, this also includes the **net-enabling start-tag**[018] and **null end-tag**[023]:

```
<para>Some <emphasis/bold words/ in text ...
```

Link type features

The link type features refer to methods of linking the SGML document to one or more style-sheet documents. This approach to adding stylistic information to SGML data is not widely used, and is not further covered in this book. Alternative approaches include the **FOSI** and **DSSSL** schemes.

Other features

The miscellaneous features of SGML are indicated by the **OTHER** keyword, followed by feature defining keywords, each in turn followed by at least a **YES** or **NO** keyword:

```
OTHER
     CONCUR   YES   12
     SUBDOC   YES   6
     FORMAL   NO
```

The **CONCUR** keyword specifies the number of concurrent document types available. If set to **NO**, only the base document type is available (a single DTD). This feature is not further explored in this book, as it is not widely used.

The **SUBDOC** keyword specifies whether at least one **SGML subdocument entity**[003] may be present, and if so how many are allowed (for example, '6').

The **FORMAL** keyword may specify that a **public identifier**[074] is checked to validate that it is also a **formal public identifier**, that the format of the public identifier name conforms to ISO rules (see the *External Entities* section of Chapter 6). By default no such check is made, as indicated by the **NO** keyword.

Application-specific information

In the final part of an SGML declaration, information of a system specific nature may be included.

Following the **APPINFO** keyword, either the keyword **NONE** is present, or a literal string appears. The parser will not check the contents of this string, if present, and its meaning is assumed to be significant to application software:

```
APPINFO
        NONE
```

Examples of its use include the ICADD initiative and HyTime; in both cases the extra information is used to inform a suitable program that the DTD supports the scheme:

```
APPINFO
      "HYTIME"
```

Standard SGML declarations

Standard declarations should be used when possible. The reference concrete syntax, core concrete syntax and CALS declaration are described and compared.

To encourage compatibility between systems, the use of standard declarations is advised. A conforming SGML application must support at least one of the two pre-defined syntaxes, named the reference concrete syntax and the core concrete syntax.

The **reference concrete syntax** is described in various places throughout this book, and is shown in full at the end of this chapter. In order to use this syntax, the **SYNTAX** keyword is followed by the public identifier shown below:

```
SYNTAX "ISO 8879:1986//SYNTAX Reference//EN"
```

The alternative is the **core concrete syntax**, which is the same as the reference concrete syntax except that short references are disallowed. In order to use this syntax, the **SYNTAX** keyword is followed by the public identifier shown below:

```
SYNTAX "ISO 8879:1986//SYNTAX Core//EN"
```

Popular use has also been made of the **CALS declaration**, which provides larger maximum values for some quantities. The **NAMELEN** value is changed from 8 to 32, the **LITLEN** value is changed from 240 to 2048 and the **ATTCNT** value is changed from 40 to 80.

```
QUANTITY     SGMLREF
             LITLEN 2048
             NAMELEN 32
             ATTCNT 80
```

This means that more attributes may be defined for an element, and element names and attribute values may be longer:

```
<thisismytag myIDattribute="thisismyID">
```

In the illustration of the **Basic Declaration** shown below, bold text refers to separately stored parts of the declaration shown later, and superscript numbers in brackets are not part of the declaration, but references to the relevant charts in the *Road Map* section:

```
[171]
<!SGML "ISO 8879-1986"
         [174]
   BASESET "ISO 646-1983//CHARSET
     International Reference Version (IRV)//ESC
     2/5 4/0
         [175]
   DESCSET 0     9     UNUSED
           9     2     9
          11     2     UNUSED
          13     1     13
          14    18     UNUSED
          32    95     32
         127     1     UNUSED
         [174]
   BASESET "ISO Registration Number 109//CHARSET
     ECMA-94 Right Part of Latin Alphabet
     Nr. 3//ESC 2/9 4/3"
         [175]
   DESCSET 128    32     UNUSED
           160     5     32
           165     1     "SGML User's Group logo"
```

```
          166    8   38   --includes 5 unused for
                              NONSGML--
          254    1   127 --move 127 to unused
                              pos. as--
          255    1   UNUSED --255 is shunned--
       (180)
CAPACITY PUBLIC "ISO 8879:1986//CAPACITY
                    Reference//EN"
       (181)
SCOPE DOCUMENT
       (182)
SYNTAX PUBLIC "ISO 8879:1986//
                    SYNTAX Reference//EN"
       (195)
FEATURES
  MINIMIZE DATATAG NO OMITTAG YES  RANK NO SHORTTAG YES
  LINK   SIMPLE NO IMPLICIT NO EXPLICIT NO
  OTHER   CONCUR NO SUBDOC NO FORMAL NO
APPINFO NONE>
```

The **reference concrete syntax**, as called from the 'SYNTAX Reference'
public identifier above (see Chapter 14 for details on pre-defined names and
quantities):

```
SYNTAX
     (184)
     SHUNCHAR CONTROLS 0 1 2 3 4 5 6 7 8 9 10 11
               12 13 14 15 16 17 18 19 20 21 22 23
               24 25 26 27 28 29 30 31 127 155
     (174)
     BASESET 0 128 0
     (186)
     FUNCTION RE          13
              RS          10
              SPACE       32
              TAB SEPCHAR 9
     (189)
     NAMING    LCNMSTRT    ""
               UCNMSTRT    ""
               LCNMCHAR    "-."
               UCNMCHAR    "-."
               NAMECASE GENERAL YES
                        ENTITY NO
     (190)
     DELIM     GENERAL   SGMLREF
               SHORTREF  SGMLREF
     (193)
     NAMES     SGMLREF
     (194)
     QUANTITY SGMLREF
```

9. Cross-references

A popular feature of electronic publishing is the ability to have software perform the otherwise time-consuming task of locating and accessing remote information from references in the text. For example, when the reader encounters such text as 'see section 9 for details,' a software link should provide instant access to the specified section.

This chapter first introduces the concept of cross-reference links, then describes how such links are implemented within an SGML document. It closes with a discussion on choosing appropriate schemes for creating and maintaining unique identification codes, including a look at the HyTime standard.

The principles

The concepts behind cross-references and supporting products are explored.

An electronic cross-reference is also known as a **hypertext link**. A link can be visualized as a length of string, attached to the document at both ends with a pin. One pin represents the **target**. This is the end-point of the link, the referenced text, table, picture etc. The other pin represents the **source**. This is the start-point of the link, usually text directing the reader's attention to the target.

An electronic document **browser** application provides a mechanism for instant traversal from source to target objects. The browser highlights source text to draw the attention of the reader, and instantly displays the desired target object if the reference is selected.

Browsers must have some means to link the source to the target. To achieve this, each target object is identified by a unique name or code, so that any reference to it will be unambiguous. All references to the target contain a copy of this code. When the browser software is active, it uses these matching codes to provide a traversable link.

Browsers that do not work with SGML as the underlying data format may require the document author to insert the links manually, by physically locating and selecting both the source text and the target objects on-screen. When a document contains many references, some to distant objects, this can be a very time-consuming activity. In addition, this task may need to be repeated each time the document is edited and re-published. The latter part of this chapter is dedicated to exploring how to avoid this expensive task when using SGML-based coding schemes.

SGML cross-references

SGML cross-references can be checked using an SGML parser by employing the dedicated attribute types, ID and IDREF.

A specific mechanism for adding cross-reference links to SGML documents is provided by the standard, and there are at least two benefits to using the approved scheme. First, many SGML-aware applications use the official technique to automatically translate this information into their own linking schemes (including electronic book browsers and DTP packages). Second, because the parser is aware of this scheme it can check the links. Each target identifier must be unique, and each source identifier must match a target identifier. If two target identifiers share a value the parser reports the duplication as an error, and if a source identifier value is not also present in a target object, the parser reports a 'hanging pointer' error (the source points to nothing).

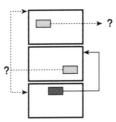

Link codes

Attributes are used to hold the link values in both source and target elements. The attribute values conform to general name limits, which can be re-defined in the SGML declaration. By default, the link code is limited to alphabetic or numeric characters, and the symbols '-' and '.', but must start with an alphabetic character. The reference concrete syntax name lengths are limited to eight characters (for this reason, the CALS declaration, which allows 32 characters, is often preferred). Valid examples include 'X-123', 'peter' and 'ABC.DEF'. By default, names are not case-sensitive, so a target value of 'mytag' will be matched with a source value of 'MyTag'.

Each object that may be the target of a link contains an attribute that holds the link value. Typical attribute names include Anchor, Target and Id. For example, a Section element may be the target of a link:

```
<section target="X123">
<title>This is Section 6</title>
...
...
</section>
```

An element is usually created specifically for the purpose of providing a platform for references, typically named Link, or Xref. This element contains an appropriately named attribute, typically Id, Ref or Target:

```
<para>Please refer to Section 6<Xref ref="X123"> for more
details</para>
...
...
<section target="X123">
<title>This is Section 6</title>
```

In the example above, the value 'X123' links the reference text to the appropriate Section element.

The document author must be aware of the unique identifier required to identify a specific target when inserting a reference element. This is the subject of the *Link Value Strategies* section later in this chapter.

Identifier (ID)

An attribute that is used to hold a link value within target elements is declared to be of type **ID** (Identifier). The parser checks a document containing ID type attributes to ensure that all the values encountered are unique. For example:

```
<!ATTLIST section  target  ID #REQUIRED>
```

The declaration above allows the following document instance to be created:

```
<section target="X123">
<title>This is Section 6</title>
...
</section>
<section target="X123">
<title>This is Section 7</title>
```

However, the parser would object to the second of these sections having an ID of 'X123', which is already assigned to another element.

Identifier reference (IDREF)

An attribute that is used to hold a link value within source elements has a type of IDREF (Identifier Reference). The parser checks a document containing IDREF type attributes to ensure that all the values encountered correspond to an ID value elsewhere in the document.

```
<!ELEMENT xref - O EMPTY>
<!ATTLIST xref  ref  IDREF #REQUIRED>
```

The declarations above allow text to be linked to the target objects using Xref elements:

```
<section target="X122">
<title>This is Section 6</title>
<para>Please refer to Section 7<xref ref="X999">
for more details.</para>
</section>
<section target="X123">
<title>This is Section 7</title>
```

However, in this example the parser would detect that the value 'X999' does not match any of the ID values found in the document, and report a suitable error message.

Reference schemes

Three schemes for adding reference markup are discussed.

The choice of approach to adding cross-reference elements to the document depends partly on the effect desired, and partly on the limitations of the electronic browsers currently available.

There are three basic methods to discuss:

- icon / push-button selection
- text selection
- auto replacement

The Icon approach was shown in the examples above. An empty element is used to identify the location of a reference. The element is placed immediately after the referencing text:

```
Refer to Section 7<xref source="SEC7"> for
details.
```

The browser converts such elements to icons (perhaps an arrow, pointing hand or bullet symbol). To traverse the link, the icon is selected:

Refer to Section 7@ for details.

The second approach encapsulates the referencing text:

```
Refer to <xref source="SEC7">Section 7</xref>
for details.
```

The browser displays the embedded text in a distinctive manner, usually colored and underlined. To traverse the link, the text is selected:

Refer to **Section 7** for details.

The third method replaces the referencing text with an empty element:

```
Refer to <xref source="SEC7"> for details.
```

In this example, the words 'Section 7' are missing. The title of the target object is inserted into the reference text as it is displayed (this is termed a **transclusion**). As before, the link is traversed by selecting this text, but this approach has the advantage that if the title or section number is changed, the amendment is automatically updated at each reference point. The disadvantage is that either the browser software must provide this facility, or pre-processing software must be written to massage the data prior to publishing. Direct viewing of the SGML document by any other means is hindered by the missing text.

Link value strategies

SGML does not specify or recommend any particular strategy for designating link values. Three general approaches are introduced and compared.

An SGML parser accepts almost any coding scheme for generating unique target values. However, document authors are usually required to generate identifiers for new objects, or refer to existing identifiers when creating a reference. The scheme adopted should not inconvenience an author, especially when many references are required.

There are three commonly used schemes to consider:

- sequential
- title text
- abbreviated reference

A sequential scheme simply assigns the next available code number to any new object. If the last object defined had an ID of 'X-77776', then the next object will have an ID of 'X-77777'. These ID numbers may be assigned automatically by authoring or database software, but authors must look up target values from a list or perform a database search when inserting references, and this can be a costly process.

The title text scheme uses the title of the target object, or an abbreviation of it:

```
<xref source="Summary">
```

This approach is suitable for small documents with distinctive titles, though standards for abbreviating longer titles must be established to avoid the need to look up the abbreviated title. Duplicate names are also a danger. For example, a chapter named 'Introduction' would be given the same identifier as an Introduction section of another chapter.

An abbreviated reference scheme uses the navigation methods devised for manual navigation, such as 'See Chapter 7, Paragraph 12,' but codifies this information to serve as an attribute value, 'ch7pa12'. This approach allows for automatic generation of target ID values, and document authors can deduce a target value from the reference text when inserting a reference element.

External links

Links to other documents can be created but not validated. There is no official scheme for external links.

The **ID/IDREF** mechanism only works within a single SGML document. A parser cannot access other documents to validate that a source value matches a target object. A link to another document is termed an **external link**, but there is no official SGML mechanism for storage of external links. An example of external links can be seen in the HTML model (see Chapter 12 for details).

When designing a DTD, some consideration should be given to exactly what *is* an SGML document. The following example is typical.

A team of authors are working on a reference book. Each author is working on a single chapter. Although some links refer to objects in the same chapter, others refer to the content of other chapters in the book. At least four approaches to inserting and checking links are possible, and each is described below.

The first approach treats each chapter as a document instance. The internal links work correctly, but another non-parsable scheme must be used for links to other chapters.

The second approach treats the entire book as a document instance, but also allows chapter instances. Links are not checked during the authoring or editing process, as errors would result. An 'internal' DTD variant is created that re-defines ID and IDREF attributes to CDATA attributes, so no errors result during parsing of a chapter (the parser does not attempt to check the values). Software merges the chapters on completion of the book, and the 'external' DTD variant, which includes ID and IDREF type attributes, is used to parse the result.

The third approach treats the entire book as a document instance throughout the authoring process. External entities are declared for each chapter. Authors can work on their own chapters (assuming that the authoring software will accept a document with no document type declaration), but all parse operations must be activated on the entire book. An entity manager merges the components for publication.

The fourth approach uses the **HyTime** standard. The HyTime scheme allows links to be made to external documents by adding another layer to the ID/IDREF mechanism. See the next section for details.

Note that the forthcoming revision to SGML is likely to include a scheme for referring to ID elements in another document. This scheme will allow an entity reference to be placed in the IDREF attribute, prior to the target name. The entity locates and identifies the other document.

HyTime

HyTime adds inter-document linking functionality to SGML documents.

HyTime is not an extension of SGML, but uses existing SGML structures to define various linking schemes. For example, processing instructions are used at the top of a document to announce that the document is HyTime compliant, and specific attribute names and values are deemed significant.

HyTime provides several techniques for creating links, including one that locates a target object by its sequential position within an element ('the target text is the phrase starting at word five and ending at word nine in the given Para element'), and another that locates a target by its position in the document hierarchical tree ('take the first branch on the left, the third sub-branch on the right, and arrive at the second twig on the left').

One of the first features of HyTime to be widely used helps solve the problem of inter-document linking described in the previous section. Each document remains a separate SGML document, but parses without error because a 'dummy' target is made *within* the source document. External HyTime links are then added to the 'dummy' targets. However, HyTime links are not part of the SGML standard, and can only be followed by HyTime-aware software (in the same way as HTML-aware Web browsers understand another means of linking between documents; see Chapter 12 for details).

HyTime linking requires the declaration of at least two specific elements, called **Name Location** (**Nameloc**), and **Name List** (**Nmlist**), as shown below:

```
<!ELEMENT NAMELOC  - O  (NMLIST*) >
<!ELEMENT NMLIST   - O  (#PCDATA)>
<!ATTLIST NAMELOC  HyTime  NAME  nameloc
     id        ID   #REQUIRED
     ... >
<!ATTLIST NMLIST   HyTime  NAME  nmlist
     nametype (entity|element)   entity
     docorsub  ENTITY      #IMPLIED
     ... >
```

In fact, it is the HyTime attributes that identify the elements that perform the respective roles, not the names of the elements themselves. If Nameloc and Nmlist are inconvenient names for these elements, they may be changed.

The element or elements used to hold the source point of a link must have a fixed attribute named HyTime, in this case specifying that the element is a 'clink' element:

```
<!ELEMENT MyRef  - -  (#PCDATA)>

<!ATTLIST MyRef  HyTime  NAME       #FIXED clink
                 id      IDREF      #REQUIRED>
```

In the example below, the Myref element encloses the source text, and targets a local Name Location element:

```
<nameloc id=CH3SE5>
...
</nameloc>
For details see <myref id=CH3SE5>Chapter 3,
Section 5</myref>.
```

The Name Location element contains a Name List element that provides the ID number of the target object. It has a **Nametype** attribute, which is used to specify that the enclosed name refers to an ID value instead of an entity name:

```
<nameloc id=CH3SE5>
  <nmlist nametype=element>CHAP-3.5</nmlist>
</nameloc>
```

In the example above, the Name Location element identified as 'CH3SE5' contains a Name List that refers to an object (possibly but not necessarily in another document) with an ID of 'CHAP-3.5'. The local Name Location element will satisfy an SGML parser because it provides a legal target for the IDREF attribute in the Myref element, and because the text 'CHAP-3.5' 'appears' to be insignificant (it is merely #PCDATA).

However, at this point the target document has not been identified. There is more than one way to do this, but perhaps the simplest is to make the Name List refer to an entity that locates the remote file. The **Docorsub** attribute is used to provide this link:

```
<!ENTITY chapter3 SYSTEM "C:\CHAPS\CHAPTER3.SGM">

<nameloc id=CH3SE5>
  <nmlist nametype=element
          docorsub="chapter3">CHAP-3.5</nmlist>
</nameloc>
```

In the example above, the Name List element refers to an entity called 'chapter3'. The named entity locates a file called 'CHAPTER3.SGM'.

To summarize, the Myref element uses an IDREF to point to the Name Location element with an ID of 'CH3SE5'. As the 'real' object required is in another document, the embedded Name List element refers to an entity identified as 'chapter3', and to an element in the file (located via this entity) with an ID of 'CHAP-3.5'.

```
...
For details see <myref id=CH3SE5>Chapter 3,
Section 5</myref>.                |
...                              /
-------------------------- /  -------------
...                        /
<section myid=CHAP-3.5>
<title>This is Chapter 3, Section 5</title>
...
```

10. CALS tables

SGML does not provide a standard model for representation of tabular material. Although an ISO model exists (in technical report **ISO/IEC TR 9573**), a different *de facto* standard has arisen from widespread use of software that supports the **CALS** DTDs, which were defined by the US Department of Defense for interchange of documentation between the DoD and its sub-contractors (the acronym currently stands for '*Continuous Acquisition and Lifecycle Support*').

The table model described in this chapter is derived from Appendix A of *MIL-M-28001B* (26 June 1993), and includes many usage recommendations from the SGML Open Committee technical memorandum TR 9502:1995, of 19 October 1995, which addresses several ambiguities in the standard.

When to use CALS tables

SGML may represent tabular material in any number of ways, so why attempt to apply conformity, and the compromises this implies? CALS is not always the best solution – it does little to meet the SGML ideal of replacing format with meaning.

In one sense, any SGML-aware application can 'understand' any SGML table model. The DTD provides enough information to ensure that the correct elements and attributes are used in the construction of a table. In this sense, a table is no different to any other structure. However, by its nature a table makes heavy use of elements or attributes, particularly if it includes border lines, straddled cells and varying text alignments. In addition, there are obvious difficulties reading text intended to be displayed in a two-dimensional grid when it is presented in a linear fashion. The solution to these problems is to 'hide' the tags, and to display the content in its true tabular form. But to do this, the composition software must be aware of the purpose of relevant elements and attributes, and a recognized standard is essential to justify the effort involved in writing WYSIWYG editing and composition routines.

The CALS model has arisen as the *de facto* solution due to its use in software developed for US defense applications.

Note: The CALS table model has been used to create all of the tables in this book.

The CALS format should not be used if the table structure is simple, and has meaningful columns or rows which need to be identified for database searching or re-formatting in non-tabular representations. In this case, specific elements should be defined for the structure, and software relied upon to translate these elements into a table layout on demand.

A good example of this is a catalog, containing tables that include an item number column and a price column. For software to update the prices, it must be able to recognize these columns. A sensible structure would be:

```
<prices>
  <item><code>XYZ-15<price>987</item>
  <item><code>XYZ-22<price>765</item>
</prices>
```

Code	Price
XYZ-15	£ 987
XYZ-22	£ 765

However, more difficulties displaying or printing this information in tabular format should be expected.

The rest of this chapter assumes that the effort of adding a sensible structure to the DTD cannot be justified, in which case the CALS model is ideal.

The table structure

The table is divided into logical segments, which in turn form grid-like structures. Column widths are also discussed.

The entire table is enclosed in a **Table** element. The Table element may contain an Identifier attribute, **Id**, which serves as the target for all cross-reference links (see Chapter 9). An optional **Orient** attribute, specifies a portrait ('port') or landscape ('land') orientation for the entire table. The default setting assumes a portrait orientation. An optional **Page Wide** attribute (**Pgwide**), specifies whether the table spans only a single column in a multi-column page (using a value of '0') or spans the entire page or display width. A value of '0' (zero) indicates no spanning. A value of '1' allows spanning. When the table is displayed in landscape it has an implied value of '1' (span all columns), simply because it would not be necessary to display the table in landscape orientation if the extra width this provides were not required.

The table is composed of one or more **Table Group** elements (**Tgroup**), which define the number of columns present using the **Cols** attribute.

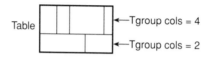

Note that some composing software will only accept a single Table Group element.

The Table Group element may contain an **Id** attribute which serves as the target for cross-reference links.

Each Table Group usually contains a **Column Specification** element (**Colspec**), for each column present. These elements are not required for very simple tables, but if present they have attributes to define column widths, column names, and defaults for border lines and text alignment.

There may also be **Span Specification** elements present (**Spanspec**), which are used to aid cell straddling, and are described in detail later.

Both the Columns Specification and Span Specification elements are empty (in the sense that they do not surround data or other elements). They exist only as containers for various attributes.

The general structure:

```
<table id="tab123">
  <tgroup cols="4">
    <colspec ...>
    <spanspec ...>
    ......
    ......
  </tgroup>
</table>
```

Column widths

Unlike most other aspects of table creation, definition of column widths can rarely be automated, as the author often needs to make a subjective decision on how to divide the available space, so the issues raised in this section must be appreciated by document authors if fundamental design mistakes are to be avoided.

The Column Specification element contains a **Colwidth** attribute to determine the width of the specific column. For example:

```
<colspec colnum="1" colwidth="2 CM">
<colspec colnum="2" colwidth="1.5 CM">
<colspec colnum="3" colwidth="4 CM">
<colspec colnum="4" colwidth="1 CM">
```

The column widths may be defined using a number of notations:

- PT (points)
- CM (centimeters)
- MM (millimeters)
- PI (picas)
- IN (inches)

If none of these are specified, 'PT' acts as the default, so a value of '12' is the same as '12 PT' (though some applications may insist on a measurement notation). Case is not significant, so 'pt' is the same as 'PT'.

However, such an approach is not suitable for multimedia publishing, where the available column widths vary (depending on the current page, column or screen width). A more neutral approach uses proportional widths, where each column is measured only as a relative comparison with the other columns.

The notation used for proportional widths is an asterisk '*'. A definition of '1*' (or just '*') specifies the smallest unit available. A width of '3*' specifies three times the smallest unit. The size of a single unit is not predefined, but is calculated whenever the table is composed to a specific screen, page or column width. The actual size of the smallest unit is determined by adding together all the unit values, then dividing the available width by this figure. If the available width is 60 millimeters, for example, and the column specification elements declare width values of '1*', '2*' and '3*', then the value of one unit is $60/(1+2+3) = 10$. The first column is therefore $1 \times 10 = 10$ mm wide, the second is $2 \times 10 = 20$ mm, and the third is $3 \times 10 = 30$ mm.

If no value is supplied for a particular column, a proportional width of '1*' is assumed.

It is not a requirement that any column be defined using the smallest unit. The previous example could be defined using the values '2*', '4*' and '6*', for example, though there would be little point in doing so. However, this fact is important because fractional values are not advised (some composing software will not recognize fractions). An example above had one column set to '1 cm' and another set to '1.5 cm'. Equivalent proportional values should be larger to avoid the decimal point. Values of '2*' and '3*' would suffice.

Much larger values can be used when necessary. If a two-column table had one column only slightly wider than the other, the proportional values could be '20*' and '21*'.

Fixed and proportional width values may be mixed, though it is not advised for the same reasons as stated previously. If used, the fixed width columns reserve the required horizontal space, and the proportional width columns must share the remaining space using the scheme outlined above.

Table segments

Each Table Group is further divided into three logical divisions; the **Table Header** segment, **Thead**, the **Table Footer** segment, **Tfoot**, and the **Table Body** segment, **Tbody**. The Table Body is the only required element of these three. If present, however, the Table Footer is placed before the Table Body in the data stream.

Table head
Table footer
Table body

This unusual configuration aids pagination software when dealing with multi-page tables (note that the element structure has no concept of pages – composing software must decide where to split large tables across pages). By placing the footer text before the body text, composing software is able to access the footer text for insertion at the base of the first page containing a reference to it.

Table Header rows are identified so that the enclosed text may be repeated at the top of each page (and possibly appear in a different style to the body text).

Note that the Table Header and Table Footer segments may include overriding Colspec elements (but not Spanspec elements), as these segments may have differing column widths to the main body of the table. If used, any missing re-definitions default to a proportional width of '1*'.

The CALS model is 'row oriented,' which means that the table is built row-by-row, with each row containing entries.

The three segments in the table group are all composed of one or more **Row** elements (even the footer segment), and each Row element contains a number of **Entry** elements:

```
<tbody>
  <row>
    <entry>Red</entry>
    <entry>Urgent</entry>
  </row>
  ...
  ...
</tbody>
```

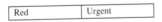

The number of rows in a segment (and ultimately in a Table Group) is determined purely by the number of Row elements present.

The number of Entries in a Row is pre-determined by the value of the **Cols** attribute in the **Tgroup** element. There may not be more Entry elements within a Row element than allowed by this value. Leading empty entries may in theory be omitted by including the **Name Start** attribute (see the next section) or **Colname** attribute in the first real Entry, though some composing software may not support this. It is known that some software requires trailing empty Entry elements to be present, though this restraint is not defined by CALS.

Straddled entries

The content of an entry may cross logical cell boundaries, both horizontally and vertically.

An **Entry** may expand horizontally to the right, and occupy the space normally reserved for other entries.

Various attributes are used to indicate the scope of the straddle. In all cases, attribute values refer to column names, as defined in the **Colspec** elements. The Column Specification element has a **Colname** attribute, which attaches a user-defined name to a logical column number. For example, column 1 may be named 'color.' Any later reference to 'color' is actually a reference to column 1:

```
<colspec colnum="1" colname="color">
<colspec colnum="2" colname="priority">
```

This indirect method of specifying a column also allows new columns to be inserted, without invalidating such references. The column named 'color' may be easily changed to column 2, for example, and all references to 'color' will be affected.

The **Entry** element has straddling attributes. The name of the first column in a spanning entry is placed in the **Name Start** attribute, **Namest**. The name of the last column in a spanning entry is placed in the **Nameend** attribute:

```
<colspec colnum="1" colname="color">
<colspec colnum="2" colname="priority">
.......
<row>
   <entry>Red<entry>Urgent
</row>
<row>
   <entry namest="color" nameend="priority">
   Blue (with no priority indicator)
</row>
```

Red	Urgent
Blue (with no priority indicator)	

Note that the second row contains only one Entry element. Normally, all the Entry elements required to fill a row will be present, even if they contain no text, but in this case composing software is expected to take account of the previous, straddling Entry. A second Entry element in the second row of the example above would be invalid according to the CALS model (though an SGML parser would not detect this error, as the structure still conforms to the DTD rules).

A more convenient mechanism for referring to ranges of columns is provided by the **Span Specification** element (**Spanspec**). This element defines a single name for a range of columns. It is of benefit when the same horizontal span is used several times, because repeated reference to the same start and end column names is a laborious task. This element includes the **Namest** and **Nameend** attributes to determine the range, and a new attribute called **Spanname** to label this range. The example below produces identical output to the previous example:

```
<colspec colnum="1" colname="color">
<colspec colnum="2" colname="priority">
<spanspec namest="color" nameend="priority"
         spanname="myspan">
.......
<row>
   <entry spanname="myspan">
   Blue (with no priority)</entry>
</row>
```

In the example above, the single name 'myspan' represents a range starting at 'color' and ending at 'priority'. These column names are defined in the Column Specification elements as column 1 and column 2 respectively. Therefore, 'myspan' ultimately indicates a span from column 1 to column 2.

Vertical straddling is achieved using the **Entry** attribute **Morerows**. The default value of this attribute is '0' (zero), indicating no vertical span. To span the Entry into lower rows, the value is changed to reflect the number of additional rows.

```
<row><entry>Red<entry>Urgent<entry>1</row>
<row>
   <entry>Blue</entry>
   <entry morerows="1">no priority indicator for
   these colors</entry>
   <entry>2</entry>
</row>
<row>
   <entry>brown</entry><!--NO ENTRY--><entry>3</entry>
</row>
```

Red	Urgent	1
Blue	no priority indi-	2
Brown	cator for these colors	3

Again, note that there are only two **Entry** elements in the final row, as the middle column is occupied by the Entry element above this position. The second Entry element is therefore deemed to occupy the third column. As before, it is incorrect to place three Entry elements here, but this rule is beyond the scope of a parser to validate.

Border lines

Border lines may surround the table, or separate specified columns, rows or entries.

There are two concepts embodied in CALS that relate to border lines. The first concerns lines around the entire table, which may be described as 'external' border lines. The second concerns lines between adjacent columns and adjacent rows, which may be described as 'internal' border lines.

The presence of external border lines is controlled by the **Frame** attribute in the **Table** element. Its value may be 'none', 'all', 'topbot', 'top', 'bottom' or 'sides'. The default setting is 'all', indicating the presence of a box around the table.

Internal border lines are defined using the **Column Separator** attribute (**Colsep**), and the **Row Separator** attribute (**Rowsep**). These attributes appear in various elements. They hold numeric values, where a value of '0' (zero) indicates no border line, and a value of '1' (one) represents the presence of a line. The value '1' is the default in both attributes, and in all affected elements, indicating that every column and every row (and therefore every cell) is surrounded by lines. Any value other than '0' may be used to indicate the presence of a border line, and some pagination systems infer further meaning from the value given (for example, '1' may represent a single line, '2' may represent a double line, '3' may represent a dashed line, and so on, though CALS does not presently make this distinction, and there are no agreed number-to-style relationships).

When the presence of a vertical border line is indicated, its position is assumed to be *to the right* of the column or entry concerned. When a horizontal border line is indicated, its position is assumed to be *below* the row or entry concerned.

It may seem that a conflict arises between the setting of the column separator of the last column, and the use of the **Frame** attribute described previously – both would seem to specify a vertical line to the right of the table. This conflict is avoided by ignoring any settings for the last column. The same principle is applied to the last row separator. In both cases, the Frame attribute must be utilized to gain the desired effect, and the default setting of 'all' places lines in these positions.

The elements that contain one or both of these attributes are Table, Table Group, Column Specification, Span Specification, Row, Entry Table and Entry. The principle adopted is that large objects indicate the majority case, and small objects override these settings. For example, the Table element may dictate that all rows have lines, but the Row element representing row six may specify that it has no line, so every row except row six will be followed by a horizontal line. This approach encourages efficient use of attributes. The document author is expected to generalize at each level of the table hierarchy, so as to avoid unnecessary work at the lower levels.

Border lines do not dissect straddled entries. This is illustrated in various examples within this chapter.

Text alignment

The position of text or other objects within the boundary of an entry can be set in various ways, both horizontally and vertically.

When the area of an entry is wider or higher than the text it encloses, the text by default appears in the top-left corner of the entry. However, the text may be re-aligned both horizontally and vertically. As with border lines and straddling entries, control of text alignment is provided by attributes, and managed by the judicious use of these attributes within the hierarchy of elements.

Several elements contain an **Align** attribute, which takes one of the following values: 'left', 'right', 'center', 'justify' or 'char'. This attribute controls horizontal alignment of text within an Entry element, and the first three settings listed above have an obvious effect. Note the American spelling of 'center' – some composing software will not recognize and apply this alignment if the attribute declaration uses the British spelling of 'centre'.

The 'justify' option aligns text both left and right, using extra inter-word spaces where necessary to achieve this effect. The 'char' option aligns text on a nominated character.

When the 'char' option is selected, further information is required. Both the character to be used for alignment, and the position of this character within the entry are needed. The significant character is specified in the **Char** attribute (typically, its value would be a full-point, '.', for alignment of decimal numbers in columns of figures). By default, this character will appear horizontally centered within the entry, but if this position is inconvenient, due to a combination of lack of space and unbalanced text, it can be changed using the **Character Offset** attribute, **Charoff**. The Charoff attribute value must be a numeric token that represents a percentage offset from the left edge of the entry. A value of '25', for example, would place the left edge of the significant character a quarter of the width of the column from the left edge of the cell.

In the following example, the first column is aligned on full-point, with a character offset of '30' percent, and the second column is aligned on comma, with a character offset of '60' percent:

465.2	6300,000
.987611	10,000
1.2345	1,250

Elements that contain the attributes described above are Table Group, Column Specification, Span Specification and Entry. In all cases, the default value is 'left'.

Vertical alignment is defined using the **Vertical Alignment** element (**Valign**), which is allowed in the Table Head element, the Table Body element, the Table Footer element, and the Row and Entry elements. The Vertical Alignment attribute may take the following values: 'top', 'bottom' and 'middle'. The default value is 'top'. As before, the Row and Entry elements may override higher level settings.

Note the Vertical Alignment option of 'middle' rather than 'center'. This is an example of the SGML restriction on name lists in attribute declarations. As explained previously, two attributes cannot share a name token value. In order to abbreviate the start-tag, as in the following example, there must be no ambiguity as to which attribute a value belongs. In this case, it is clear that Vertical Alignment is being defined:

```
<entry middle>
```

Entry content and inner tables

The entry element may contain further element structures, or be replaced by an embedded table.

Previous examples demonstrated that an Entry element may contain normal characters, but tables may be more complex than this. The CALS definition does not restrict the content of an Entry element to simple text, the DTD may define any required subelement structures. It may, for example, be necessary to allow multiple Paragraphs:

| This is the first paragraph. | |
| This is the second paragraph. | |

The Entry element content may be re-defined for specific purposes (no other element in a CALS table should be re-defined, because this would confuse software developed to deal with the standard).

Some applications require the further ability to contain tables within tables. A cell may need to contain a complete embedded table. The CALS standard does not allow a Table element to be contained within an Entry belonging to another Table, but instead defines a new element called **Entrytbl**, which is used in place of the Entry element.

The Entry Table element has most of the same attributes as the Entry element, but also has an additional Columns attribute, **Cols**, which works in the same way as the Columns attribute in the Table element.

An Entry Table is similar to a Table, in that it may contain Columns Specification, Span Specifications, Table Header and Table Body elements (though not footers):

```
<row><entry>Red</><entry>DANGER</><entry>1</>
<row>
    <entry>Amber</>
    <entrytbl cols="2">
        <tbody>
            <row><entry>flashing</>
            <entry>URGENT</></row>
            <row><entry>steady</>
            <entry>IMPORTANT</></row>
        </tbody>
    </entrytbl>
    <entry>2</entry>
</row>
<row><entry>Green</><entry>NORMAL</><entry>3</>
```

Red	DANGER		1
Amber	flashing	URGENT	2
	steady	IMPOR-	
		TANT	
Green	NORMAL		3

An Entry Table cannot be used in header and footer segments.

Although CALS provides this facility, extreme caution is advised as many applications do not support this feature. It is also possible to produce the same effect artificially (without using Entry Table elements), by defining the extra columns and rows required, and using the spanning feature to hide these columns and rows in surrounding entries. Although cumbersome, this method is guaranteed to be compatible with all CALS-aware applications (and was actually used to produce the table shown above, which therefore has four columns and four rows).

11. ISO 9573 math

Of various proposals for a standard scheme to represent mathematical formulae, the original **ISO** recommendations (embodied in the **ISO/IEC TR 9573** technical report) are now well supported by a range of SGML-aware applications, so may be seen as at least one of the main contenders. This model was incorporated into the CALS standard.

In theory, the 9573 standard has been superseded by another ISO standard, **ISO 12083:1991**. The newer version is more thorough, and meets a greater number of needs, but is not yet well supported by SGML-aware application software, and is not fully drafted at the time of writing.

Note: The ISO/IEC TR 9573 technical report also recommends a scheme for representing tabular material, but the **CALS table** scheme has since become the *de facto* standard (and is described in the previous chapter).

The rationale for having a standard coding scheme for mathematical formulae is the same as for tabular material – to make it feasible for application developers to develop composing software for **WYSIWYG** authoring, editing and publishing of such structures. Tools that hide complex coding from the author are vital for widespread acceptance of SGML.

Formula identification structures

The DTD fragment concerned has four outermost elements (when the fragment is included in a larger DTD, only four of the elements described in this chapter should be inserted directly into the 'wider' document, as all other elements described are child elements to these four). A mathematical formula may be defined as an **Inline Formula** (**F**), or as a **Display Formula** (**Df**), a number of which may be numbered within a **Display Formula Group** (**Dfg**). A **Display Formula Reference** element (**Dfref**) may be used within the general text to locate a referenced formula.

The difference between inline and display is simply that inline formulae do not force line-breaks, so remain embedded in the surrounding text. Display formulae break surrounding text into separate paragraphs. The possible content of the two types is identical, though it would be unwise to code a large, multi-layered structure as an inline formula:

```
<p>The sum <f>2 + 2 = 4</f> is correct.</p>

<p>The following sum:
<df>x = <fence>
<pile>a<above>b<above>c</pile>
</fence></df>
would not be viable as an inline sum.</p>
```

$$x = \begin{pmatrix} a \\ b \\ c \end{pmatrix}$$

The Display Formula element has three attributes, an **Identifier** (**Id**), an **Alignment** (**Align**) and a **Formula Number** (**Num**). The Identifier is used to create a **target** for cross-references from other elements (see Chapter 9), and must be unique. The Align attribute specifies how the formula is to be formatted in relation to the borders of the page or column, and takes a value of 'left' (the default), 'right' or 'center'.

The Display Formula Group element contains the same three attributes as the Display Formula element. If both elements contain a formula number, then the embedded display formula number is appended to the group number when composed. For example, a display formula group numbered '[1]' may contain two display formulae, numbered '[1a]' and '[1b].'

The Display Formula Reference element is an empty element that contains a **Reference Identifier** attribute (**Refid**). The value of this attribute must match an identifier value of a Display Formula element or a Display Formula Group element (see Chapter 9).

```
Please refer to formula<dfref refid="DF013"> for details.
```

Break

The **Break** element either forces or advises a line break in the formula, depending on the value of the **Type** attribute, which defaults to 'required' but may be set to 'optional':

```
<df> z  = x + 6y + <break type="optional"> 12x - 3y </df>
```

$$z = x + 6y +$$

$$+ 12x - 3y$$

Mark and Mark Reference

The **Mark** element is used to specify a horizontal position for alignment of subsequent lines. It is placed next to the character to be aligned. For later identification, the Mark element has an Identifier attribute, **Id**, which must hold a unique value:

```
<df> z =<mark id=F123> x + 6y + 12x - 3y </df>
```

In the example above, the equals character will be aligned with the same symbol in further formulae (that refer to identifier 'F123').

The **Mark Reference** element (**Markref**) is used to align a display formula with a previous formula. It has a **Reference Identifier** attribute (**Refid**), which must hold a value matching the relevant Mark element Identifier value:

```
<df> z <mark id=X123> = x + 6y + 12x - 3y </df>
<df> <markref refid=X123> = y - 3 </df>
```

$$z = x + 6y + 12x - 3y$$
$$= y - 3$$

Superscript and Subscript

The **Superscript** element (**Sup**) is used to display superscript text, either before, directly above or after the preceding item, depending on the value of the **Pos** attribute, which has a default value of 'post' (after), but which can also take values of 'pre' (prior) and 'mid' (middle):

```
x<sup>2</sup> and y<sup pos="pre">3</sup>
```

$$x^2 \, and \, {}^3y$$

Likewise, the **Subscript** element (**Sub**) is used to display subscript text, either before, directly below or after the preceding item, again depending on the value of the **Pos** attribute.

Box

The **Box** element is used to surround part of a formula inside a box shape:

```
<box>a+b</box>
```

Over

The Over-character element, **Over**, is used to add accents or diacritic marks to a character or characters.

The default is a single bar over the selected character or characters. Other marks are added by use of the **Type** attribute, which can take values of 'dot', 'dotdot', 'dot3', 'dot4', 'tie', 'tiebrace', 'hat', 'caron', 'acute', 'grave', 'cedil', 'ring', 'macron', 'ogonek', 'dblac', 'breve', 'tilde', 'vec', 'rvec', 'dyad' or the default, 'bar'. The position of the mark is specified using the **Pos** attribute, which can take values of 'mid' (through the character), 'above' (the default) or 'below'. The style of the mark is defined by the **Style** attribute, which can take a value of 'single' (the default), 'double', 'triple', 'dash', 'dots' or 'bold'.

```
<over type="bar" pos="below">
a+b</over>
```

$$\underline{a + b}$$

Tensor

The **Tensor** element defines tensor characters, by default standing above the character, though this can be changed using the **Position First** attribute (**Posf**) taking a value of 'sub' (the default being 'sup'). The tensor characters are held in the **Suffix** attribute. A space in this attribute indicates a switch between subscript and superscript positioning:

```
<tensor posf="sub" suffix="a bc d">Z</tensor>
```

$$z_a{}^{bc}{}_d$$

Function

Text in a formula is normally displayed in italic typeface. One exception is the **Function** element (**Mfn**), which specifies a function type and encloses a value.

Two attributes are used to hold the function type name, simply because the reference quantity set only allows 32 tokens in a group. The attribute **Type1** allows specification of the type names 'and', 'antilog', 'arc', 'arccos', 'arcsin', 'arctan', 'arg', 'colog', 'cos', 'cosh', 'cot', 'coth', 'csc', 'ctn', 'deg', 'det', 'dim', 'exp', 'for', 'gcd', 'glb', 'hom', 'if', 'Im', 'ker', 'lg', 'lim', 'ln', 'log', 'lub', 'max' and 'min'. The attribute **Type2** allows specification of the type names 'mod', 'Re', 'sec', 'sin', 'sinth', 'tan', 'tanh'. Use of attribute minimization techniques means that it is not necessary to remember which group holds a particular type name:

```
<mfn cos>x</mfn>
```

$$\cos(x + y)$$

If the function name is not one of those listed above, an alternative coding scheme allows the user to define a new function name. The **Function Name** attribute (**Fname**) holds the new function name. The **Of** attribute holds the argument:

```
<mfn><fname>myfunc</fname><of>x+y</of></mfn>
```

$$myfunc(x + y)$$

Roman and italic

There are occasions where it is convenient to present text in a normal roman typeface. The **Roman** element contains normal style text. The **Italic** element has the opposite effect in circumstances where text normally appears in roman typeface within a formula.

Vectors

Vectors in a formula are identified by the **Vec** element. The output is either italic with an arrow above, or bold:

```
<vec>v</vec>
```

$$\vec{v}$$

Fraction

Fractions in a formula are identified by the **Frac** element. The numerator and denominator alignment are set by the **Align** attribute, which can take values of 'left', 'right' or 'center' (the default). The numerator is contained within the **Numer** element. The denominator is contained within the **Over** element:

```
<frac align="left">
<numer>x</numer><over>y+z</over>
</frac>
```

$$\frac{x}{y+z}$$

Typical element minimization omits the Numerator tags and the Over end-tag:

```
<frac align="left">X<over>Y+Z</frac>
```

Derivative

The **Diff** element identifies a differential. The **Type** attribute specifies one of two possible differential types, 'normal' (the default) or 'partial'. The numerator is contained within the **Diffof** element, and the denominator is contained within the **By** element:

```
<diff><diffof>y</diffof><by>x</by></diff>
```

$$\frac{dy}{dx}$$

The Diffof element is required, so should be omitted by minimization:

```
<diff type="partial">x<by>y</diff>
```

Limit

The **Plex** element allows any character to be used as a limit. It includes the **Operator** element, which contains the limit character, and upper- and lower-limit values are specified by the **From** and **To** elements. The **Of** element completes the structure:

```
<plex><operator>&cup;</operator>
<from>i=1</from><to>10</to><of>x-i</of></plex>
```

$$\bigcup_{i=1}^{10} x - i$$

The Operator element, being compulsory, may be omitted by minimization. Other end-tags may also be omitted:

```
<plex>&cup;<from>i=1<to>10<of>a</plex>
```

Specific limit types are available using the elements **Sum, Integral** and **Product**:

```
<sum><from>i=1<to>10<of>a</sum>
```

$$\sum_{i=1}^{10} a$$

Pile

The **Pile** element places portions of a formula over each other. The **Align** attribute can take values of 'left', 'centre' (the default – also note British spelling) and 'right'. Each row is held in **Above** elements, except for the first row, which is enclosed in an **Above1** element:

```
<pile>
<above1>a</above1>
<above>b</above>
<above>c</above>
</pile>
```

$$a$$
$$b$$
$$c$$

As the Above1 element is required, it may be omitted through minimization, as may the Above end-tags:

```
<pile>a<above>b<above>c</pile>
```

Matrix

Matrices are identified by the **Matrix** element. The matrix is arranged in columns, using the **Col** element. Within each column, rows are arranged as described for the Pile structure, using **Above1** and **Above** elements:

```
<matrix>
<col>
<above1>1</above1>
<above>2</above>
</col>
<col>
<above1>3</above1>
<above>4</above>
</col>
</matrix>
```

$$1\ 3$$
$$2\ 4$$

As before, minimization should be employed to omit the Above1 element tags and Above element end-tags:

```
<matrix>
<col>1<above>2</col>
<col>3<above>4</col>
</matrix>
```

Roots and Power

The **Square Root** element (**Sqrt**) is used to hold a square root:

```
<sqrt>a+b</sqrt>
```

When the root is anything other than a square, the **Root** element is used in place of the Sqrt element. The **Degree** element specifies the degree of root, and the **Of** element specifies the operand:

```
<root><degree>4</degree><of>a+b</of></root>
```

```
<root>4<of>a+b</root>
```

The **Square** element is used to contain a square:

```
<square>a+b</square>
```

If the power is anything other than a square, the **Power** element is used in place of the Square element. The Degree and Of elements are used as described for the Root element:

```
<power><degree>3</degree><of>a+b</of></power>
```

```
<power><degree>3<of>a+b</power>
```

Fence

The **Fence** element contains a fenced formula. The **Type** attribute specifies the type of fence, and takes the values 'paren' (the default), 'bracket', 'angbrack', 'brace', 'bar' and 'none'. The **Style** attribute specifies the style of the fence, and takes the values 'single' (the default), 'double', 'triple', 'dash', 'dots' and 'bold':

```
<fence type="brace" style="bold">
<frac>x<over>y</frac>
</fence>
```

$$\left\{ \frac{x}{y} \right\}$$

When the required fences do not match, the Type attribute is replaced by the **Open** and **Close** attributes, which hold single character values representing the fence styles:

```
<fence open="{" close="]">
<frac>x<over>y</frac>
</fence>
```

$$\left\{ \frac{x}{y} \right]$$

A post is represented by the **Middle** element, which has a **Style** attribute as described above:

```
<fence open="{" close="]">
<frac>X<over>Y</frac><middle style="bar">1
</fence>
```

$$\left\{ \frac{x}{y} \middle| \right]_{1}$$

12. HTML

HTML (the *HyperText Markup Language*) originated in 1990, specifically for use with the **World Wide Web** (henceforth to be termed the **Web**), and has become hugely popular within this and other arenas. Publishing with HTML is a large topic in its own right, and there are many books dedicated to the standard. This chapter introduces the subject, explores the relationship between HTML and SGML, and describes the use of each HTML tag. Issues of communication between browsers, servers and scripts are not covered.

Knowledge of HTML tags is important for originating new material. Although many HTML authoring packages hide the formatting tags, their meaning must still be understood so as to access the correct item from selection menus. Knowledge of HTML tags is also important for converting existing material. Format converters are not perfect; some manual correction and enhancement is usually required.

The rate of change in the HTML world is rapid. The phrase 'at the time of writing' has been largely avoided in the following text, as it would be used too frequently. However, backward compatibility has *so far* remained a priority, so the material in this chapter should be relevant for the foreseeable future.

Background

This section discusses the reasons for HTML's existence and its limitations.

HTML is an application of SGML, and is therefore defined by a DTD. It is a markup language that has the ability to link documents using a simple **hypertext** scheme. Although devised for delivery of documents over the **World Wide Web** (an **Internet** service), it is also widely used within organizations, utilizing Internet communication protocols or the file systems of local area networks (where it forms the basis of an **Intranet** service).

A **Web server** provides access to HTML documents, where they are also known as '**pages**'. The page first made available to users accessing a Web server is known as the '**home page**' (and often has the default filename of 'index.html' or 'home.html'). The home page is expected to welcome the user and contain the links required to access other pages.

The user accesses the Web server and views HTML documents using an **HTML browser**. The browser copies the HTML file to the user's own system, then composes the document from the HTML tags. This approach makes efficient use of limited wide area network bandwidth, as each screenful of information is represented by approximately 1Kb of text and markup (except where graphics are included).

HTML is a simple markup language that from the start took a position halfway between format and structure. It defines style tags such as Italic, where the output format is explicit, but also defines generalized objects such as Emphasis, where output format is left to the browser software. Initially, its relationship to SGML was purely its visual appearance (the format of the tags and character entities). Later, a DTD was created for HTML, making it a true SGML application.

The rationale for creating a standard set of tags for document delivery over the Internet is that browsers can be developed with the DTD 'hard-wired' in, along with default styles and formats for each tag. Note that this approach may one day be surpassed by a method that includes delivery of a DTD and associated style-sheet along with the document (possibly utilizing the **DSSSL Online** standard), and products that take this general approach have already appeared.

A note of caution: Just because HTML is now an SGML application, it should not be assumed that it provides a viable model for any particular document type. HTML is a relatively weak, general-purpose format, that should only be considered as a source format for one-off publications, such as marketing material. When the information has longevity, a richer structure is desirable, if only to take advantage of future, more flexible versions of HTML. The current version of HTML should be viewed as an output format, and data should be converted into HTML format from a more appropriate DTD.

There are have been four versions of HTML, known as **HTML Level One**, **HTML Level Two**, **HTML+** and **HTML Level Three**, of which HTML+ was an interim to Level Three that included tables. The respective DTDs are named **HTML 1.0**, **HTML 2.0** and **HTML 3.0** accordingly. Level Two is currently the most widely implemented version. In particular, it adds the 'forms' feature to the original standard. Level Three (which adds tables and text alignment options) is still being perfected, but is supported by a few browsers. To be precise, version 3.0 never proceeded beyond draft status, but version 3.2 was released in May 1996. The DTDs are released by the **W³C** (the *World Wide Web Consortium*). For information regarding the latest version of HTML, access 'http://www.w3/org'.

This chapter first describes HTML 2.0, then covers the additional features in HTML 3.2. Finally, some non-standard extensions, such as frames, are explained.

Note that the **IETF** (*Internet Engineering Task Force*) working group responsible for HTML decided to disband after the release of HTML 3.2. This is probably due to the fact that browser developers are increasingly adding their own tags to gain commercial advantage. The **WG8** working group of the ISO is considering adopting one version of HTML (probably 3.2) as an ISO standard.

HTML 2.0

This section introduces the elements used in HTML Level Two documents.

The public identifier for this version of HTML is '-//IETF//DTD HTML 2.0//EN', though use of the following document type declaration is only encouraged, not enforced:

```
<!DOCTYPE HTML PUBLIC "-//IETF//DTD HTML 2.0//EN">
```

As indicated in the declaration above, an HTML conforming document has a document element of **Html**. This element encloses a **Head** section and a main **Body** section. The header contains a **Title**, which appears in the title bar of the browser. The Body element may contain any of a number of other elements, but will usually begin with the title repeated in a header-one element, **H1**.

An **Address** element encloses details of the author of the document, and is usually inserted at the end of the document, where it is displayed in italic, possibly indented or centered.

The broad structure of an HTML document:

```
<html>
   <head>
      <title>What is HTML?</title>
   </head>
```

```
   <body>
      <h1>What is HTML?</h1>
      ......
      <address>Neil Bradley
      (http://neil@bradley.co.uk)</address>
   </body>
</html>
```

Basic formatting

The most basic tag used in the Body is the **Paragraph** element (**P**). As line-feed characters in an HTML document are not preserved, but converted into spaces so that the browser can paginate the text to the available screen width, the Paragraph element is used to identify and separate paragraphs.

Early versions of HTML used the Paragraph tag to end a paragraph. It was placed at the end of the last sentence in the paragraph. In HTML 2.0 it has been re-defined to use SGML conventions, by adding an optional end-tag; and making the start-tag begin a paragraph instead of end a paragraph. Documents coded to the original specification may still be composed successfully, regardless of interpretation, as most Paragraph tags are placed between two paragraphs (a blank line is created either way). However, spacing between paragraphs and other elements will not always match expectations:

```
HTML 1.0                    HTML 2.0

   This is the first          <p>This is the first
   paragraph.<p>              paragraph</p>

   This is the second         <p>This is the second
   paragraph<p>               paragraph</p>

                              <h2>Header</h2>

<h2>Header</h2>
```

In the example fragments above, the first and second paragraphs are separated, in both cases, by a Paragraph open tag, but in the earlier version of HTML the gap between the second paragraph and the header may be widened in a browser expecting HTML 2.0 conventions, because they are separated by both a Paragraph tag and a Header two tag.

Element groups

A number of parameter entities are used to group elements as follows:

HEADING Definition:

- **H1** (Header one)
- **H2** (Header two)
- **H3** (Header three)
- **H4** (Header four)
- **H5** (Header five)
- **H6** (Header six)

LIST Definition:

- **Ul** (Unordered List)
- **Ol** (Ordered List)
- **Dir** (Directory List)
- **Menu** (Menu List)

FONT Definition:

- **Tt** (Teletype – mono-spaced)
- **B** (Bold typeface)
- **I** (Italic)

PHRASE Definition:

- **Em** (Emphasis)
- **Strong** (Strong Text – possibly Bold)
- **Code** (Computer code – mono-spaced)
- **Samp** (Sample text)
- **Kbd** (Keyboard)
- **Var** (Variable – computer text)
- **Cite** (Citation – possibly Italic)

TEXT Definition:

- normal characters
- **A** (Anchor for cross-reference source and/or target)
- **Img** (Image – inline reference to picture)
- all PHRASE definitions
- all FONT definitions

All of the elements defined by the FONT and PHRASE entities may enclose the elements defined in the TEXT definition, which may in turn contain further FONT and PHRASE elements. For example, Sample text (Samp) may contain an Anchor (A), which may contain Keyboard (Kbd) Elements. The HEADING elements may also contain any TEXT elements.

Heading elements

The heading elements, **H1** to **H6**, hold title text with varying degrees of highlighting. H1 is the most important, and is typically used only for the title of the document (perhaps in conjunction with the Center element, described later). At the other extreme, H6 is the least important header, and should only be used when six levels of heading are strictly necessary.

Each header element is a block, separated from preceding and following objects, including paragraphs and other headers:

```
<h1>This is Header One</h1>
<h2>This is Header Two</h2>
<h3>This is Header Three</h3>
<h4>This is Header Four</h4>
<h5>This is Header Five</h5>
<h6>This is Header six</h6>
```

Although no specific formatting style is indicated, typically the header elements are all displayed in bold typeface. The point size of the text varies, increasing with the level of importance.

This is Header One
This is Header Two
This is Header Three
This is Header Four
This is Header Five
This is Header Six

Headers can be used to create crude section and subsection divisions in the document, or to define outliner levels.

List elements

The most basic type of list is the **Unordered List** type (**Ul**). It contains a number of **List Item** elements (**Li**), each of which contains text and is automatically preceded by a bullet, dash or other symbol:

```
<ul>
<li>First Item
<li>Second Item
<li>Third Item
</ul>
```

- First Item
- Second Item
- Third Item

The Unordered List is used when the items do not form a logical sequence or series of steps.

The **Ordered List** type (**Ol**), is similar to the Unordered List, but each item is preceded by a sequential, automatically generated number. It is used in preference to the Unordered List when the items describe a series of steps, or are referred to individually elsewhere:

```
<ol>
<li>First Item
<li>Second Item
<li>Third Item
</ol>
```

1. First Item
2. Second Item
3. Third Item

A further list type is available, though not grouped with the others in the LIST entity (for no apparent reason). The **Definition List** element (**Dl**), contains a number of items (but not Item elements), each one consisting of two parts, a **Definition Term** element (**Dt**) and a **Definition Entry** element (**Dd** – not 'De'!). Typically, these elements are used to hold glossary items and keys to labeled diagrams:

```
<dl>
<dt>SGML<dd>Standard Generalized Markup
Language
<dt>DTD<dd>Document Type Definition
</dl>
```

SGML Standard Generalized Markup Language
DTD   Document Type Definition

There are two other variants of unordered list, called Menu and Directory. Both are intended for brief items and may be omitted from future versions of HTML, so their use should be carefully considered.

The **Directory List** element (**Dir**), is intended to hold directory listings, very short items that may be formatted in columns (as in UNIX file listings):

```
<dir>
<li>MYBOOK.DEC
<li>MYBOOK.DTD
<li>MYBOOK.SGM
<li>PARSER.EXE
<li>REPORT.DAT
</dir>

MYBOOK.DEC     PARSER.EXE
MYBOOK.DTD     REPORT.DAT
MYBOOK.SGM
```

The **Menu** list is intended to be used to represent software menu selections. The content of each item is assumed to be short, and the browser is likely to indent them and omit the bullet:

```
<menu>
<li>Option One
<li>Option Two
<li>Help
<li>Exit
</menu>

        Option One
        Option Two
        Help
        Exit
```

All of the above list types may have more closely formatted items using a **Compact** attribute. This implied attribute has a single value option of 'compact', and the attribute name does not appear:

```
<ul compact>
```

Font elements

The font elements are all inline elements (they do not form a new paragraph block). They specify a change of character style. The **Teletype** element (**Tt**) specifies a mono-spaced font such as Courier. The **Bold** element (**B**) specifies a bold typeface. The **Italic** element (**I**) specifies an italic typeface:

```
<p>This paragraph contains <b>bold</b>, <i>italic</i>
and <b><i>bold/italic</i></b> text.</p>
```

This paragraph contains **bold**, *italic* and ***bold/italic*** text.

Phrase elements

The phrase elements are all inline elements that do not specify an output format. However, many have obvious style mappings. **Strong** normally maps to bold typeface and **Emphasis (Em)** to italic typeface. The computer sample elements **Code** and **Var**, as well as the **Keyboard** element (**Kbd**), normally map to a mono-spaced font. The **Sample** element (**Samp**) and **Citation** element (**Cite**) may both map to italic typeface:

```
<em>Emphasized text</em>
<strong>Strong text</strong>
<code>Computer text</code>
<kbd>Keyboard text</kbd>
<var>Variable text</var>
<samp>Sample text</samp>
<cite>Citation text</cite>
```

Emphasized text

Strong text

Computer text

Keyboard text

Variable text

Sample text

Citation text

Text elements

Text elements are all inline elements. All the elements described as font elements and as phrase elements are included in this category. Other elements in this group are described below.

The **Image** element (**Img**) identifies an image file, the content of which is to appear within the current line of text. This is an empty element; there is no end-tag. A **Source** attribute (**Src**) specifies the name and location of an image file (often stored in **GIF** format):

```
...there is a GIF file<img src="myimage.gif">
here.
```

The image name alone, as shown above, can be used when the image resides in the same directory as the HTML document. The rules for specifying an image file stored in another location are the same as for hypertext links, described later, so need not be covered here. By default the base of the image is likely to be aligned with the baseline of the text. Image alignment can be made specific using the **Align** attribute, which takes a value of 'top', 'middle' or 'bottom'. As some browsers are not able to display images, an **Alternative** attribute (**Alt**) may be used to display alternative text. The second example below demonstrates its use:

```
...there is a GIF file
<img src="myimage.gif" align="top" alt="No Piccy"> here.

...there is a GIF file   --------   here.
                         |        |
                          --------

...there is a GIF file [no piccy] here.
```

An increasing number of image formats are supported by some browsers, including **XBM**, **JPEG** and the original **GIF**.

The **Anchor** element is also included in this group of elements. This element is the subject of *Internal and External Links* below.

Other elements

The **Isindex** element, which appears in the Head element, simply indicates that the Web server will accept a search request from the browser. The browser displays a text entry box for entry of the term to be searched for. A more powerful facility, termed 'forms,' is discussed later.

The **Line Break** element (**Br**) forces a new line. This is very useful for semi-formatting text, such as lines of poetry. It is an empty element:

```
<p>Break this line here <br>so this is line 2
```

The **Blockquote** element contains a block of text quoted from another source, which is typically indented by the browser.

A more powerful, though visually less pleasing, approach to formatting uses the **Preformatted** element (**Pre**), which composes the content in a mono-spaced font. All spaces and line-feed characters are retained, making it possible to use these characters to create simple character-based diagrams, or columns of text:

```
<pre>
Here is a face:    ---
                  /   \
                  [ o o ]
                  \ - /
                   ---

</pre>
```

The **Horizontal Rule** element (**Hr**) draws a line across the screen. It is an empty element.

```
<p>The next para is in another section</p>
<hr>
<p>New section of the document</p>
```

Internal and external links

HTML does not use the standard SGML hypertext link scheme (see Chapter 9), partly because Web functionality requires the use of inter-document links, as well as internal links. HTML browsers are designed to understand the scheme described below, not the official SGML linking scheme.

The **Anchor** element (**A**) is the only element that is used to create a link. It is therefore used to locate both the source and target ends of the link. When used as a source element it contains the referencing text. When used as a target element it usually contains the title of the referenced text (in order that it may be highlighted on completion of a link to that item).

When used as a target element, the Anchor contains a **Name** attribute value:

```
<h3>
<a name="details">The Details</a>
</h3>
```

When used as a source element, the Anchor contains a **Hypertext Reference** attribute (**Href**) which holds either the name of a target Anchor, or a file specification for inter-document linking. When a link is made to an object in the same file, the Anchor contains the name of the target object, preceded by a hash symbol:

```
<a href="#details">See details</a>
```

A single Anchor may be both the source of a link, and also the target of a link:

```
<a name="summary" href="#details">See details</a>
```

Characters allowed in the Name and Hypertext Reference attributes are not set by the SGML standard, but by HTML conventions. The DTD specifies these attributes to be of type CDATA. HTML further restricts the content to upper case and lower case letters, digits and the symbols '$', '+', '.', '-' and '_'. All other characters are represented by a special code, comprising a percent symbol, '%', followed by a hexadecimal two-digit ASCII character value ('%00' to '%FF'). For example, '%20' represents a space:

```
<a href="#More%20Details">See More Details</a>
<h3>
<a name="More%20Details">More Details</a>
</h3>
```

Links to other documents use the same element and attributes, but involve a file specification that includes at least a file name, but may also include a path to the file. UNIX conventions are used, including the use of '/' (directory separator) and '..' (parent directory).

The full path to the file may be supplied, starting at the root directory, '/':

```
<a href="/html/myfiles/detail.html">See details</a>
```

However, the use of relative path names is more flexible (as well as generally briefer), as this means that a collection of documents and directories can be moved to another system, without editing the HTML files. A relative link to a file in an embedded directory may appear as follows:

```
<a href="myfiles/detail.html">See details</a>

    /html/source.html        ------------\
          /myfiles/detail.html          <--\
```

A relative link to a file in a directory which shares the same parent directory as the source document may appear as follows:

```
<a href="../myfiles/detail.html">See details</a>

    /html/source/source.html        ------------\
          /myfiles/detail.html          <---------\
```

The target document does not require an Anchor element, because the entire file is the target. However, it is possible to link to an anchored item in the other file by appending the hash symbol and item name:

```
<a href="../myfiles/detail.html#part3">See
details, part 3</a>
```

Note: MS-DOS based systems should name HTML files with an extension of '.HTM', due to the three-letter limit on file name extensions.

Links to documents on other systems must be preceded by the protocol and host name. The most common protocol used for Web page delivery is **HTTP** (*HyperText Transfer Protocol*), specified using 'http:'. A double solidus, '//', separates the protocol from the server name, and a single solidus separates the server name from the file specification:

```
<a href="http://www.myserve.com/myfiles/
detail.html#part3">See details, part 3</a>
```

If the path ends with a solidus, the target Web server supplies the name of the default home page:

```
<a href="http://www.myserver.com/myfiles/">
See My Server</a>
```

To target a browser at a home page held on the reader's own system, or another system visible over a local area network, the protocol becomes 'file:' and a triple solidus may be required (the third one being part of the file path specification):

```
<a href="file:///myserver/myfiles/me.html">
See My Server Home Page</a>
```

Image maps

Following on the theme of hypertext links, a popular feature of HTML is the ability to create links from parts of an image. This is called an **image map**. For example, a map of the world could be linked to other HTML documents that describe some characteristic of each country. The source of the link is therefore an area of the image. In the well-supported concept of a 'server-sided' image map, the browser simply passes the coordinates of the mouse-click to the Web server, which calls a script that decides which HTML document to return to the browser depending on the coordinate values.

The **Image** element (**Img**) takes an additional attribute, **Ismap**, to indicate that the coordinates of the mouse-click should be sent to the Web server. This implied attribute has a single legal value of 'ISMAP' (the attribute name never appears):

```
<img src="myimage.gif" ISMAP>
```

However, the Web server must also be told which script to activate when the mouse is clicked on this image. To do this, the Img element is enclosed in an **Anchor** element (**A**) which uses a **URL** to locate the appropriate script:

```
<a href="/cgi-bin/imagemap/my.map">
<img src="myimage.gif" ISMAP>
</a>
```

This scheme relies upon the use of the **HTTP** protocol, a Web server and **CGI** scripts, so is not particularly suitable for Intranet solutions, or for publishing HTML files on a CD-ROM. The concept of 'client-sided' image maps overcomes this problem, and is introduced later.

Meta-data

The **Meta** element is not used for document markup, and is of interest to those involved in browser/server communications. The Meta element is placed within the **Head** element to add meta-information not covered by attributes of other elements. The content of Meta is not to be displayed in the document, but may be read by the browser or server. Its use is not standardized. It has three attributes, HTTP-Equiv, Name and Content. The **Name** attribute provides the name of the meta-information (almost an attribute name in itself). The **Content** attribute provides the current value for the named meta-data. For example:

```
<meta name="Index" content="cycle">
```

If more than one Meta element is present, with the same Name attribute value, the various contents are accumulated into a comma separated list; for example 'cycle, bus, car'. The third attribute, **HTTP-Equiv**, allows the Contents to be inserted into an **HTTP** header field (a topic not explored further in this book).

Forms

The remainder of this section deals with **forms**, the major new feature of HTML 2.0. The forms concept allows the receiver of an HTML document to send information back to the Web server. The document may contain a questionnaire, for example, which the user fills in and returns. This book does not describe how the Web server receives and interprets the content of forms.

A **Form** element encloses the entire form. It has an attribute called **Action**, which identifies a script that can process the form when it is submitted.

The Form element may contain a number of **Input** elements, of which exactly one must have an attribute **Type** value of 'submit':

```
<form method="POST"
action="../mydir/myscript.cgi">
   <input type="submit" value="Send Form">
   ...
</form>
```

The example above sends the data entered into the form to the 'myscript.cgi' script running on the Web server when the 'Send Form' button is selected by the user of the browser.

Note: The Form element has another attribute called Method, which in the example has a value of 'POST'. It may also take a value of 'GET'. These values define the means by which the form sends information back to the server, a subject which is not covered further here.

Another Input element may be used to define a button that resets the default settings of the form, using a Type attribute value of 'reset'.

The **Input** element is also used to provide a selection of 'radio buttons,' 'check boxes' and 'text fields.'

A **Type** value of 'radio' indicates that radio buttons will appear in the form. The browser ensures that only the last radio button selected is highlighted at any one time within a group of buttons. The Name attribute is used to define groups of radio buttons. All Input elements sharing the same **Name** value are part of a single group:

```
<input type="radio" name="vehicle" value="car">
<input type="radio" name="vehicle" value="truck">
<input type="radio" name="vehicle" value="van">
<input type="radio" name="color" value="Red">
<input type="radio" name="color" value="Blue">
```

In the example above two groups are defined, 'vehicle' and 'color'. From the vehicle group the user may select the radio button labeled 'car', 'truck' or 'van', and from the color group the user may select 'Red' or 'Blue'. The user may therefore select, for example, a blue car or a red van. However, the user will not be able to see which buttons to select unless descriptive names also appear near the Input element, perhaps within List Item elements:

```
<li>
<input type="radio" name="color" value="red">
Red option.
<li>
<input type="radio" name="color" value="blue">
Blue option.
```

   (*) Red option.
   ( ) Blue option.

The browser is likely to pre-select the first item when the form is displayed, as in the example above, because one option must always be selected, but it is the value selected when the 'submit' button is used that matters.

The **Input** element can also be used to provide 'check boxes,' which differ from radio buttons in that more than one can be selected at any one time. The **Type** attribute contains 'checkbox' and the **Name** attribute contains the name of the item that may be selected. An item can be pre-selected by including the **Checked** attribute, holding the single legal value of 'checked' (the attribute name not appearing):

```
<li>
<input type="checkbox" name="car"
value="leather">
Leather
<li>
<input type="checkbox" name="car"
value="CD" checked>
CD-player
```

```
[ ] Leather
[X] CD-player
```

In the example above, the user is presented with two options, 'leather' (seats) and 'CD' (player), and the CD item is already selected. The user can de-select CD player, select leather seats, select both or select neither.

The **Input** element can also be used to provide text entry areas. The **Type** attribute either holds a value of 'text', or may be absent as this is the default value for the Type attribute. The **Name** attribute holds the label for the text field. The **Size** attribute may be used to determine the length in characters of the text field, and if not present defaults to 20 characters. Also, the attribute **Maxlength** can be used to strictly limit the number of characters that can be entered, and may be smaller or larger than the text field size:

```
<input type="text" size="25" maxlength="15">
```

```
Fifteen chars !▓▓▓▓▓▓▓▓▓
```

To allow for multiple lines of text, the **Textarea** element is used. Each text area is identified using the **Name** attribute. The attributes **Rows** and **Cols** set the height and width of the visible text area in character sized units. Scroll bars or other devices may allow extra characters or lines of text to be displayed within this area:

```
<textarea name="mybox" rows="3" cols="10">Here
is some
content</textarea>
```

All line-feed characters in the data are retained, including one between the start-tag and the first word, if present (the example above would begin with a blank line if there were a line-feed before 'Here').

Selection menus are available using the Select and Option elements. The **Select** element encloses the menu. It uses the **Name** attribute to identify the menu. Each option in the menu is defined using the **Option** element.

```
<select name="mymenu">
<option>Car
<option selected>Truck
<option>Van
</select>
```

HTML 3.2 enhancements

An overview of the changes and new tags included in the latest DTD.

The precise specification for HTML is almost impossible to define. There is a conflict between the methodical deliberations of the **W³C** steering group, releasing DTDs for each version, and the browser developers seeking to gain an edge over their competitors.

At the time of writing, however, **HTML 3.2** had just been released, and there was public support for this DTD by all of the most influential developers. It seems hopeful that this standard, and its successors, will at least form the basis of a common set of tags supported by all browsers. For more information on this and future versions, see 'http://www.w3.org/pub/'.

The public identifier for this version of HTML is '-//W3C//DTD HTML 3.2//EN', though use of the following document type declaration is only encouraged, not enforced:

```
<!DOCTYPE HTML PUBLIC "-//W3C//DTD HTML 3.2//EN">
```

General

There are additional text style options, including the **Underline** element (**U**), the **Strikethrough** element (**Strike**), the **Subscript** element (**Sub**), the **Superscript** element (**Sup**) and the font size change tags, **Big** and **Small**, all of which are self-explanatory.

The **Center** element has been added to center any other structure or group of structures. The **Division** element (**Div**) extends this idea, surrounding segments of the document that share an alignment option. It takes an **Align** attribute, with a value of 'left', 'center' or 'right'. The Center element is, therefore, no different to a Division element with an Align value of 'center'.

As an alternative to Center or Div, several elements now have an **Align** attribute, with a value of 'left', 'center' or 'right', including **P**, **H1**, **H2**, **H3**, **H4**, **H5** and **H6**.

The **Horizontal Rule** element (**Hr**) has attributes that specify the thickness of the line (the **Size** attribute); the width of the line in pixels or as a percentage of the screen width (the **Width** attribute); the alignment of a line smaller than the screen width (the **Align** attribute); and that dictate that the line must be solid (the **Noshade** attribute). The Noshade attribute has a single legal value of 'noshade', and the attribute name does not appear:

```
<hr Noshade size="4" width="50%" align="center">
```

In the example above, the line must be solid, occupy half the width of the window and be centered.

A **Type** attribute has been added to the **Ordered List** element, the **Unordered List** element and the **List Item** element. An Ordered List can take values of 'A' (capital letters), 'a' (small letters), 'I' (large Roman letters), 'i' (small Roman letters) or '1' (digits), which is the default. An Unordered List can take values of 'DISC' (bullet), 'CIRCLE' (hollow bullet) or 'SQUARE' (a square hollow bullet). The List Item can take the same values, depending which list type it is within, and overrides the current setting for the list within all remaining items. In addition, the Ordered List has a **Start** element, which indicates a start value for the first item when it is not '1' (or equivalent), and the List Item has a **Value** attribute that can only be used within Ordered Lists to reset the current calculated value:

```
<ol Type="A" Start="4">
   <li>First Item
   <li Value="G">Second Item
   <li>Third Item
</ol>
```

   D First Item
   G Second Item
   H Third Item

The formatting of text has been enhanced with two new elements, the **No Break** element (**Nobr**) and the **Word Break** element (**Wbr**). The Nbr element encloses text which should not be split over lines by the browser. The Wbr element indicates points in the text where a break may be made if necessary:

```
<nobr>THIS LINE OF TEXT<WBR> MAY BE BROKEN AT ONE POINT</nobr>
```

THIS LINE OF TEXT MAY BE BROKEN AT ONE POINT

THIS LINE OF TEXT
MAY BE BROKEN AT ONE POINT

Text and page style

The document background color and foreground text color can be specified in the **Body** element, using the new **Background Color** attribute (**Bgcolor**) and the new **Text** attribute. In both cases, the format of the attribute value comprises either the name of a color, or a coded RGB (red, green, blue) mix. Available color names are 'aqua', 'black', 'fuchsia', 'gray', 'green', 'lime', 'maroon', 'navy', 'olive', 'purple', 'red', 'silver', 'teal', 'white' and 'yellow'. The RGB scheme uses three hexadecimal (two-digit) values, preceded by a hash symbol; for example '#FF2250'. The first two digits indicate the amount of Red, the next two digits indicate the amount of Green, and the final two digits indicate the amount of Blue to be mixed to create the desired color:

```
<body bgcolor="#000000" text="#F0F0F0">
```

The example above produces a document with light-gray text on a black background.

As an alternative, the background can be composed from a picture, often in GIF format. The new **Background** attribute provides a **URL** to the desired picture. When the picture is smaller than the display area, it is repeated across and down until it fills the display area:

```
<body background="/piccies/mybackgr.gif">
```

A change to the document background or text color may affect the visibility of **hypertext** links, so three additional attributes are used to set the color of linking text. The **Link** attribute sets the color of a link that is not active and has not been visited. The **Visited Link** attribute (**Vlink**) sets the color of all links that have been activated in the (recent) past. The **Active Link** attribute (**Alink**) sets the color of the currently selected link. The format of the values are as described above for the document foreground and background color.

The font size may be varied using the new **Font** element. The **Size** attribute dictates the new font size, either absolutely, as a value between '1' and '7' (the default being '3'), or relatively as a size change from the current value. An initial '+' or '-' character indicates a relative size:

```
This text is <font size="+1">bigger</font> than
normal.
```

An additional **Color** attribute uses the scheme described for changing the document color in the Body element. Font elements can also be embedded within each other.

The new **Basefont** element is used to specify a new default font size for the whole document, and should therefore be placed at the top of the Body segment. It also uses a **Size** attribute to set the font size:

```
<basefont size="2">Text size is smaller than
normal but <font size="+1">is now as
expected</font>.
```

Image handling

The **Image** element (**Img**) takes additional alignment options using the **Align** attribute. In addition to the standard 'middle', 'top' and 'bottom' options, the new 'left' and 'right' options create **floating images** in the left or right margin. New attributes include **Border**, which specifies the thickness of the image border line, the **Vertical Space** attribute (**Vspace**) and the **Horizontal Space** attribute (**Hspace**) which create extra space around the image, and **Width** and **Height**, which tell the browser in advance the dimensions of the image so as to speed-up downloading:

```
<img border="3" vspace="2" hspace="2"
align="left">
```

Due to the new floating images described above, the **Break** element (**Br**) has been extended to allow the break to force the next line to appear below large, horizontally adjacent floating images. Account can be taken of images that appear in just one of the margins. The **Clear** attribute takes a value of 'all' (an image in either or both margins), 'left' (an image in the left margin only) or 'right' (an image in the right margin only):

```
<br clear="left">
```

The concept of a 'client-sided image map' was introduced earlier. The browser uses HTML tags to identify image areas and associated URLs to other documents or parts of the same document. This approach provides the benefits of less interaction with the server (making the process more efficient) and independence from the HTTP protocol (making it suitable for Intranet use as well as Internet use), as well as giving prior warning of the effect of clicking on any part of the image (the target URL is displayed as the pointer is moved over the image). The **Usemap** attribute is added to the Img element, and holds the name of a **Map** element that defines areas of the image:

```
<IMG SRC="/images/myimage.gif" usemap="#mymap">

<map name="mymap"> ..... </map>
```

Within the Map element, each area and associated URL is defined using an **Area** element. This element contains attributes to define the shape of the area, the coordinates of the area and the URL associated with the area. The **Coords** attribute defines the coordinates of the area and the **Href** attribute provides the URL. Consider an example of an image showing a new model of motor car. Each area of interest, such as the wheels, or the engine, could be located and attached to an appropriate HTML document:

```
<map name="mymap">
    <area coords="50, 150, 150, 250"
    href="wheels/back.html">
    <area shape="circle" coords="350 200 50"
    href="wheels/front.html">
</map>
```

The default shape is assumed to be a rectangle, with four coordinates representing in pixels the left edge, top edge, right edge and bottom edge of the area. The first example above defines an area for the back wheel – '50' pixels in, '150' pixels down for the left and top edges, and as the diameter of the wheel is 100 pixels, '150' in and '250' down for the right and bottom edges. The optional **Shape** attribute may be used to make this area type explicit, 'shape="rect"'. Another shape option is 'circle', which requires three values, the horizontal and vertical coordinate for the center of the circle, followed by a radius value. The second example defines the area of the front wheel as a circle with a radius of '50' pixels, '350' pixels across and '200' down.

Backward compatibility can be provided for the benefit of browsers not able to use this facility. Both schemes for creating image maps (client-sided and server-sided) can co-exist by including both the Ismap attribute and the Usemap attribute in the same Img element. In the example below, a browser that does not support the client-sided map scheme uses the Anchor to pass coordinates to 'myscript.cgi':

```
<a href="myscript.cgi">
    <IMG SRC="/images/myimage.gif" usemap="#mymap"
    ISMAP>
</a>

<map name="mymap"> ..... </map>
```

Tables

The **Table** element encloses all tabular material, and starts a new line in the page.

The cells may be separated by border lines. The original specification included a simple optional **Border** attribute, which if present indicated that border lines surround all cells in the table. There being no value, the actual word 'border' appeared in the tag. In SGML terms this can be seen as a minimized attribute, the attribute name not being visible. If the word 'border' is missing, no border lines are drawn, but the space they would take remains blank. This approach is still in use, but now the border can take a value that defines the thickness of the border line, such as 'border=3'. A value of '0' indicates no border and no space for a border (which is different from the effect of not including the word 'border' in the tag). This confusing arrangement only makes sense in SGML terms if the word 'border' is seen to be a single option value of another attribute, actually named 'Dummy', which is never included:

```
<table>              no borders, space for them remains

<table border=0>  no borders, no space for them

<table border>     same as 'border=1' using 'dummy'

<table border=10> very thick border lines
```

The space between cells can be adjusted. The **Cellspacing** attribute takes a numeric value that states how much space there is between cells (including their borders). It has a default value of '2':

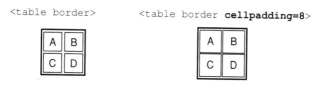

```
<table border>                  <table border cellspacing=8>
```

If a value of zero is used, the border lines overlap each other.

The space between the cell contents and the borders of the cell can also be adjusted using the **Cellpadding** attribute, which takes a numeric value. The default value is '1':

```
<table border>              <table border cellpadding=8>
```

The width and height of the table is often left under the control of the browser, which composes the table within the restrictions of the available window area. The **Width** attribute may be used to 'encourage' the browser to take into account the wishes of the document author. This attribute takes a numeric value that dictates how many pixels wide the table should be, or what percentage of the available screen width it should occupy. A pure number is interpreted as a pixel value. A percentage symbol indicates a proportion of the screen dimensions.

```
<table border width=800>
```

The table may have a title, which is contained within a **Caption** element. This element is placed within the Table element, but before the elements described later. The content is by default displayed above the main table grid, but may be explicitly displayed below the table using the **Align** attribute, with a value of 'bottom':

```
<table>
   <caption align="bottom">Title Below</caption> ...
</table>
```

The table structure is row-oriented, which means that the grid is built by first defining each row, then separating each cell within a row. Each row of data is enclosed in a **Table Row** element (**Tr**), and each cell is enclosed in either a **Table Header** element (**Th**) or a **Table Data** element (**Td**), the only difference being one of emphasis – the Th element content is usually displayed in bold (and centered). Th and Td elements may be mixed within the same row, possibly to create side headings:

```
<tr><th>Color<th>Status<th>Level</tr>
<tr><th>Red<td>Danger<td>1</tr>
<tr><th>Green<td>Normal<td>3</tr>
```

Colour	Status	Level
Red	Danger	1
Green	Normal	3

As shown above, a cell may directly contain text. It may also contain any document body elements, including a complete embedded table. The Line Break element is particularly useful for formatting text within the cell. If a cell is empty, no border lines are drawn (assuming that border lines are in use).

The content of individual cells, or all the cells in a row, may be aligned horizontally and vertically in various ways. The default horizontal alignment is 'left' in Td elements, and 'center' in Th elements, as shown in the example above. The default vertical alignment is 'middle' for both types of cell. The **Align** attribute allows horizontal alignment to be set to 'left', 'right' or 'center'. The **Valign** attribute allows vertical alignment to be set to 'top', 'middle', 'bottom' or 'baseline' (where all cells in the row are horizontally aligned by last line, after the cell with the most lines is aligned to 'top'). An alignment set in the Tr element provides a default for all cells in the row, but individual cells may override this setting.

By default each cell occupies an area dissected by one column and one row, forming a simple position within the table grid, but may be expanded across or down using the **Colspan** and **Rowspan** attributes. These attributes take numeric values, and have implied values of '1' (zero is not a legal option). Higher values than '1' stretch the cell over adjoining areas:

```
<tr><th>Color<th>Status<th>Level</tr>
<tr><th>Red<td>Danger<td>1</tr>
<tr><th>Blue<td colspan=2>No Priority<td>2</tr>
<tr><th>Brown</th><td>3</td></tr>
```

Colour	Status	Level
Red	Danger	1
Blue	No	2
Brown	Priority	3

Note that the final row in the example above has only two cell elements, containing 'Brown' and '3', because the middle cell has effectively been replaced by the cell above it.

The content of a cell is normally formatted by the browser as it is composed to fit the available screen width. The **Nowrap** attribute may be used in the Th and Td elements to prevent lines being split. This is another example of a minimized attribute with a single value, in this case 'nowrap':

```
<td nowrap>This line must not be broken</td>
```

Java

Some HTML browsers are now able to access and execute **Java** programs (or **applets**). Java code is only semi-compiled into **byte code** in advance; the local browser interprets the byte code so that it can be activated on the user's computer (regardless of the processor and operating system in use).

The HTML document contains an element called **Applet**, which identifies the file containing the Java program. An attribute called **Code** holds the **URL** of the program, but as it cannot be an absolute URL, the optional **Codebase** attribute provides the base for relative paths (and if not present, the URL of the HTML document is assumed). The **Name** attribute identifies the applet for inter-communication between active applets. An area of the screen is set aside to display any output from the program when it is activated, using the **Width** and **Height** attributes, which indicate the number of pixels to reserve:

```
<applet code="MyJava.class" height="150" width="300">
   ...
</applet>
```

The remaining attributes, **Align**, **Alt**, **Hspace** and **Vspace** have the same function as described for the Img element.

The **Parameter** element (**Param**) is used to send parameter values to the program. The **Name** attribute identifies a particular parameter, and the **Value** attribute assignes a value to the named parameter:

```
<applet code="MyJava.class" height="150" width="300">
   <param name="myparam1" value="12345">
   <param name="myparam2" value="XYZ">
</applet>
```

Browsers that are not Java-aware should simply ignore the Applet element.

Netscape extensions

Frames are used to provide further control over the presentation of information.

The Netscape browser has preceded, and helped to define, the latest versions of HTML. There are one or two features in this browser that arguably go beyond the current standard. Whether they will be incorporated into later versions of HTML remains to be seen.

General

The **Image** element (**Img**) takes additional alignment options using the **Align** attribute. In addition to 'middle', 'top' and 'bottom', there are subtly distinct variants of 'absmiddle', 'texttop' and 'absbottom'. The absolute middle option positions the middle of the image against the middle of the line of text, instead of the bottom of the line of text.

Frames

Using the **Frame** element, the screen is divided into areas, with each area possibly displaying a different document that may be scrolled independently. Among other uses, frames facilitate the use of table of contents and button bars that do not scroll off the screen. It is probable that frames will be incorporated into the standard (though not necessarily exactly as described below).

A frame-based document replaces the Body element with a **Frameset** element:

```
<html>
<head>...</head>
<frameset>...</frameset>
</html>
```

The Frame Set defines an area which generally fills the end user's screen. This area is divided into frames using the **Cols** or **Rows** attribute. These attributes take a value that specifies the width or height of the sub-areas. This value specifies the height or width using one of three methods, the number of pixels (not advised), a percentage of the available space or a proportion of the available space. Values are separates by commas, which also therefore specify the number of columns or rows in the set:

```
<frameset rows="1500, 1000, 500">

<frameset rows="3*, 2*, *">

<frameset rows="50%, 33%, 16%">
```

The first example above specifies a height of 1500 pixels for the first row, the second example reserves three proportional units for the first row (the asterisk character alone is equivalent to '1*'), and the third example specifies that the first row should occupy half the available height ('50%'). If the available height were 3000 pixels, then all three examples above would be equivalent (a discussion of proportional units is presented in Chapter 10). These value types may be mixed:

```
<frameset cols="50%, 100, 2*, *">
```

When value types are mixed, fixed values have precedence, followed by percentage values, then proportional values. In the example above, the second column is assigned exactly 100 pixels of horizontal space, the first column is then assigned half of the remaining space, and the remainder is divided among the proportional columns (the third column taking twice the space of the last column):

2nd (percentage)	**1st**	**3rd** (proportional)	
50% of remaining area	100 pixels	2*	1*

A Frame Set can contain further embedded Frame Sets. Each embedded Frame Set occupies the space reserved for it by the enclosing Frame Set. Taking the example above, a Frame Set embedded in the first column is restricted to the left half of the screen, and will define subdivisions of this area:

```
<frameset cols="50%, 100, 2*, *">
   <frameset cols="60%, 40%">
   ...
   </frameset>
   ...
</frameset>
```

|-------- **60 %** -------|--- **40 %** ---|	100 pixels	2*	1*

A Frame Set may contain a **Noframes** element. This element is intended to hold information to be displayed by a browser that cannot interpret the frames. Its function is therefore similar to the Alt attribute in the Image element. Its content, which may include normal blocks such as paragraphs and lists, is not displayed in frame-aware browsers:

```
<noframes><p>If you see this, you can't see
FRAMES!</noframes>
```

Of course, a browser that does not understand frames is unlikely to be aware of the Noframes element. But, as such browsers simply remove all unknown tags, the text enclosed by this element will be displayed anyway.

Finally, a Frame Set may contain a **Frame** element. This is an empty element, so has no end-tag. It is used to identify the document to be displayed within the frame, to identify the frame itself (so that it can be made the target of links from other frames or documents), to determine whether the width and height of the frame can be altered by the end user, to determine whether scroll bars are used and to specify the margin widths.

The Frame element has a **Source** attribute (**Src**) which contains the **URL** of the HTML document to be displayed in the frame. If no URL is provided, the area is left blank. The Frame element also has a **Name** attribute, which contains the name of the frame, so that it can be the target of a link from another frame, or from another document:

```
<frame name="myarea" url="../areas/myarea.html">
```

The Frame element has a **Scrolling** attribute, which indicates whether horizontal and vertical scroll bars are always present, present as required or never present. A value of 'yes' forces scroll bars to appear even if not needed. A value of 'auto' displays scroll bars when necessary, and is the default value. A value of 'no' disables scroll bars, even when they would be useful.

The Frame element has a **Resize** attribute, which, if present, prevents the end user from changing the height or width of the frame. By default it is absent, and resizing is allowed. In SGML terms, this must be seen as an attribute called Resize that has an optional, single value of 'RESIZE', and that minimization is in use to avoid stating the attribute name:

```
<frame url="../areas/myarea.html" RESIZE>
```

Finally, the Frame element has **Marginwidth** and **Marginheight** attributes, which specify the space to reserve between the borders of the frame and the enclosed text. Width settings affect the space between the left and right edges. Height settings affect the space above and below the content. Values are in pixels, and if present must be at least '1', and not so large that content cannot be displayed. If absent, the browser provides default settings.

13. SGMLS and NSGMLS parsers

This chapter describes two related and freely available SGML parsers, the *SGMLS* parser and the *NSGMLS* parser. The prefix 'N' stands for 'New.' In both cases the suffix 'S' stands for 'Structured.' They are the only software products described in this book, and are featured because they are free, and are of great benefit to programmers who need to process SGML documents.

These parsers are public domain utilities, developed by James Clark. *SGMLS* is based on the *ARCSGML* parser developed by Charles F. Goldfarb. In contrast, *NSGMLS* is built using *SP*, a portable SGML parser C++ library also developed by James Clark. *NSGMLS* itself adds the command line interface and the ESIS and RAST output formats described later. Details of *SP* are available from 'http://www.jclark.com/sp.html'.

The main text describes *SGMLS* but includes notes on any important additions or changes implemented in the newer product.

The *SGMLS* parser performs three roles:

- it replaces entity references with the entity text
- it checks the DTD for ambiguities and errors, and checks the document instance against both the DTD and the SGML declaration
- it transforms the data into a standardized output format

The first two features combine to provide the parsing facility. A built-in **entity manager** locates entities so that the **parser** can compile the complete document for checking. The output from the parser comprises, as one would expect, of any warnings or error messages resulting from problems with the DTD or document instance.

ESIS output

SGMLS is able to output the content of a document instance using a scheme called **ESIS** (*Element Structure Information Set*), which is defined by **ISO/ IEC 13673** (although the actual format described below is bespoke to the two parsers described here). It is a simpler and more rigid format than

SGML, and is therefore easier to process. Take the following SGML document:

```
<!DOCTYPE list [
      <!ELEMENT list - - (item+)>
      <!ELEMENT item - o (#PCDATA)>
      <!ATTLIST list     offset (no|yes) "no"
                         sepchar CDATA #IMPLIED>
]>
<list offset="no" sepchar="+">
<item>This is item one</item>
<item>This is item two</item>
</list>
```

When read by the *SGMLS* parser, the example above is checked for validity, then output as:

```
AOFFSET TOKEN NO
ASEPCHAR CDATA +
(LIST
(ITEM
-This is item one
)ITEM
(ITEM
- This is item two
)ITEM
)LIST
C
```

This format is described in detail later. For now, the most important point to consider is that the output shown above is generated regardless of any choice of minimization technique applied, and regardless of the exact use of markup separating characters such as spaces and line-feed codes. The following example would generate identical ESIS output to the example above:

```
<!DOCTYPE list SYSTEM "C:\DTDS\LIST.DTD">
<list   no   sepchar="+"><item>
This is item one</>
<item>This is item two
</list>
```

When the exact nature of SGML input is so unpredictable, prior conversion to a simpler format is of great benefit to the developer of **down-conversion** or **normalization** filters. Note, however, that a utility called *SPAM* (also developed using *SP*) performs markup normalization.

ESIS syntax

ESIS format is based on ASCII. Each line begins with a significant character, known as a 'command.' As the command is always a single character,
it is *not* separated from any following parameters or data. This makes it easy
for software to read the file, but is not very clear to the human reader.

The table below shows each command, along with the names of any parameters:

Command	Description	After	Before
(*gi*	Generic identifier open (start-tag), e.g. '(MYELEM'		
)*gi*	Generic identifier close (end-tag), e.g. ')MYELEM'		
-*data*	Normal text, e.g. '-my text'		
&*name*	External entity reference, e.g. '&myent;'	D	
?*pi*	Processing instruction, e.g. '?new_page'		
A*name val*	Attribute name and value, e.g. 'AMY-ATT CDATA Hello There'	D or N or none	
D*ename name val*	Data attribute for external entity	E	A or &
N*nname nname*	Notation declaration	P or S	A or E
E*ename typ nname*	External data entity	F	
I*ename typ text*	Internal data entity		
S*ename*	Subdocument entity	P, F or S	{ or A
s*sysid*	System identifier		E, S or N
p*pubid*	Public identifier		N
f*filename*	File name of identifier		E or S
}*ename*	Subdocument entity open	S	
{*ename*	Subdocument entity close		
L*lineno file*	Line number		
#*text*	Application info (**APPINFO**)	L	
C	Conforming document	*All*	*None*

Within text data, backslash delimited codes are used to specify special characters:

\\	Single slash '\'
\n	Record end (convert to line end)

∖ǀ (vertical bar)	Internal SDATA entity (start and end)
∖_nn_	Octal character value ('∖012' should be deleted)

For example:

```
-here is an \|internal entity\| merged-in.
```

Some of these commands were illustrated in the example above. The following example shows more complex combinations:

```
<!DOCTYPE embed [
     <!NOTATION TEX
                 PUBLIC "-//ME//NOTATION TeX//EN"
                 SYSTEM "TEXREADME.DAT">
     <!NOTATION PS  SYSTEM "">
     <!ELEMENT embed  - - (#PCDATA)>
     <!ATTLIST embed  nota NOTATION (TEX|PS) "PS">
]>
<embed nota=TEX>
$${Gamma(J/\psi \rightarrow \eta_c \gamma)}.....
</embed>
```

The ESIS output:

```
P-//ME//NOTATION TeX//EN
sTEXREADME.DAT
NTEX
ANOTA NOTATION TEX
(EMBED
-$${Gamma(J/\psi \rightarrow \eta_c \gamma)}.....
)EMBED
C
```

Note that the 'PS' notation declaration does not appear in the output because it is not used in the document instance.

Using SGMLS

In its simplest form, where a single file contains an entire SGML document, _SGMLS_ is activated as follows:

```
SET SGML_PATH = C:\ENTS\%N.ENT;
SGMLS  switches MYDOC.SGM
```

Note that the entity manager looks for entities in directories specified by the SGML_PATH environment variable. The methods of mapping an entity declaration to an external file are extensive, and detailed in accompanying documentation. The form shown above maps an entity name to a file, using the variable '%N' ('%N%' if in an MS-DOS batch file). In the example, an entity declaration named 'ISOlat1' would be mapped to a file named 'ISOLAT1.ENT' in the 'ENTS' directory.

NSGMLS also builds on the **SGML Open** defined **catalog** format, as described in Chapter 6, adding a mechanism for matching a system identifier to a system file, among other extensions.

The command line may specify several files, which are concatenated in the order provided, and which together must complete an SGML document entity[002]. Typically, a variant SGML declaration is held in a separate file:

```
SGMLS switches  CALS.DEC  MYDOC.SGM
```

The default *SGMLS* settings include:

- parsing of both the DTD and document instance
- error reporting to standard error
- ESIS formatting to standard output

This means that error messages and output data are mixed together, which may be useful for tracking the location of errors. If this effect is not desired, ESIS output may be suppressed using the '-s' switch, or error messages may be sent to a separate file using the '-fname' switch.

The exact nature and scope of warning and error messages is adjusted using further command line switches:

- *-g* show all open elements (the hierarchy)
- *-e* show all open entities
- *-d* warn of duplicate entity declarations (also '-wduplicate' in *NSGMLS*)
- *-r* warn of defaulted references (entity not found) (also '-wdefault' in *NSGMLS*)
- *-w* warn of undefined elements (referenced but not declared) (note: *NSGMLS* variant is '*-wundefined*')

Other options controlled by switches include:

- *-cfile* report capacity usage to 'file' (including maximum capacities) (note: not available in *NSGMLS*)
- *-p* parse prolog only (check DTD)
- *-v* display *SGMLS* version number
- *-iname* makes 'name' an entity set to 'INCLUDE' (see *Choosing a DTD variant* below)
- *-l* output line number commands (also '-oline' in *NSGMLS*)

Choosing a DTD variant

Marked sections may be used to create several variants of a DTD within one file. The '-iname' feature allows one variant to be 'switched-on' only for the duration of the parse operation. For example:

```
<!ENTITY % standard "IGNORE">
<!ENTITY % variant "IGNORE">
<![ %standard; [
     <!ELEMENT mybook - - (chapter+)>
          ]>
<![ %variant;  [
     <!ELEMENT yourbook - - (chapter+)<
          ]>
```

In this example, the DTD contains two document definitions, one for MyBook and one for YourBook, both contained in marked sections which, via entity declarations, are set to be ignored. To make MyBook active, the Standard entity must be re-defined to hold 'INCLUDE'. Instead of editing the DTD, this can be achieved using the *SGMLS* switch as follows:

```
-iStandard
```

This produces the same effect as if the following declaration had been entered in the document type declaration subset:

```
<!ENTITY Standard "INCLUDE">
```

As re-definitions are ignored, this overrides the entity declaration for Standard in the DTD, and therefore switches-on the marked sections controlled by the entity called Standard. To use the other variant of the DTD, the switch is simply changed to '-ivariant'.

NSGMLS additional features

A **catalog** file containing mappings between public or system identifiers and the physical location and file names is specified using the '-m' switch, as in '-mmycatal.dat' (see Chapter 6 for details on the SGML Open standard for the syntax of catalog entries). Alternatively, the '-D' switch specifies the directory containing files specified in a **system identifier**. These techniques may be used in combination.

The '-C' switch indicates that the following file names a catalog file which contains a DOCUMENT entry specifying the SGML document to parse. For example, 'NSGMLS -C MYCAT.DAT'. In this example, the catalog file 'MYCAT.DAT' will contain an entry such as:

```
DOCUMENT C:\SGML\DOCS\MYDOC.SGM
```

The '-t' switch specifies a file to which **RAST** output should be directed. The RAST format is an alternative format to **ESIS** standardized under **ISO/IEC 13673**. If used, the ESIS output is suppressed.

The '-w' switch specifies various warning and error reporting conditions, in some cases duplicating existing switches used in *SGMLS*, as previously described. In addition, the switch '-wno-idref' switches-off checking of IDREF values, which can be useful when parsing a document that will eventually become part of a larger document, and removes the need to produce an 'internal' DTD that re-defines these attributes to NAME or CDATA types. The switch '-wmixed' warns of ambiguous content caused by mixed data models not using the OR connector, such as '(name,#PCDATA)'. The switch '-wsgmldecl' warns about errors in the SGML declaration and the switch '-wundefined' warns of elements referred to in the DTD but not defined there. Other '-w' switches are also allowed to warn of various minimization techniques in use in the document instance.

14. Charts and tables

The charts and tables included in this chapter are:

- Reference quantity set
- Attribute types
- ISO 639 language codes
- This book DTD
- ISO 8859/1 – 8-bit character set
- ISO Latin 1 character entities (ISOlat1)
- ISO Greek 1 character entities (ISOgrk1)
- ISO Numeric and Special Graphic entities (ISOnum)

Reference quantity set

The limits set on various quantities in the implied settings for the Basic SGML declaration.

ATTCNT	40	Number of attribute names and name tokens in an attribute definition list
ATTSPLEN	960	Normalized length of a start-tag attribute specifications list
BSEQLEN	960	Length of a blank sequence in a short reference string
DTAGLEN	16	Length of a data tag
DTEMPLEN	16	Length of a data tag template or pattern template (undelimited)
ENTLVL	16	Nesting level of entities (other than primary)
GRPCNT	32	Number of tokens in a group
GRPGTCNT	96	Grand total of content tokens at all levels of a content model
GRPLVL	16	Nesting level of model groups (including first level)
LITLEN	240	Length of a parameter literal or attribute value literal (interpreted and undelimited)
NAMELEN	8	Length of a name, name token, number etc.
NORMSEP	2	Used in lieu of counting separators in calculating normalized lengths
PILEN	240	Length of a processing instruction (undelimited)
TAGLEN	960	Length of a start-tag (undelimited)
TAGLVL	24	Nesting level of open elements

Attribute types

The names of **types** that may be declared for an attribute in an **attribute definition list**[142].

Keyword	Description	Characters	Example
CDATA	Character data	ALL	J. Smith
ENTITY	Entity name	*same as NAME*	FIG1
ENTITIES	Entity names	*same as NAMES*	FIG1 FIG2
ID	Identifier (unique)	a...Z 0...9 .-	Z-123.98
IDREF	Identifier reference	a...Z 0...9 .-	Z-123.98
IDREFS	Identifier references	a...Z 0...9 .-	Par54 Par78
NAME	SGML name	a...Z then a...Z .- **default 8 char length**	Lucas
NAMES	SGML names	a...Z then a...Z .- **default 8 char length**	Lucas Kettle
NMTOKEN	SGML name token	a...Z .- **default 8 char length**	-Lucas
NMTOKENS	SGML name tokens	a...Z .- **default 8 char length**	-Lucas .Kettle
NOTATION	Pre-defined Notation Name	*same as NAME*	CGM
NUMBER	Numeric value	0...9	123
NUMBERS	Numeric values (separated by '+')	0...9+0...9	123+987+456
NUTOKEN	Numeric token	0...9 then a...Z 0...9 .-	6zz
NUTOKENS	Numeric tokens (separated by '+')	0...9 then a...Z 0...9 .-	6zz+9yy+4-X+2

ISO 639 language codes

These language codes are used in **public identifiers**.

Code	Language
EN	English
FR	French
DE	German
GR	Greek
IT	Italian
NL	Dutch
ES	Spanish
PT	Portuguese
AR	Arabic
HE	Hebrew
RU	Russian
CH	Chinese
JA	Japanese
HI	Hindi
UR	Urdu
SA	Sanskrit

This book DTD

The DTD used for this book is included as an illustration of the concepts described in Chapter 7:

```
<!-- The Concise SGML Companion DTD v 1.3-->
<!-- ENTITY DECLARATIONS -->

<!ENTITY % CALStable SYSTEM "C:\CALS\TABLE.DTD">
%CALStable;
<!ENTITY % ISOnum
        PUBLIC "ISO 8879:1986//ENTITIES
                Numeric and Special Graphic//EN">
%ISOnum;
<!ENTITY % ISOlat1
        PUBLIC "ISO 8879:1986//ENTITIES
                Added Latin 1//EN">
%ISOlat1;
<!ENTITY % ISOgrk1
        PUBLIC "ISO 8879:1986//ENTITIES
                Greek Letters//EN">
%ISOgrk1;
<!ENTITY % ISOpub
        PUBLIC "ISO 8879:1986//ENTITIES
                Publishing//EN">
%ISOpub;

<!ENTITY % Examples  "Markup | Rendered" >
<!ENTITY % SuperSub  "Super | Sub" >
<!ENTITY % Titletext "#PCDATA | %SuperSub | Keyword" >
<!ENTITY % Hilite    "Emph | Stress | Keyword | Name" >

<!-- MAIN STRUCTURE -->

<!ELEMENT SGML-Book   - - (Chapter+) +(Xref | Pref)>
<!ELEMENT Chapter     - - (ChapTitle,
                          (Glossary | Roadmap | Para |
                           Random-list | Markup-para |
                           SecTitle | Sub-title |
                           Tabular | Graphic | Chap-toc |
                           Sect-toc | Breakpage)* |
                           Dedicate+) >
<!ATTLIST Chapter         Target    ID        #REQUIRED>
<!-- Dedications on front page -->
<!ELEMENT Dedicate    - - (#PCDATA | Emph)*
                          -- Dedication -->
<!-- Glossary item para's displayed differently -->
<!ELEMENT Glossary    - - (Para | Markup-para |
                           Breakpage)*
                          -- Glossary Items -->
<!-- Roadmap charts have different pagination and
     font size rules -->
```

```
<!ELEMENT Roadmap      - - (Para | Markup-para)*>

<!-- HEADINGS -->

<!-- Chapter Titles, such as "DTD" -->
<!ELEMENT ChapTitle    - - (%Titletext;)*
                            --Chapter Title-->
<!-- Section Title, such as "Model Groups" -->
<!ELEMENT SecTitle     - - (%Titletext;)*
                            --Section Title-->
<!ATTLIST SecTitle       Target    ID      #REQUIRED>
<!ELEMENT Sub-title    - - (%Titletext;)*
                            --Sub-Section Title-->
<!ATTLIST Sub-title      Target    ID      #REQUIRED>

<!-- TEXT BLOCKS -->

<!ELEMENT Para         - - ((#PCDATA | Markup |
                            %hilite; | Sup | Sub |
                            Keyword)*, Paralist?)>
<!-- A simple list at the end of a Paragraph -->
<!ELEMENT Paralist     - - (Paralitem+)>
<!ELEMENT Paralitem    - - (#PCDATA | %hilite |
                            Markup | %SuperSub)*
                            -- Paragraph List It>
<!ELEMENT Random-list  - - (Item*)>
<!ELEMENT Item         - - (Para*)>
<!-- Text block dislayed in mono-space -->
<!ELEMENT Markup-para  - - (Markup-line*)>
<!ELEMENT Markup-line  - - ((#PCDATA | %hilite | Rendered
                            | %SuperSub)*>

<!-- INLINE STRUCTURES -->

<!ELEMENT Rendered     - - (#PCDATA | %examples | %hilite
                            | Sup | Sub)* -(Rendered)>
<!ELEMENT Markup       - - (#PCDATA | %hilite |%SuperSub)*
 --SGML text-->
<!-- Proper name displayed in italic -->
<!ELEMENT Name         - - (#PCDATA)*
                            --Proper Name-->
<!-- Emphasized text is shown in bold -->
<!ELEMENT Emph         - - (#PCDATA | %examples | Stress |
                            %SuperSub | Keyword)* -(Emph)
                            --Emphasis (gloss items)-->
<!-- Stresses text is shown in italic -->
<!ELEMENT Stress       - - (#PCDATA | Markup | Emph |
                            %SuperSub | Keyword)*
                            --Stressed (names)-->
<!-- SGML Keywords are shown in small-caps -->
<!ELEMENT Keyword      - - (#PCDATA | %SuperSub)*
                            --SGML Keyword-->
<!ELEMENT Sup          - - (#PCDATA)
```

```
                          --Superscript-->
<!ELEMENT Sub          - - (#PCDATA)
                          --Subscript-->

<!-- MISCELLANEOUS -->

<!-- Forced page break for "pretty" effects (used in the
     "Charts and Tables" chapter -->
<!ELEMENT Breakpage    - O EMPTY>
<!ELEMENT Graphic      - O EMPTY>
<!ATTLIST Graphic           Ident  ENTITY   #REQUIRED>
<!-- Structures for building Table of Contents (TOC) -->
<!ELEMENT Chap-toc     - - (#PCDATA | Stress)*>
<!ELEMENT Sect-toc     - - (#PCDATA | Stress)*>
<!-- Page reference to generate page numbers in TOC -->
<!ELEMENT Pref         - - #PCDATA>
<!-- Cross-references to other text in the book -->
<!ELEMENT Xref         - - #PCDATA>
<!ATTLIST Xref              Source  IDREF   #REQUIRED>
```

ISO 8859/1 – 8-bit character set

The character set describing European letters, numbers and symbols. This character set is used by HTML, and forms the basis of Microsoft Windows fonts (although reserved places are filled with extra characters in the Windows version) and UNIX fonts (for example, Open Windows).

The first 128 characters are derived from the **ISO/IEC 646** version of **ASCII**. The remaining 128 characters cover European accented characters, and further common symbols. The official ISO name for each character is placed in brackets, for example, 'Solidus (slash).'

The ISO SGML Character Entity sets, **ISOnum**, **ISOlat1** and **ISOdia**, provide an alternative means of specifying most of the characters in this set. Each entity reference is identified as belonging to one of these sets as follows:

- N = ISOnum
- L = ISOlat1
- D = ISOdia

For example, '< N' indicates that entity reference '<' belongs to the ISOnum set. Those not covered by any ISO entity set are shown as numeric entities, '&#...;'. When an entry appears in italic, the character is easily available from the keyboard, and has no significance in any SGML context (so the entity reference is not generally needed), or it is unused within an SGML context (mainly redundant control codes).

HTML format uses all of the **ISOlat1** character entities, plus those **ISOnum** entities commented '(use in HTML).'

Decimal and Hex		Character Entities	Description
000 00		&#00;	*NUL - no effect*
001 01		&#01;	*SOH - Start of Heading*
002 02		&#02;	*STX - Start of Text*
003 03		&#03;	*ETX - End of Text*
004 04		&#04;	*EOT - End of Transmission*
005 05		&#05;	*ENQ - Enquiry*
006 06		&#06;	*ACK - Acknowledge*
007 07		&#07;	*BEL - Bell*
008 08		&#08;	*BS - Backspace*
009 09		&#09;	HT - Horizontal Tab, **HTML** Tab

010 0A		&#10;	LF - Line Feed, **HTML** new-line (with or without '013'), **record start** (**RS**)
011 0B		*&#11;*	*VT - Vertical Tabulation*
012 0C		&#12;	FF - Form Feed
013 0D		&#13;	CR - Carriage return, **HTML** new-line (with or without '010'), **record end** (**RE**)
014 0E		*&#14;*	*SO - Shift Out*
015 0F		*&#15;*	*SI - Shift In*
016 10		*&#16;*	*DLE - Data Link Escape*
017 11		*&#17;*	*DC1 - Device Control (1)*
018 12		*&#18;*	*DC2 - Device Control (2)*
019 13		*&#19;*	*DC3 - Device Control (3)*
020 14		*&#20;*	*DC4 - Device Control (4)*
021 15		*&#21;*	*NAK - No Acknowledge*
022 16		*&#22;*	*SYN - Synchronize*
023 17		*&#23;*	*ETB - End of Transmission Block*
024 18		*&#24;*	*CAN - Cancel*
025 19		*&#25;*	*EM - End of Medium*
026 1A		*&#26;*	*SUB - Substitute Character*
027 1B		*&#27;*	*ESC - Escape*
028 1C		*&#28;*	*FS - File Separator*
029 1D		*&#29;*	*GS - Group Separator*
030 1E		*&#30;*	*RS - Record Separator*
031 1F		*&#31;*	*US - Unit Separator*
032 20		&#32;	Space (space)
033 21	!	*!* N	Exclamation (exclam), **markup declaration open** ('<!mymarks>')
034 22	"	" N (use in HTML)	Quotation (quotedbl), **Literal** (use " in attributes with literal delimiters)
035 23	#	*#* N	Number sign (numbersign), **reserved name indicator** ('#PCDATA')
036 24	$	*$* N	Dollar sign (dollar)
037 25	%	*%* N	Percent sign (percent), **parameter entity reference open** ('%ent;')
038 26	&	& N	Ampersand (ampersand), **and connector** ('a & b'), **entity reference open** ('&ent;'), **character reference open** ('&#26;')
039 27	'	*'* N	Apostrophe sign (-), **literal alternative** (use ' in attributes with literal alternative delimiters)
040 28	(	(N	Left parenthesis (parenleft), **group open** ('(a, b)')
041 29	)	) N	Right parenthesis (parenright), **group close** ('(a, b)')
042 2A	*	*** N	Asterisk (asterisk), **optional and repeatable** ('a, b*')

043 2B	+	+ N	Plus sign (plus), **required and repeatable** ('a, b+'), **inclusion** (' +(a,b)')
044 2C	,	, N	Comma (comma), **sequence connector** ('a, b, c')
045 2D	-	‐ N	Hyphen (hyphen), **exclusion, comment** ('--my comment--')
046 2E	.	. N	Full point (period)
047 2F	/	/ N	Solidus (slash), **null end-tag** ('</>'), **end-tag open** ('</tag>')
048 30	0	&#48;	Zero (zero)
049 31	1	&#49;	One (one)
050 32	2	&#50;	Two (two)
051 33	3	&#51;	Three (three)
052 34	4	&#52;	Four (four)
053 35	5	&#53;	Five (five)
054 36	6	&#54;	Six (six)
055 37	7	&#55;	Seven (seven)
056 38	8	&#56;	Eight (eight)
057 39	9	&#57;	Nine (nine)
058 3A	:	: N	Colon (colon)
059 3B	;	; N	Semicolon (semicolon), **reference close** ('&ent;')
060 3C	<	< N (use in HTML)	Less than (less), **start tag open, markup declaration open** ('<!'), **end-tag open** ('</'), **processing instruction open** ('<?')
061 3D	=	= N	Equals (equal), **value indicator** ('attrib="value"')
062 3E	>	> N (use in HTML)	Greater than (greater), **markup declaration close** ('<!.......>'), **processing instruction close** ('<?proc>', **tag-close** ('<tag>')
063 3F	?	? N	Question mark (question), **optional occurrence indicator** ('a ǀ b'), **processing instruction open** ('<?')
064 40	@	@ N	Commercial at (at)
065 41	A	&#65;	A
066 42	B	&#66;	B
067 43	C	&#67;	C
068 44	D	&#68;	D
069 45	E	&#69;	E
070 46	F	&#70;	F
071 47	G	&#71;	G
072 48	H	&#72;	H
073 49	I	&#73;	I
074 4A	J	&#74;	J
075 4B	K	&#75;	K

076 4C	L	&#76;	L
077 4D	M	&#77;	M
078 4E	N	&#78;	N
079 4F	O	&#79;	O
080 50	P	&#80;	P
081 51	Q	&#81;	Q
082 52	R	&#82;	R
083 53	S	&#83;	S
084 54	T	&#84;	T
085 55	U	&#85;	U
086 56	V	&#86;	V
087 57	W	&#87;	W
088 58	X	&#88;	X
089 59	Y	&#89;	Y
090 5A	Z	&#90;	Z
091 5B	[	[N	Left square bracket (bracketleft), **declaration subset open** ('<!DOCTYPE ... [...]>'), **data tag group open**
092 5C	\	&#92;	Reverse solidus (backslash)
093 5D	]	] N	Right square bracket (bracketright), **declaration subset close** ('<!DOCTYPE ... [...]>'), **data tag group close**, **marked section close** (']]')
094 5E	^	ˆ D	Caret (asciicircum)
095 5F	_	― N	Underscore (underscore)
096 60	`	` D	Grave accent (-)
097 61	a	&#97;	a
098 62	b	&#98;	b
099 63	c	&#99;	c
100 64	d	&#100;	d
101 65	e	&#101;	e
102 66	f	&#102;	f
103 67	g	&#103;	g
104 68	h	&#104;	h
105 69	i	&#105;	i
106 6A	j	&#106;	j
107 6B	k	&#107;	k
108 6C	l	&#108;	l
109 6D	m	&#109;	m
110 6E	n	&#110;	n
111 6F	o	&#111;	o
112 70	p	&#112;	p
113 71	q	&#113;	q
114 72	r	&#114;	r

115 73	s	`&#115;`	s
116 74	t	`&#116;`	t
117 75	u	`&#117;`	u
118 76	v	`&#118;`	v
119 77	w	`&#119;`	w
120 78	x	`&#120;`	x
121 79	y	`&#121;`	y
122 7A	z	`&#122;`	z
123 7B	{	`&lcub;` N	Left curly brace (braceleft)
124 7C	|	`&verbar;` N	Vertical bar (bar), **or connector**
125 7D	}	`&rcub;` N	Right curly brace (braceright)
126 7E	~	`&tilde;` D	Tilde (asciitilde)
127 7F		`&#127;`	Delete (del), Checkerboard effect
128 80			WINDOWS CHARS, delete (del)
....			...
....			...
....			...
159 9F			WINDOWS CHARS
160 A0		` ` N (use in HTML 3)	NBS - Non break space (-)
161 A1	¡	`&iexcl;` N	Inverted exclamation (exclamdown)
162 A2	¢	`&cent;` N	Cent sign (cent)
163 A3	£	`&pound;` N	Pound sterling (pound)
164 A4	¤	`&curren;` N	General currency symbol (currency)
165 A5	¥	`&yen;` N	Yen sign (yen)
166 A6	≠	`&verbar;` N	Broken vertical bar (pipe)
167 A7	§	`&sect;` N	Section sign (section)
168 A8	¨	`&uml;` D	Umlaut (dieresis)
169 A9	©	`&copy;` N (use in HTML 3)	Copyright (copyrightserif)
170 AA	ª	`&ordf;` N	Feminine ordinal (ordfeminine)
171 AB	«	`&laquo;` N	Left angle quote (guillemotleft)
172 AC	¬	`&not;` N	Not sign (logicalnot)
173 AD	-	`&#173;`	Soft hyphen (hyphen)
174 AE	®	`&reg;` N (use in HTML 3)	Registered trademark (registerserif)
175 AF	¯	`&macr;` D	Macron accent (macron)
176 B0	°	`&deg;` N	Degree sign (ring)
177 B1	±	`&plusmn;` N	Plus or minus (plusminus)
178 B2	Σ	`&sup2;` N	Superscript two (Reserved)
179 B3	Π	`&sup3;` N	Superscript three (Reserved)
180 B4	´	`&acute;` D	Acute accent (acute)
181 B5	µ	`&micro;` N	Micro sign (Reserved)

182 B6	¶	¶ N	Paragraph sign (paragraph)
183 B7	·	· N	Middle dot (periodcentered)
184 B8	¸	¸ D	Cedilla (cedilla)
185 B9	∂	¹ N	Superscript one (Reserved)
186 BA	º	º N	Masculine ordinale (ordmasculine)
187 BB	»	» N	Right angle quote (guillemotright)
188 BC	π	¼ N	Fraction one-fourth (Reserved)
189 BD	∫	½ N ½ N	Fraction one-half (Reserved)
190 BE	Ω	¾ N	Fraction three-fourths (Reserved)
191 BF	¿	¿ N	Inverted question mark (questiondown)
192 C0	À	À L	Capital A grave (Agrave)
193 C1	Á	Á L	Capital A acute (Aacute)
194 C2	Â	Â L	Capital A circumflex (Acircumflex)
195 C3	Ã	Ã L	Capital A tilde (Atilde)
196 C4	Ä	Ä L	Capital A umlaut (Adieresis)
197 C5	Å	Å L	Capital A ring (Aring)
198 C6	Æ	Æ L	Capital AE dipthong (AE)
199 C7	Ç	Ç L	Capital C cedilla (Ccedilla)
200 C8	È	È L	Capital E grave (Egrave)
201 C9	É	É L	Capital E acute (Eacute)
202 CA	Ê	Ê L	Capital E circumflex (Ecircumflex)
203 CB	Ë	Ë L	Capital E umlaut (Edieresis)
204 CC	Ì	Ì L	Capital I grave (Igrave)
205 CD	Í	Í L	Capital I acute (Iacute)
206 CE	Î	Î L	Capital I circumflex (Icircumflex)
207 CF	Ï	Ï L	Capital I umlaut (Idieresis)
208 D0	√	Ð L	Capital Eth Icelandic (Reserved)
209 D1	Ñ	Ñ L	Capital N tilde (Ntilde)
210 D2	Ò	Ò L	Capital O grave (Ograve)
211 D3	Ó	Ó L	Capital O acute (Oacute)
212 D4	Ô	Ô L	Capital O circumflex (Ocircumflex)
213 D5	Õ	Õ L	Capital O tilde (Otilde)
214 D6	Ö	Ö L	Capital O umlaut (Odieresis)
215 D7	×	× N	Multiply sign (Reserved)
216 D8	Ø	Ø L	Capital O slash (Oslash)
217 D9	Ù	Ù L	Capital U grave (Ugrave)
218 DA	Ú	Ú L	Capital U acute (Uacute)
219 DB	Û	Û L	Capital U circumflex (circumflex)
220 DC	Ü	Ü L	Capital U umlaut (Udieresis)
221 DD	≈	Ý L	Capital Y acute (Reserved)
222 DE	◊	Þ L	Capital THORN Icelandic (Reserved)

223 DF	ß	ß L	Small sharp s, sz ligature (germandbls)
224 E0	à	à L	Small a grave (agrave)
225 E1	á	á L	Small a acute (aacute)
226 E2	â	â L	Small a circumflex (acircumflex)
227 E3	ã	ã L	Small a tilde (atilde)
228 E4	ä	ä L	Small a umlaut (adieresis)
229 E5	å	å L	Small a ring (aring)
230 E6	æ	æ L	Small ae dipthong, ligature (ae)
231 E7	ç	ç L	Small c cedilla (ccedilla)
232 E8	è	è L	Small e grave (egrave)
233 E9	é	é L	Small e acute (eacute)
234 EA	ê	ê L	Small e circumflex (ecircumflex)
235 EB	ë	ë L	Small e umlaut (edieresis)
236 EC	ì	ì L	Small i grave (igrave)
237 ED	í	í L	Small i acute (iacute)
238 EE	î	î L	Small i circumflex (icircumflex)
239 EF	ï	ï L	Small i umlaut (idieresis)
240 F0	≤	ð L	Small eth Icelandic (Reserved)
241 F1	ñ	ñ L	Small n tilde (ntilde)
242 F2	ò	ò L	Small o grave (ograve)
243 F3	ó	ó L	Small o acute (oacute)
244 F4	ô	ô L	Small o circumflex (ocircumflex)
245 F5	õ	õ L	Small o tilde (otilde)
246 F6	ö	ö L	Small o umlaut (odieresis)
247 F7	÷	÷ N	Division sign (Reserved)
248 F8	ø	ø N	Small o slash (oslash)
249 F9	ù	ù N	Small u grave (ugrave)
250 FA	ú	ú N	Small u acute (uacute)
251 FB	û	û N	Small u circumflex (ucircumflex)
252 FC	ü	ü N	Small u umlaut (udieresis)
253 FD	Δ	ý N	Small y acute (Reserved)
254 FE		þ N	Small thorn Icelandic (Reserved)
255 FF	ÿ	ÿ N	Small y umlaut (ydieresis)

ISO Latin 1 character entities (ISOlat1)

Latin alphabet characters (covering most Western European languages) are represented by the entity set **ISOlat1**:

	Entity	Description		Entity	Description
á	&aacute;	Small a acute	ï	&iuml;	Small i dieresis (umlaut)
Á	&Aacute;	Capital A acute	Ï	&Iuml;	Capital I dieresis (umlaut)
â	&acirc;	Small a circumflex	ñ	&ntilde;	Small n tilde
Â	&Acirc;	Capital A circumflex	Ñ	&Ntilde;	Capital N tilde
à	&agrave;	Small a grave	ó	&oacute;	Small o acute
å	&aring;	Small a ring	Ó	&Oacute;	Capital O acute
Å	&Aring;	Capital A ring	ô	&ocirc;	Small o circumflex
ã	&atilde;	Small a tilde	Ô	&Ocirc;	Capital O circumflex
Ã	&Atilde;	Capital A tilde	ò	&ograve;	Small o grave
ä	&auml;	Small a umlaut	Ò	&Ograve;	Capital O grave
Ä	&Auml;	Capital A umlaut	ø	&oslash;	Small o slash
æ	&aelig;	Small ae dipthong	Ø	&Oslash;	Capital O slash
ç	&ccedil;	Small c cedilla	õ	&otilde;	Small o tilde
Ç	&Ccedil;	Capital C cedilla	Õ	&Otilde;	Capital O tilde
≤	&eth;	Small eth Icelandic	ö	&ouml;	Small o dieresis (umlaut)
√	&ETH;	Capital Eth Icelandic	Ö	&Ouml;	Capital O dieresis
é	&eacute;	Small e acute	ß	&szlig;	Small s sharp (sz ligature)
É	&Eacute;	Capital E acute		&thorn;	Small thorn Icelandic
ê	&ecirc;	Small e circumflex	◊	&THORN;	Capital THORN Icelandic
Ê	&Ecirc;	Capital E circumflex	ú	&uacute;	Small u acute
è	&egrave;	Small e grave	Ú	&Uacute;	Capital U acute
È	&Egrave;	Capital E grave	û	&ucirc;	Small u circumflex

ë	&euml;	Small e dieresis (umlaut)	Û	&Ucirc;	Capital U circumflex
Ë	&Euml;	Capital E dieresis (umlaut)	ù	&ugrave;	Small u grave
í	&iacute;	Small i acute	Ù	&Ugrave;	Capital U grave
Í	&Iacute;	Capital I acute	ü	&uuml;	Small u dieresis (umlaut)
î	&icirc;	Small i circumflex	Ü	&Uuml;	Capital U dieresis (umlaut)
Î	&Icirc;	Capital I circumflex	Δ	&yacute;	Small y acute
ì	&igrave;	Small I grave	≈	&Yacute;	Capital Y acute
Ì	&Igrave;	Capital I	ÿ	&yuml;	Small y dieresis (umlaut)

ISO Greek 1 character entities (ISOgrk1)

Greek alphabet characters are represented by the entity set **ISOgrk1** (for use in formulae see ISOgrk2):

	Entity	Description		Entity	Description
α	&agr;	Small alpha	ξ	&xgr;	Small xi
A	&Agr;	Capital Alpha	Ξ	&Xgr;	Capital Xi
β	&bgr;	Small beta	o	&ogr;	Small omicron
B	&Bgr;	Capital Beta	O	&Ogr;	Capital Omicron
γ	&ggr;	Small gamma	π	&pgr;	Small pi
Γ	&Ggr;	Capital Gamma	Π	&Pgr;	Capital Pi
δ	&dgr;	Small delta	ρ	&rgr;	Small rho
Δ	&Dgr;	Capital Delta	P	&Rgr;	Capital Rho
ε	&egr;	Small epsilon	σ	&sgr;	Small sigma
E	&Egr;	Capital Epsilon	Σ	&Sgr;	Capital Sigma
ζ	&zgr;	Small zeta		&sfgr;	final small sigma
Z	&Zgr;	Capital Zeta	τ	&tgr;	Small tau
η	&eegr;	Small eta	T	&Tgr;	Capital Tau
H	&EEgr;	Capital Eta	υ	&ugr;	Small upsilon
θ	&thgr;	Small theta	Y	&Ugr;	Capital Upsilon
Θ	&THgr;	Capital Theta	φ	&phgr;	Small phi
ι	&igr;	Small iota	Φ	&PHgr;	Capital Phi
I	&Igr;	Capital Iota	χ	&khgr;	Small chi
κ	&kgr;	Small kappa	X	&KHgr;	Capital Chi
K	&Kgr;	Capital Kappa	ψ	&psgr;	Small psi
λ	&lgr;	Small lambda	Ψ	&PSgr;	Capital Psi
Λ	&Lgr;	Capital Lambda	ω	&ohgr;	Small omega
μ	&mgr;	Small mu	Ω	&OHgr;	Capital Omega
M	&Mgr;	Capital Mu			
ν	&ngr;	Small nu			
N	&Ngr;	Capital Nu			

ISO Numeric and Special Graphic entities (ISOnum)

Common symbols found in character sets not covered by ASCII or by ISOlat1, including alternatives for special characters '<' and '&', are represented by the entity set **ISOnum**:

	Entity	Description		Entity	Description
⌠	&half;	Fraction one-half	°	&degree	Degree sign
⌠	&frac12;	Fraction one-half	º	&ordm;	Ordinal masculine
π	&frac14;	Fraction one-quarter	ª	&ordf;	Ordinal feminine
Ω	&frac34;	Fraction three-quarters	§	&sect;	Section sign
1/8	&frac18;	Fraction one-eighth	¶	&para;	Pilcrow (paragraph sign)
3/8	&frac38;	Fraction three-eighths	·	&middot;	Middle dot
5/6	&frac56;	Fraction five-sixths	←	&larr;	Leftward arrow
7/8	&frac78;	Fraction seven-eighths	→	&rarr;	Rightward arrow
¹	&sup1;	Superscript one	↑	&uarr;	Upward arrow
²	&sup2;	Superscript two	↓	&darr;	Downward arrow
³	&sup3;	Superscript three	©	&copy;	Copyright sign
+	&plus;	Plus sign	®	&reg;	Registered sign
±	&plusmn;	Plus-or-minus sign	™	&trade;	Trademark sign
<	&lt;	Less-than sign	≠	&brvbar;	Broken vertical bar
=	&equals;	Equals sign	¬	&not;	Not sign
>	&gt;	Greater-than sign		&sung;	Musical note
÷	&divide;	Divide sign	!	&excl;	Exclamation mark
×	&times;	Multiply sign	¡	&iexcl;	Inverted exclamation mark
¤	&curren;	General currency sign	"	&quot;	Quotation mark
£	&pound;	Pound sign	'	&apos;	Apostrophe
$	&dollar;	Dollar sign	(	&lpar;	Left parenthesis

¢	&cent;	Cent sign	)	&rpar;	Right paren-thesis
¥	&yen;	Yen sign	,	&comma;	Comma
#	&num;	Number sign	_	&lowbar;	Low line
%	&percnt;	Percent sign	-	&hyphen;	Hyphen
&	&amp;	Ampersand	.	&period;	Full stop
*	&ast;	Asterisk	/	&sol;	Solidus
@	&commat;	Commercial at	:	&colon;	Colon
[	&lsqb;	Left square bracket	;	&semi;	Semicolon
\	&bsol;	Backslash (reverse solidus)	?	&quest;	Question mark
]	&rsqb;	Right square bracket	¿	&iquest;	Inverted ques-tion mark
{	&lcub;	Left curly bracket	«	&laquo;	Angle quota-tion left
–	&horbar;	Horizontal bar	»	&raquo;	Angle quota-tion right
|	&verbar;	Vertical bar	'	&lsquo;	Single quota-tion mark left
}	&rcub;	Right curly bracket	'	&rsquo;	Single quota-tion mark right
µ	&micro;	Micro sign	"	&ldquo;	Double quota-tion mark left
Ω	&ohm;	Ohm sign	"	&rdquo;	Double quota-tion mark right
					No break space (required)
				&shy;	Soft hyphen (end line split word)

Road Map

This section is intended to be used as an aid to navigation through the **ISO 8879** standard, and is referenced from terms appearing in the main text and the Glossary. Note that for the sake of brevity, little used features of the language are not illustrated (including the link, rank and datatag features, and the system declaration). The full ISO standard is still required for a thorough specification of SGML.

Syntactic productions

The 'road map' is derived from the **syntactic production** charts appearing in ISO 8879. This is essentially a hierarchy of definitions. Each syntax production defines a **syntactic variable**, such as 'SGML document,' using an expression composed of syntactic tokens.

```
syntactic variable = expression
                      /         \
               syntactic      syntactic
                 token          token
```

Each **syntactic token** must be one of the following:

- another syntactic variable, such as 'SGML document entity' (which would have its own defining expression)
- a **syntactic literal**, such as 'PUBLIC'
- a **delimiter role**, such as 'TAGC' or 'AND'
- a **terminal variable** or **terminal constant** name, such as 'EE,' 'RE' and 'LCletter'

Chart format

Every syntactic variable begins a new chart, and is identified with a number in brackets, such as '(171)' (this is the official syntactic production number). The chart then shows the constituent syntactic tokens using a simple structure format:

```
(171) token one

----- token two ... (172)
        |
      token three ... (180)
```

In the example above, token one includes both token two and token three, and token three follows token two. The substructures are displayed in charts '(172)' and '(180).'

The production charts appear in numeric order. Note that an alphabetically ordered listing (and definition) of these productions appears in the *Glossary*.

Some obscure features of SGML are not covered (link, rank, datatag and the system declaration), leaving gaps in the numbers. When referred to, such features are displayed in italics, and are not further elaborated:

```
----- token two ... (172)
         |
      token three
```

The connecting lines can be followed across to the right and down only, starting from the top-left corner of the chart. In the example above, token two leads down to token three. The content of token two, indicated using '...(172),' can be implied to be part of this structure, not an alternative to token three.

The next example shows how optional structures are represented:

```
----- token two ... (172)
   |
   --- token three ... (180)
          |
       token four ... (013)
```

In this example, the expression contains either token two *or* token three followed by token four. The path divides across to token two, or down to token three.

Occurence rules for each token are shown using the official convention, '?' for optional, '+' for repeatable and '*' for optional and repeatable.

After most of the charts, there follows an example of its use. The example appears in italic style. For example:

```
----- start-tag ... (014)
          |
       content ... (024)
          |
       end-tag ... (019)
<mytag> ..... </mytag>
```

However, it should be noted that production charts show a hierarchy of *concepts*, which also just happen to specify and dictate the order of physical objects. It should not be assumed that each syntactic token directly relates to a unique object in the data stream. For example, a 'document element' is defined in chart (012) as consisting of an 'element' token. A 'document element' is simply a special category of 'element,' defined by its context, not by any additional characters in the data. The example for a document element may therefore be identical to the example for any other element.

Most examples only show typical usage, and should not be assumed to cover all possibilities. In some cases, however, several examples are employed to show various options. In this case, the examples are numbered:

```
1. <!ENTITY myentity "my text">
2. <!ENTITY myentity CDATA "my text">
3. <!ENTITY % myentity CDATA "my text">
4. <!ENTITY % myentity STARTTAG "chapter">
5. <!ENTITY % myentity SYSTEM "C:\MYENT.DAT"
```

Linking charts

All tokens are identified, using a combination of the chart number and a sequence number. This allows backward cross-referencing from other charts. For example:

```
(005) . . . . . . . . . . . . .
                | (005.8)       <-------------
                token ten ... (010)   >--    |
(007) ...                             |   |
                                      |   |
  /-----------------------------------   |
 /                                       |
                                         |
(010) token ten (005.8)        >-------------
                (010.1)
     ----- token fifteen ... (015)
           |   (010.2)
         token twenty ... (020)
           |   (010.3)
         token six ... (006)
```

The chart for token ten is numbered '(010)', and contains three tokens labelled '(010.1)', '(010.2)' and '(010.3)'. Token ten itself appears in chart '(005)', at precise location '(005.8)'. A token may be referenced from more than one other location, in which case there will be multiple references, such as '(005.8) (019.12)'. When a token is referenced several times from another single token, an abbreviated format is used. Instead of '(005.8) (005.11)', the format '(005.8 .11)' is used.

Chart groupings

001–006   Entity Structure

007–043   Element Structure

044–045   Processing Instruction

046–064   Common Constructs

065–109   Markup Declarations: General

110–153   Markup Declarations: DTD *(rank and datatag not covered)*

154–170   Markup Declarations: link (not covered)

171–199   SGML Declaration

200–204   Conformance (not covered)

(001) SGML document *(not part of any other structure)*

```
              (001.1)
----- SGML document entity ... (002)
          |
     (optional)
     (repeatable)
          |              (001.2)
          --- SGML subdocument entity... (003)
          |              (001.3)
          --- SGML text entity ... (004)
          |              (001.4)
          --- character data entity ... (005a)
          |              (001.5)
          --- specific character data entity ... (005b)
          |              (001.6)
          --- non-SGML data entity ... (006)
<!SGML ISO 8879:1986.......>
<!DOCTYPE mybook ( ... ]>
<mybook>.....</mybook>[EE]
a text entity(EE]a specific entity[EE]
```

(002) SGML document entity (001.1):

```
           (002.1)
----- s * ... (005)
       | (002.2)
       SGML declaration ... (171)
       | (002.3)
       prolog ... (007)
       | (002.4)
       document instance set ... (010)
       | (002.5)
       EE (entity end)
```

```
<!SGML ISO 8879:1986.......>
<!DOCTYPE mybook ......>
<mybook>.....</mybook>[EE]
```

(003) SGML subdocument entity (001.2):

```
           (003.1)
----- prolog ... (007)
       | (003.2)
       document instance set ... (010)
       | (003.3)
       EE (entity end)
```

(004) SGML text entity (001.3):

```
           (004.1)
----- SGML character * ... (050)
       | (004.2)
       EE (entity end)
```

```
This is an SGML text entity![EE]
```

(005) s (002.1) (008.3) (014.5) (017.5) (018.4) (019.4) (022.4) (026.3) (032.1 .3 .5) (065.1) (070.1) (071.1) (091.3) (149b.4):

```
           (005.1)
----- RE
   |       (005.2)
   --- RS
   |       (005.3)
   --- SPACE
   |       (005.4)
   --- SEPCHAR (separator character)
```

(005a) character data entity (001.4):

```
           (005a.1)
----- SGML character * ... (050)
       | (005a.2)
       EE (entity end)
```

```
This is a character data entity![EE]
```

(005b) specific character data entity (001.5):

```
          (005b.1)
----- SGML character * ... (050)
      | (005b.2)
      EE (entity end)
```

This is a specific character data entity![EE]

(006) non-SGML data entity (001.6):

```
          (006.1)
----- character * ... (049)
      | (006.2)
      EE (entity end)
```

@@<<<!%$£^&<<<)£&^&*[EE]

(007) prolog (002.3) (003.1):

```
              (007.1)
----- other prolog * ... (008)
          | (007.2)
      base document type declaration ... (009)
              |
      (repeatable)
          |           (007.3)
          --- document type declaration ... (110)
          |           (007.4)
          --- other prolog ... (008)
                  |
              (repeatable)
                  |           (007.5)
                  --- link type declaration
                  |           (007.6)
                  --- other prolog ... (008)
```

<!DOCTYPE mytag ....>

(008) other prolog (007.1 .4 .6) (010.2):

```
                  (008.1)
----- comment declaration ... (091)
   |              (008.2)
   --- processing instruction ... (044)
   |              (008.3)
   --- s (separator) ... (005)
```

<!-- this is the rest of the prolog -->

(009) base document type declaration (007.2):

```
                  (009.1)
----- document type declaration ... (110)
```

<!DOCTYPE mybook ....>

(010) document instance set (002.4) (003.2):

```
            (010.1)
----- base document element ... (011)
      |  (010.2)
      other prolog * ... (008)

<mybook> ..... </mybook>
<!-- the other prolog comment -->
<? the other prolog processing instruction>
```

(011) base document element (010.1):

```
                (011.1)
----- document element ... (012)

<mybook> ..... </mybook>
```

(012) document element (011.1):

```
          (012.1)
----- element ... (013)

<mybook> ..... </mybook>
```

(013) element (012.1) (025.2) (026.1):

```
              (013.1)
----- start-tag ? ... (014)
      |  (013.2)
      content ... (024)
      |  (013.3)
      end-tag ? ... (019)

1. <mytag...>
2. <mytag> ..... </mytag>
```

(014) start-tag (013.1):

```
            (014.1)
----- STAGO (start-tag open) ... "<"
  |   |  (014.2)
  |   document type specification ... (028)
  |   |  (014.3)
  |   generic identifier specification ... (029)
  |   |  (014.4)
  |   attribute specification list ... (031)
  |   |  (014.5)
  |   s * (separator) ... (005)
  |   |  (014.6)
  |   TAGC (tag close) ... ">"
  |   (014.7)
  --- minimized start-tag ... (015)

1. <(dtd2)mytag>
2. <mytag>
3. <mytag myattr="1">
4. <>
5. <mytag<...
6. <mytag/...
```

(015) minimized start-tag (014.7):

```
            (015.1)
----- empty start-tag ... (016)
  |        (015.2)
  --- unclosed start-tag ... (017)
  |        (015.3)
  --- net-enabling start-tag ... (018)

1. <>
2. <mytag <...
3. <mytag/
```

(016) empty start-tag (015.1):

```
            (016.1)
----- STAGO (start-tag open) ... "<"
      |  (016.2)
      TAGC (tag close) ... ">"

<>
```

(017) unclosed start-tag (015.2):

```
            (017.1)
----- STAGO (start-tag open) ... "<"
      |  (017.2)
      document type specification ... (028)
      |  (017.3)
      generic identifier specification ... (029)
      |  (017.4)
      attribute specification list ... (031)
      |  (017.5)
      s * (separator) ... (005)

1. <mytag<...
2. <mytag <...
3. <mytag myattr=1 <...
4. <(dtd2)mytag <...
```

(018) net-enabling start-tag (015.3):

```
            (018.1)
----- STAGO (start-tag open) ... "<"
      |  (018.2)
      generic identifier specification ... (029)
      |  (018.3)
      attribute specification list ... (031)
      |  (018.4)
      s (separator) * ... (005)
      |  (018.5)
      NET ... "/"

1. <mytag/
2. <mytag /
```

(019) end-tag (013.3):

```
          (019.1)
----- ETAGO (end-tag open) ... "</"
   |     |  (019.2)
   |     document type specification ... (028)
   |     |  (019.3)
   |     generic identifier specification ... (029)
   |     |  (019.4)
   |     s * (separator) ... (005)
   |     |  (019.5)
   |     TAGC (tag-close) ... ">"
   |        (019.6)
   --- minimized end-tag ... (020)

1. </mytag>
2. </>
3. /
```

(020) minimized end-tag (019.6):

```
          (020.1)
----- empty end-tag ... (021)
   |     (020.2)
   --- unclosed end-tag ... (022)
   |     (020.3)
   --- null end-tag ... (023)

1. </>
2. </mytag <othertag>
3. /
```

(021) empty end-tag (020.1):

```
          (021.1)
----- ETAGO (end-tag open) ... "<"
   |  (021.2)
      TAGC (tag close) ... ">"

</>
```

(022) unclosed end-tag (020.2):

```
          (022.1)
----- ETAGO (end-tag open) ... "<"
   |  (022.2)
      document type specification
   |  (022.3)
      generic identifier specification ... (029)
   |  (022.4)
      s * (separator) ... (005)

1. </mytag<othertag>
2. </mytag <othertag>
```

(023) null end-tag (020.3):

```
      (023.1)
----- NET ... "/"

/
```

(024) content (013.2):

```
                (024.1)
----- mixed content ... (025)
   |           (024.2)
   --- element content ... (026)
   |           (024.3)
   --- replaceable character data ... (046)
   |           (024.4)
   --- character data ... (047)
```

```
1. Water is H<sub>2</sub>O &amp; nothing else!
2. <title>...</title><p>...</p>
3. The caf&eacute; is open
4. The cafe is open (with no accent!)
```

(025) mixed content (024.1):

```
----|
  (optional)
 (repeatable)
     |           (025.1)
     --- data character ... (048)
     |           (025.2)
     --- element ... (013)
     |           (025.3)
     --- other content ... (027)
```

```
Water is H<sub>2</sub>O &amp; nothing else!
```

(026) element content (024.2):

```
----|
  (optional)
 (repeatable)
     |           (026.1)
     --- element ... (013)
     |           (026.2)
     --- other content ... (027)
     |           (026.3)
     --- s (separator) ... (005)
```

```
<title>...</title><p>...</p>
```

(027) other content (025.3) (026.2):

```
           (027.1)
 ----- comment declaration ... (091)
   |      (027.2)
   --- short reference use declaration ... (152)
   |      (027.3)
   --- link set use declaration
   |      (027.4)
   --- processing instruction ... (044)
   |      (027.5)
   --- shortref (short reference character) ... ("&#TAB;")
   |      (027.6)
   --- character reference ... (062)
   |      (027.7)
   --- general entity reference ... (059)
   |      (027.8)
   --- marked section declaration ... (093)
   |      (027.9)
   --- EE (entity end)

 <? PAGE_BREAK>&#126;
 <!-- A New Section! -->
 &commonparas;
```

(028) document type specification (014.2) (017.2) (019.2):

```
           (028.1)
 ----- name group ? ... (069)

 (dtd2)
```

(029) generic identifier specification (014.3) (017.3) (018.2) (019.3) (022.3):

```
           (029.1)
 ----- generic identifier ... (030)
   |      (029.2)
   --- rank stem

 mytag
```

(030) generic identifier (029.1) (072.1) (111.1) (117.1) (130.1):

```
         (030.1)
 ----- name ... (055)

 mytag
```

(031) attribute specification list (014.4) (017.4) (018.3) (149b.3):

```
                  (031.1)
 ----- attribute specification * ... (032)

 myattrib="X&amp;123" another="abc"
```

(032) attribute specification (031.1):

```
            (032.1)
----- s * (separator) ... (005)
      |        (032.2)
      ----- name ... (055)
      |       | (032.3)
      |       s * (separator) ... (005)
      |       | (032.4)
      |       VI (value indicator) ... "="
      |       | (032.5)
      |       s * (separator) ... (005)
      |       |
      |------|
              | (032.6)
              attribute value specification ... (033)
```

1. *MyValue*
2. *"My Value"*
3. *myattrib="X&123"*

(033) attribute value specification (032.6) (147.4):

```
            (033.1)
----- attribute value ... (035)
    |       (033.2)
    --- attribute value literal ... (034)
```

1. *myvalue*
2. *"My Value"*

(034) attribute value literal (033.2):

```
            (034.1)
----- LIT (literal delimiter) ... " " "
    |     | (034.2)
    |     replaceable character data * ... (046)
    |     | (034.3)
    |     LIT (literal delimiter) ... " " "
    |       (034.4)
    --- LITA (literal alternative) ... " ` "
          | (034.5)
          replaceable character data * ... (046)
          | (034.6)
          LITA (literal alternative) ... " ' "
```

1. *"X&123"*
2. *'X&123'*

(035) attribute value (033.1):

```
        (035.1)
----- character data ... (047)
  |     (035.2)
  --- general entity name ... (103)
  |     (035.3)
  --- general entity name list ... (035.a)
  |     (035.4)
  --- id value ... (036)
  |     (035.5)
  --- id reference value ... (038)
  |     (035.6)
  --- id reference list ... (037)
  |     (035.7)
  --- name ... (055)
  |     (035.8)
  --- name list ... (039)
  |     (035.9)
  --- name token ... (057)
  |     (035.10)
  --- name token list ... (040)
  |     (035.11)
  --- notation name ... (041)
  |     (035.12)
  --- number ... (056)
  |     (035.13)
  --- number list ... (042)
  |     (035.14)
  --- number token ... (058)
  |     (035.15)
  --- number token list ... (043)
```

myvalue

(035a) general entity name list (035.3):

```
        (035a.1)
----- name list ... (039)
```

entity1 entity2

(036) id value (035.4):

```
        (036.1)
----- name ... (055)
```

ThisID

(037) id reference list (035.6):

```
        (037.1)
----- name list ... (039)
```

thatID anothID

(038) id reference value (035.5):

```
          (038.1)
----- name ... (055)
```

myname

(039) name list (035.8) (035a.1) (037.1):

```
          (039.1)
----- name ... (055)
        |
   (optional)
   (repeatable)
       |   (039.2)
       SPACE ... " "
       |   (039.3)
       name ... (055)
```

myname Name2 Name3

(040) name token list (035.10):

```
          (040.1)
----- name token ... (057)
        |
   (optional)
   (repeatable)
       |   (040.2)
       SPACE ... " "
       |   (040.3)
       name token ... (057)
```

mytoken Token2 Token3

(041) notation name (035.11) (109.6) (148.4) (149a.4):

```
          (041.1)
----- name ... (055)
```

MyNota

(042) number list (035.13):

```
          (042.1)
----- number ... (056)
        |
    (optional)
    (repeatable)
       |  (042.2)
       SPACE ... " "
       |  (042.3)
       number ... (056)
```

123 987 555

(043) number token list (035.15):

```
          (043.1)
----- number token ... (058)
        |
    (optional)
    (repeatable)
        | (043.2)
      SPACE ... (" ")
        | (043.3)
      number token ... (058)
```

123 97X 1z

(044) processing instruction (008.2) (027.4) (071.5):

```
          (044.1)
----- PIO (processing instruction open) ... "<?"
        | (044.2)
      system data ... (045)
        | (044.3)
      PIC (processing instruction close) ... ">"
```

<? page_break >

(045) system data (044.2) (75.2 .5):

```
          (045.1)
----- character data ... (047)
```

page_break

(046) replaceable character data (024.3) (034.2 .5):

```
-----
        |
    (optional)
    (repeatable)
        |        (046.1)
      --- data character ... (048)
        |        (046.2)
      --- character reference ... (062)
        |        (046.3)
      --- general entity reference ... (059)
        |        (046.4)
      --- EE (entity end)
```

page_break

(047) character data (024.4) (035.1) (045.1):

```
          (047.1)
----- data character * ... (048)
```

a <tag> and some text

(048) data character (025.1) (047.1) (046.1) (067.1):

```
          (048.1)
----- SGML character ... (050)
```

(049) character (006.1):

```
        (049.1)
----- SGML character ... (050)
  |      (049.2)
  --- NONSGML (non SGML character)
```

(050) SGML character (004.1) (005a.1) (005b.1) (048.1) (049.1) (092.2) (096.1):

```
        (050.1)
----- markup character ... (051)
  |      (050.2)
  --- DATACHAR
```

(051) markup character (050.1):

```
        (051.1)
----- name character ... (052)
  |      (051.2)
  --- function character ... (054)
  |      (051.3)
  --- DELMCHAR
```

(052) name character (051.1) (055.2) (057.1) (058.2):

```
        (052.1)
----- name start character ... (053)
  |      (052.2)
  --- DIGIT ... ("7")
  |      (052.3)
  --- LCNMCHAR (lower case name character) ... ("-")
  |      (052.4)
  --- UCNMCHAR (upper case name character) ... ("-")
```

(053) name start character (052.1) (055.1):

```
        (053.1)
----- LC LETTER (lower case letter)... ("e")
  |      (053.2)
  --- UC LETTER (upper case letter)... ("E")
  |      (053.3)
  --- LCNMSTRT (lower case name start)... ("")
  |      (053.4)
  --- UCNMSTRT (upper case name start) ... ("")
```

(054) function character (051.2):

```
          (054.1)
----- RE (record end)
   |      (054.2)
   --- RS (record start)
   |      (054.3)
   --- SPACE ...  "  "
   |      (054.4)
   --- SEPCHAR ...  ("[tab]")
   |      (054.5)
   --- MSOCHAR (markup-scan-out character)
   |      (054.6)
   --- MSICHAR (markup-scan-in character)
   |      (054.7)
   --- MSSCHAR (markup-scan-suppress character)
   |      (054.8)
   --- FUNCHAR (function character)
```

(055) name (030.1) (032.2) (035.7) (036.1) (038.1) (039.1 .3) (041.1) (059.3) (060.3) (063.4) (069.3 .7) (086.1) (088.1) (103.1) (104.3) (144.1) (150 .8) (151.1) (180.8) (187.1) (191.5) (193.5) (194.5):

```
          (055.1)
----- name start character ... (053)
      | (055.2)
      name character * ... (052)
```

```
1. Mytag
2. X-1.8
```

(056) number (035.12) (042.1 .3) (064.1) (179.1) (180.10) (191.7) (198.8 .15):

```
          (056.1)
----- DIGIT + ... ("9")
```

```
95768
```

(057) name token (035.9) (040.1 .3) (068.3 .7):

```
          (057.1)
----- name character + ... (052)
```

```
mytoken
```

(058) number token (035.15) (043.1 .3):

```
          (058.1)
----- DIGIT ... ("9")
      | (058.2)
      name character * ... (052)
```

```
97X
```

(059) general entity reference (027.7) (046.3):

```
        (059.1)
----- ERO (entity reference open) ... "&"
      | (059.2)
      name group ? ... (069)
      | (059.3)
      name ... (055)
      | (059.4)
      reference end ... (061)
```

&myentity;

(060) parameter entity reference (065.3) (067.3) (070.3) (071.3):

```
        (060.1)
----- PERO (parameter entity reference open) ... "%"
      | (060.2)
      name group ? ... (069)
      | (060.3)
      name ... (055)
      | (060.4)
      reference end ... (061)
```

%myentity;

(061) reference end (059.4) (060.4) (062.4):

```
---
  |
(optional)
  |      (061.1)
  --- REFC (reference close) ... ";"
  |      (061.2)
  --- RE (record end)
```

;

(062) character reference (027.6) (046.2) (067.2):

```
        (062.1)
----- CRO (character reference open) ... "&#"
      |
      |----------------------------
      | (062.2)                    | (062.3)
      character number ... (064)   function name ... (063)
      |                            |
      ----------------------------|
                                   | (062.4)
                                   reference end ... (061)
```

1. &#109
2. &#SPACE;

(063) function name (062.3):

```
        (063.1)
----- "RE"
  |     (063.2)
  --- "RS"
  |     (063.3)
  --- "SPACE"
  |     (063.4)
  --- name ... (055)
```

SPACE

(064) character number (062.2) (177.1) (178.1) (183.7 .9) (184.5 .7) (186.5 .9 .13 .19):

```
        (064.1)
----- number ... (056)
```

109

(065) ps (073.2 .5 .7) (097.1 .3) (101.3 .5 .7) (104.2) (106.4) (107.5) (108.2) (109.5) (110.3 .5 .7 .11) (116.3 .5 .7 .9 .12) (122.2) (126.2 .5) (138.2) (141.3 .5 .7.10 .12) (142.2) (143.2 .4) (146.2) (147.3) (148.3 .5 .7) (149a.3) (149b.1) (150.3 .5 .7 .9) (152.3 .5 .7) (171.3 .6 .8 .10 .12 .14 .16) (172.2) (173.3 .5) (174.2) (175.2) (176.2 .4) (180.2 .4 .7 .9) (181.2) (182.2 .5 .7 .9 .11 .13 .15) (183.2 .4 .6 .8) (184.2 .6) (186.2 .4 .6 .8 .10 .12 .14 .16 .18) (189.2 .4 .6 .8 .10 .12 .14 .16 .19 .21 .24 .26) (189.2 .4 .6 .8 .10 .12 .14 .16 .19 .21 .24 .26) (190.2 .4) (191.2 .4 .6) (192.2 .6) (193.2 .4 .6) (194.2 .4 .6) (195.2 .4 .6) (196.2 .4 .7 .9 .12 .14 .17 .19) (198.2 .4 .7 .9 .11 .14 .16 .18) (199.2):

```
        (065.1)
----- s (separator) ... (005)
  |     (065.2)
  --- EE (entity end)
  |     (065.3)
  --- parameter entity reference ... (060)
  |     (065.4)
  --- comment ... (092)
```

SPACE

(066) parameter literal (105.1) (106.5) (107.6) (150.6) (189.5 .9 .13 .17)
(191.7) (192.7) (193.7):

```
            (066.1)
  ----- LIT (literal) ... " " "
    |     | (066.2)
    |     replaceable parameter data ... (067)
    |     | (066.3)
    |     LIT (literal) ... " " "
    |       (066.4)
    --- LITA (literal alternative) ... " " "
          | (066.5)
          replaceable parameter data ... (067)
          | (066.6)
          LITA (literal alternative) ... " " "

1. "Smith &#23; Son"
2. 'Smith &#23; Son'
```

(067) replaceable parameter data (066.2 .5):

```
  -----
    |
  (optional)
  (repeatable)
    |      (067.1)
    --- data character ... (048)
    |    (067.2)
    --- character reference ... (062)
    |    (067.3)
    --- parameter entity reference ... (060)
    |    (067.4)
    --- EE (entity end)

  Smith &#23; Son are owned by %MyCorp;.
```

(068) name token group (145.16):

```
            (068.1)
----- GRPO (group open) ... "("
      |  (068.2)
      ts * (token separator) ... (070)
      |  (068.3)
      name token ... (057)
      |
      |-----
      |     |
      | (optional)
      | (repeatable)
      |     | (068.4)
      |     ts * (token separator) ... (070)
      |     | (068.5)
      |     connector ... (131)
      |     | (068.6)
      |     ts * (token separator) ... (070)
      |     | (068.7)
      |     name token ... (057)
      |     |
       --------
               | (068.8)
               ts * (token separator) ... (070)
               | (068.9)
               GRPC (group close) ... ")"
```

(name1 | name2)

(069) name group (028.1) (059.2) (060.2) (072.2) (117.2) (139.2) (140.2) (146.3) (149a.5):

```
            (069.1)
----- GRPO (group open) ... "("
      | (069.2)
      ts * (token separator) ... (070)
      | (069.3)
      name ... (055)
      |
       -----
      |     |
      | (repeatable)
      |     | (069.4)
      |     ts * (token separator) ... (070)
      |     | (069.5)
      |     connector ... (131)
      |     | (069.6)
      |     ts * (token separator) ... (070)
      |     | (069.7)
      |     name ... (055)
      |     |
       ------
               | (069.8)
               ts * (token separator) ... (070)
               | (069.9)
               GRPC (group close) ... ")"
```

(quote | emphasis | %myelems)

(070) ts (token separator) (068.2 .4 .6 .8) (069.2 .4 .6 .8) (127.2 .4 .6 .8):

```
             (070.1)
----- s (separator) ... (005)
  |       (070.2)
  --- EE (entity end)
  |       (070.3)
  --- parameter entity reference ... (060)
```

(071) ds (113.2) (114.4) (115.4):

```
             (071.1)
----- s (separator) ... (005)
  |       (071.2)
  --- EE (entity end)
  |       (071.3)
  --- parameter entity reference ... (060)
  |       (071.4)
  --- comment declaration ... (091)
  |       (071.5)
  --- processing instruction ... (044)
  |       (071.6)
  --- marked section declaration ... (093)
```

(072) associated element type (141.4) (152.6):

```
             (072.1)
----- generic identifier ... (030)
  |       (072.2)
  --- name group ... (069)
```

```
1. MyElem
2. ( MyElem | Another )
```

(073) external identifier (108.1) (110.6) (149.1):

```
               (073.1)
------- "SYSTEM"
  |       |  (073.2)
  |       ps * (parameter separator) ... (065)
  |       |  (073.3)
  |       system identifier ? ... (075)
  |          (073.4)
  ----- "PUBLIC"
            |  (073.5)
            ps + (parameter separator) ... (065)
            |  (073.6)
            public identifier ... (074)
            |  (073.7)
            ps + (parameter separator) ... (065)
            |  (073.8)
            system identifier ? ... (075)
```

```
1. SYSTEM
2. SYSTEM "mybook.dtd"
3. PUBLIC "-//NB//DTD MyBook//EN"
4. PUBLIC "-//NB//DTD MyBook//EN" "mybook.dtd"
```

(074) **public identifier** (073.6) (174.3) (180.5) (183.3):

```
              (074.1)
----- minimum literal ... (076)
```

"-//NB//DTD MyBook//EN"

(075) **system identifier** (073.3 .8):

```
              (075.1)
----- LIT (literal) ... " " "
  |      | (075.2)
  |   system data ... (045)
  |      | (075.3)
  |   LIT (literal) ... " " "
  |      (075.4)
   --- LITA (literal alternative) ... " " "
         | (075.5)
      system data ... (045)
         | (075.6)
      LITA (literal alternative) ... " " "
```

1. *"mybook.dtd"*
2. *'mybook.dtd'*

(076) **minimum literal** (074.1) (176.6) (199.4):

```
              (076.1)
----- LIT (literal) ... " " "
  |      | (076.2)
  |   minimum data ... (077)
  |      | (076.3)
  |   LIT (literal) ... " " "
  |      (076.4)
   --- LITA (literal alternative) ... " " "
         | (076.5)
      minimum data ... (077)
         | (076.6)
      LITA (literal alternative) ... " " "
```

"ISO 8879:1986"

(077) **minimum data** (076.2 .5) (081.1) (082.2) (083.2) (087.2) (087a.1) (089.1) (090.1):

```
              (077.1)
----- minimum data character * ... (078)
```

ISO 8879:1986

(078) minimum data character (077.1):

```
          (078.1)
----- RS (record start)
  |       (078.2)
  --- RE (record end)
  |       (078.3)
  --- SPACE ... " "
  |       (078.4)
  --- LC LETTER (lower case letter) ... ("a")
  |       (078.5)
  --- UC LETTER (upper case letter) ... ("A")
  |       (078.6)
  --- DIGIT ... ("9")
  |       (078.7)
  --- SPECIAL
```

(079) formal public identifier (*no enclosing structures – this is a **minimum literal**(076) value in a **public identifier**(074)*):

```
          (079.1)
----- owner identifier ... (080)
      |  (079.2)
      "//"
      |  (079.3)
      text identifier ... (084)
```

-//MyCorp//DTD My document type//EN

(080) owner identifier (079.1):

```
          (080.1)
----- ISO owner identifier ... (081)
  |       (080.2)
  --- registered owner identifier ... (082)
  |       (080.3)
  --- unregistered owner identifier ... (083)
```

1.ISO 8879-1986
2.+//MyCorp
3.-//MyCorp

(081) ISO owner identifier (080.1):

```
          (081.1)
----- minimum data ... (077)
```

ISO 8879-1986

(082) registered owner identifier (080.2):

```
          (082.1)
----- "+//"
      |  (082.2)
      minimum data ... (077)
```

+//MyCorp

(083) unregistered owner identifier (080.3):

```
        (083.1)
----- "-//"
     | (083.2)
     minimum data ... (077)

-//MyCorp
```

(084) text identifier (079.3):

```
        (084.1)
----- public text class ... (086)
     | (084.2)
     SPACE ... " "
     | (084.3)
     unavailable text indicator ? ... (085)
     | (084.4)
     public text description ... (087)
     | (084.5)
     "//"
     |
     --------------------
     | (084.6)              |      (084.7)
     public text           public text
     language ... (088)    designating sequence ... (089)
     |                     |
     --------------------|
                         |---
                         |  | (084.8)
                         |  "//"
                         |  | (084.9)
                         |  public text
                         #  display version ... (090)
```
```
1. DTD My document type//EN
2. CHARSET International Reference Version//ESC 2/5 4/0
```

(085) unavailable text indicator (084.3):

```
        (085.1)
----- "-//"

-//
```

(086) public text class (084.1):

```
        (086.1)
----- name ... (055)

DTD
```

(087) public text description (084.4):

```
        (087.1)
----- ISO text description ... (087.a)
     | (087.2)
     minimum data ... (077)

My document type
```

(087a) ISO text description (087.1):

```
        (087a.1)
----- minimum data ... (077)

  Clear text encoding
```

(088) public text language (084.6):

```
        (088.1)
----- name ... (055)

  EN
```

(089) public text designating sequence (084.7):

```
        (089.1)
----- minimum data ... (077)

  ESC 2/5 4/0
```

(090) public text display version (084.9):

```
        (090.1)
----- minimum data ... (077)
```

(091) comment declaration (008.1) (027.1) (071.4):

```
          (091.1)
----- MDO (markup declaration open) ... "<!"
        |
        -----
        |   |  (091.2)
        |   comment ... (092)
        |   |
        |   -----
        |   |   |
        |   |  (optional)
        |   | (repeatable)
        |   |   | (091.3)
        |   |   --- s (separator)... (005)
        |   |   | (091.4)
        |   |   --- comment ... (092)
        |   |   |
        -------------
                    | (091.5)
                    MDC (markup declaration close) ... ">"

  <!-- my comment -- -- another comment -- >
```

(092) comment (065.4) (091.2 .4):

```
        (092.1)
----- COM (comment) ... "--"
       | (092.2)
       SGML character * ... (050)
       | (092.3)
       COM (comment) ... "--"

  -- my comment --
```

(093) marked section declaration (027.8) (071.6):

```
            (093.1)
----- marked section start ... (094)
        | (093.2)
      status keyword specification ... (097)
        | (093.3)
      DSO (declaration subset open)... "("
        | (093.4)
      marked section ... (096)
        | (093.5)
      marked section end ... (095)
```

<?!(IGNORE (This text is not kept!]]>

(094) marked section start (093.1):

```
            (094.1)
----- MDO (markup declaration open)... "<!"
        | (094.2)
      DSO (declaration subset open)... "("
```

<?!(

(095) marked section end (093.5):

```
            (095.1)
----- MSC (markup section close) ... "]]"
        | (095.2)
      MDC (markup declaration close)... ">"
```

]]>

(096) marked section (093.4):

```
            (096.1)
----- SGML character * ... (050)
```

This text is not kept!

(097) status keyword specification (093.2):

```
   ------
        |
   (repeatable)
        | (097.1)
      ps + (parameter separator) ... (065)
        |
        |----------
        | (197.4) | (097.2)
      "TEMP"      status keyword ... (100)
        |          |
      ----------|
                  | (097.3)
                ps * (parameter separator) ... (065)
```

1. *TEMP*
2. *IGNORE*

(098–099) *not in use*

(100) status keyword (097.2):

```
          (100.1)
----- "CDATA"
  |       (100.2)
  --- "IGNORE"
  |       (100.3)
  --- "INCLUDE"
  |       (100.4)
  --- "RCDATA"
```

IGNORE

(101) entity declaration (113.1) (115.1):

```
             (101.1)
----- MDO (markup declaration open) ... "<!"
      |   (101.2)
      "ENTITY"
      |   (101.3)
      ps + (parameter separator) ... (065)
      |   (101.4)
      entity name ... (102)
      |   (101.5)
      ps + (parameter separator) ... (065)
      |   (101.6)
      entity text ... (105)
      |   (101.7)
      ps * (parameter separator) ... (065)
      |   (101.8)
      MDC (markup declaration close) ... ">"
```

```
1. <!ENTITY myentity "my text">
2. <!ENTITY myentity CDATA "my text">
3. <!ENTITY % myentity CDATA "my text">
4. <!ENTITY % myentity STARTTAG "mybook">
5. <!ENTITY % myentity SYSTEM "C:\MYENT.DAT">
```

(102) entity name (101.4):

```
          (102.1)
----- general entity name ... (103)
  |       (102.2)
  --- parameter entity name ... (104)
```

```
1. myentity
2. % myentity
```

(103) general entity name (035.2) (102.1):

```
          (103.1)
----- name ... (055)
  |       (103.2)
  --- RNI (reserved name indicator) ... "#"
      |  (103.3)
      "DEFAULT"
```

myentity

(104) parameter entity name (102.2):

```
          (104.1)
----- PERO (parameter entity reference open) ... "%"
        | (104.2)
        ps + (parameter separator) ... (065)
        | (104.3)
        name ... (055)
```

% *myentity*

(105) entity text (101.6):

```
          (105.1)
----- parameter literal ... (066)
    |   (105.2)
    --- data text ... (106)
    |   (105.3)
    --- bracketed text ... (107)
    |   (105.4)
    --- external entity specification ... (108)
```

1. *"Smith &#23; Son"*
2. *CDATA "my text"*
3. *STARTTAG "chapter"*
4. *SYSTEM "C:\ENTS\MyEnt.DAT"*

(106) data text (105.2):

```
            (106.1)
----- "CDATA"
  |     |
  |     ----------
  |     (106.2)  |
  --- "SDATA"    |
  |     |        |
  |     ----------|
  |     (106.3)  |
  --- "PI"       |
        |        |
        ----------|
                  | (106.4)
                 ps + (parameter separator) ... (065)
                  | (106.5)
                 parameter literal ... (066)
```

CDATA "my text"

(107) bracketed text (105.3):

```
            (107.1)
-----  "STARTTAG"
   |       |
   |    -----------
   |      (107.2)  |
  --- "ENDTAG"     |
   |    |          |
   |    -----------|
   |      (107.3)  |
  --- "MS"         |
   |    |          |
   |    -----------|
   |      (107.4)  |
  --- "MD"         |
        |          |
        -----------|
                   |  (107.5)
                  ps + (parameter separator) ... (065)
                   |  (107.6)
                  parameter literal ... (066)

   STARTTAG "chapter"                          .
```

(108) external entity specification (105.4):

```
            (108.1)
-----  external identifier ... (073)
       |  (108.2)
       --- ps + (parameter separator) ... (065)
       |   |  (108.3)
       #     entity type ... (109)

   1. SYSTEM "C:\MYENT.DAT"
   1. SYSTEM "C:\MYENT.DAT"   CDATA TeX
```

(109) entity type (108.3):

```
               (109.1)
-------  "SUBDOC"
   |           (109.2)
-----  "CDATA"
   |       |
   |    --------------
   |       (109.3)    |
-----  "NDATA"        |
   |       |          |
   |    --------------|
   |       (109.4)    |
-----  "SDATA"        |
           |          |
        --------------|
                      |  (109.5)
                     ps + (parameter separator) ... (065)
                      |  (109.6)
                     notation name ... (041)
                      |  (109.7)
                     data attribute specification ... (149b)
```

```
1. CDATA TeX
2. NDATA MyFormat [pixels="horizontal" resolution="400"]
```

(110) document type declaration (007.3) (009.1):

```
          (110.1)
--- MDO (markup declaration open) ... "<!"
      | (110.2)
    "DOCTYPE"
      | (110.3)
    ps + (parameter separator) ... (065)
      | (110.4)
    document type name ... (111)
      | (110.5)
    --- ps + (parameter separator) ... (065)
    |     | (110.6)
    |   external identifier ... (073)
    |     |       (110.7)
    ------- ps + (parameter separator) ... (065)
        |     |   (110.8)
        |   DSO (declaration subset open) ... "("
        |     |   (110.9)
        |   document type declaration subset ... (112)
        |     |   (110.10)
        |   DSC (declaration subset close) ... "]"
        |     |
        ----|
            | (110.11)
          ps * (parameter separator) ... (065)
            | (110.12)
          MDC (markup declaration close) ... ">"
```

```
1. <!DOCTYPE mybook SYSTEM "book.dtd" >
2. <!DOCTYPE mybook SYSTEM "book.dtd" [ ..... ]>
```

(111) document type name (110.4):

```
          (111.1)
----- generic identifier ... (030)
```

(112) document type declaration subset (110.9):

```
-----
    |
 (optional)
 (repeatable)
    |     (112.1)
    --- entity set ... (113)
    |     (112.2)
    --- element set ... (114)
    |     (112.3)
    --- short reference set ... (115)
```

```
<!ENTITY ......>
<!ELEMENT ......>
```

(113) entity set (112.1):

```
-----
     |
  (optional)
  (repeatable)
     |           (113.1)
     --- entity declaration ... (101)
     |           (113.2)
     --- ds (declaration separator) ... (071)

<!ENTITY ......>  <!ENTITY ......>
```

(114) element set (112.2):

```
-----
     |
  (optional)
  (repeatable)
     |           (114.1)
     --- element declaration ... (116)
     |           (114.2)
     --- attribute definition ... (141)
     |    list declaration
     |           (114.3)
     --- notation declaration ... (148)
     |           (114.4)
     --- ds (declaration separator)... (071)
```

(115) short reference set (112.3):

```
-----
     |
  (optional)
  (repeatable)
     |           (115.1)
     --- entity declaration ... (101)
     |           (115.2)
     --- short reference mapping declaration ... (150)
     |           (115.3)
     --- short reference use declaration ... (152)
     |           (115.4)
     --- ds (declaration separator)... (071)
```

(116) element declaration (114.1):

```
            (116.1)
--- MDO (markup declaration open) ... "<!"
     |   (116.2)
    "ELEMENT"
     |   (116.3)
     ps + (parameter separator) ... (065)
     |   (116.4)
     element type ... (117)
     |        (116.5)
     -- ps + (parameter separator) ... (065)
     |   |   (116.6)
     |   omitted tag minimization ... (122)
     |   |
     -----
        |   (116.7)
        ps + (parameter separator) ... (065)
        |        (116.8)
        --- declared content ... (125)
        |   |  (116.9)
        |   ps * (parameter separator) ... (065)
        |   |  (116.10)
        |   MDC (markup declaration close) ... ">"
        |        (116.11)
        --- content model ... (126)
             |  (116.12)
             ps * (parameter separator) ... (065)
             |  (116.13)
             MDC (markup declaration close) ... ">"
```

1. *<!ELEMENT chapter - - (section+)>*
2. *<!ELEMENT quote   CDATA>*

(117) element type (116.4):

```
            (117.1)
----- generic identifier ... (030)
 |        (117.2)
 --- name group ... (069)
 |
 --- ranked element
 |
 --- ranked group
```

1. *chapter*
2. *(quote | emphasis)*

(118–121) *rank feature (not covered)*

(122) omitted tag minimization (116.6):

```
            (122.1)
----- start-tag minimization ... (123)
     |  (122.2)
     ps + (parameter separator) ... (065)
     |  (122.3)
     end-tag minimization ... (124)
```

```
1. - -
2. - O
```

(123) start-tag minimization (122.1):

```
          (123.1)
----- "O"
  |    (123.2)
  --- MINUS ... ("-")

1. -
2. O
```

(124) end-tag minimization (122.3):

```
          (124.1)
----- "O"
  |    (124.2)
  --- MINUS ... ("-")
```

(125) declared content (116.8):

```
            (125.1)
----- "CDATA"
  |         (125.2)
  --- "RCDATA"
  |         (125.3)
  --- "EMPTY"

EMPTY
```

(126) content model (116.11):

```
            (126.1)
----- model group ... (127)
  |   |         (126.2)
  |   --- ps + (parameter separator) ... (065)
  |   |   | (126.3)
  |   # exceptions ... (138)
  |       (126.4)
  --- "ANY"
      |         (126.5)
      --- ps + (parameter separator) ... (065)
      |   | (126.6)
      # exceptions ... (138)

1. (sections | #PCDATA | (title, para+)) +(xref)
2. ANY -(mybook)
```

(127) model group (126.1) (128.2):

```
            (127.1)
----- GRPO (group open) ... ")("
      |   (127.2)
      ts * (token separators) ... (070)
      |   (127.3)
      content token ... (128)
      |
      -------
      |  (optional)
      |  (repeatable)
      |     |   (127.4)
      |     ts * (token separators) ... (070)
      |     |   (127.5)
      |     connector ... (131)
      |     |   (127.6)
      |     ts * (token separators) ... (070)
      |     |   (127.7)
      |     content token ... (128)
      |     |
      -------
            |   (127.8)
            ts * (token separators) ... (070)
            |   (127.9)
            GRPC (group close) ... ")"
            |   (127.10)
            occurrence indicator ? ... (132)

(sections | (title, para+))
```

(128) content token (127.3 .7):

```
      (128.1)
----- primitive content token ... (129)
 |    (128.2)
 --- model group ... (127)

1. #PCDATA
2. para
3. (emphasis | quote)
```

(129) primitive content token (128.1):

```
          (129.1)
----- RNI (reserved name indicator) ... "#"
 |    |   (129.2)
 |    "PCDATA"
 |        (129.3)
 --- element token ... (130)
 |        (129.4)
 --- data tag group

1. #PCDATA
2. para
```

(130) element token (129.3):

```
            (130.1)
----- generic identifier ... (030)
       | (130.2)
       occurrence indicator ? ... (132)

1. section
2. para+
```

(131) connector (068.5) (069.5) (127.5):

```
            (131.1)
----- AND ... "&"
   |        (131.2)
   --- OR ... "|"
   |        (131.3)
   --- SEQ (sequence) ... ","

1. title, para+
2. section | (.....)
```

(132) occurrence indicator (127.10) (130.2):

```
            (132.1)
----- OPT (optional) ... "?"
   |        (132.2)
   --- PLUS ... "+"
   |        (132.3)
   --- REP (repeatable) ... "*"

1. para+
2. (.....)*
```

(133–137) *data tag feature (not covered)*

(138) exceptions (126 .3 .6):

```
            (138.1)
----- exclusions ... (140)
   |    |        (138.2)
   |    --- ps + (parameter separator) ... (065)
   |    |    | (138.3)
   |    #   inclusions ... (139)
   |        (138.4)
   --- inclusions ... (139)

1. ..... -(xref) +(figure)
2. ..... +(figure)
```

(139) inclusions (138.3 .4):

```
            (139.1)
----- PLUS ... "+"
       | (139.2)
       name group ... (069)

..... +(figure)
```

(140) exclusions (138.1):

```
            (140.1)
----- MINUS ... "-"
      |   (140.2)
      name group ... (069)

..... -(xref)
```

(141) attribute definition list declaration (114.2):

```
            (141.1)
----- MDO (markup declaration open) ... "<!"
      |   (141.2)
      "ATTLIST"
      |   (141.3)
      ps + (parameter separator) ... (065)
      |         (141.4)
      --- associated element type ... (072)
      |   |  (141.5)
      |   ps + (parameter separator) ... (065)
      |   |  (141.6)
      |   attribute definition list ... (142)
      |   |  (141.7)
      |   ps * (parameter separator) ... (065)
      |   |  (141.8)
      |   MDC (markup declaration close) ... ">"
      |       (141.9)
      --- associated notation name ... (149a)
          |  (141.10)
          ps + (parameter separator) ... (065)
          |  (141.11)
          attribute definition list ... (142)
          |  (141.12)
          ps * (parameter separator) ... (065)
          |  (141.13)
          MDC (markup declaration close) ... ">"
```

<!ATTLIST MyElem MyAttr1 CDATA "MyValue">

(142) attribute definition list (141.6 .11):

```
            (142.1)
----- attribute definition ... (143)
            |
   (optional)
   (repeatable)
         |   (142.2)
      ps + (parameter separator) ... (065)
      |   (142.3)
      attribute definition ... (143)
```

1. *MyAttr1 CDATA "MyValue"*
2. *MyAttr2 NUMBER #IMPLIED*

(143) attribute definition (142.1 .3):

```
          (143.1)
----- attribute name ... (144)
      |   (143.2)
      ps + (parameter separator) ... (065)
      |   (143.3)
      declared value ... (145)
      |   (143.4)
      ps + (parameter separator) ... (065)
      |   (143.5)
      default value ... (147)
```

MyAttr1 CDATA "MyValue"

(144) attribute name (143.1):

```
          (144.1)
----- name ... (055)
```

MyAttr1

(145) declared value (143.3):

```
          (145.1)
----- "CDATA"
   |    (145.2)
   --- "ENTITY"
   |    (145.3)
   --- "ENTITIES"
   |    (145.4)
   --- "ID"
   |    (145.5)
   --- "IDREF"
   |    (145.6)
   --- "IDREFS"
   |    (145.7)
   --- "NAME"
   |    (145.8)
   --- "NAMES"
   |    (145.9)
   --- "NMTOKEN"
   |    (145.10)
   --- "NMTOKENS"
   |    (145.11)
   --- "NUMBER"
   |    (145.12)
   --- "NUMBERS"
   |    (145.13)
   --- "NUTOKEN"
   |    (145.14)
   --- "NUTOKENS"
   |    (145.15)
   --- notation ... (146)
   |    (145.16)
   --- name token group ... (068)
```

1. *CDATA*
2. *TeX*
3. *(left | right | center)*

(146) notation (145.15):

```
            (146.1)
----- "NOTATION"
        |  (146.2)
      ps + (parameter separator) ... (065)
        |  (146.3)
      name group ... (069)
```

MyAttr1

(147) default value (143.5):

```
                 (147.1)
--------- RNI (reserved name indicator) ... ("#")
   |   |     |   (147.2)
   |   |   "FIXED"
   |   |     |   (147.3)
   |   |   ps + (parameter separator) ... (065)
   |   |     |
   |   ------
   |         |   (147.4)
   |       attribute value specification ... (033)
   |             (147.5)
   ------- RNI (reserved name indicator) ... ("#")
             |   (147.6)
             --- "REQUIRED"
             |   (147.7)
             --- "CURRENT"
             |   (147.8)
             --- "CONREF"
             |   (147.9)
             --- "IMPLIED"
```

1. *#FIXED "My Fixed Value"*
2. *"My Default Value"*
3. *#IMPLIED*

(148) notation declaration (114.3):

```
            (148.1)
----- MDO (markup declaration open) ... "<!"
        |  (148.2)
      "NOTATION"
        |  (148.3)
      ps + (parameter separator) ... (065)
        |  (148.4)
      notation name ... (041)
        |  (148.5)
      ps + (parameter separator) ... (065)
        |  (148.6)
      notation identifier ... (149)
        |  (148.7)
      ps * (parameter separator) ... (065)
        |  (148.8)
      MDC (markup declaration close) ... ">"
```

<!NOTATION MyNota SYSTEM "MYNOTA.NOT">

(149) notation identifier (148.6):

```
        (149.1)
----- external identifier ... (073)
```

SYSTEM "MYNOTA.NOT"

(149a) associated notation name (141.9):

```
        (149a.1)
----- RNI (reserved name indicator) ... ("#")
     |  (149a.2)
     "NOTATION"
     |  (149a.3)
     ps + (parameter separator) ... (065)
     |  (149a.4)
     --- notation name ... (041)
     |  (149a.5)
     --- name group ... (069)
```

```
1. #NOTATION myNotat
2. #NOTATION ( myNotat | OtherNot )
```

(149b) data attribute specification (109.7):

```
        (149b.1)
----- ps + (parameter separator) ... (065)
     |  (149b.2)
     DSO (declaration subset open) ... "["
     |  (149b.3)
     attribute specification list ... (031)
     |  (149b.4)
     s * (separator) ... (005)
     |  (149b.5)
     DSC (declaration subset close) ... "]"
```

[pixels="horizontal" resolution="400"]

(150) short reference mapping declaration (115.2):

```
         (150.1)
----- MDO (markup declaration open) ... "<!"
      | (150.2)
      "SHORTREF"
      | (150.3)
      ps + (parameter separator) ... (065)
      | (150.4)
      map name ... (151)
      |
      -----
      |   |
      | (repeating)
      |   | (150.5)
      |   ps + (parameter separator) ... (065)
      |   | (150.6)
      |   parameter literal ... (066)
      |   | (150.7)
      |   ps + (parameter separator) ... (065)
      |   | (150.8)
      |   name ... (055)
      |   |
      |   |
      ----| (150.9)
          ps * (parameter separator) ... (065)
          | (150.10)
          MDC (markup declaration close) ... ">"

<!SHORTREF  MyMap   "....."  MyEnt1
                    "....."  MyEnt2
```

(151) map name (150.4) (153.1):

```
         (151.1)
----- name ... (055)
```

(152) short reference use declaration (027.2) (115.3):

```
         (152.1)
----- MDO (markup declaration open) ... "<!"
      | (152.2)
      "USEMAP"
      | (152.3)
      ps + (parameter separator) ... (065)
      | (152.4)
      map specification ... (153)
      |
      -----
      |   | (152.5)
      |   ps + (parameter separator) ... (065)
      |   | (152.6)
      |   associated element type ... (072)
      |   |
      ----|
          | (152.7)
          ps * (parameter separator) ... (065)
          | (152.8)
          MDC (markup declaration close) ... ">"
```

```
1. <!USEMAP  MyMapSp >
2. <!USEMAP  MyMapSp MyElem >
3. <!USEMAP  MyMapSp (Book | Manual | MyElem) >
4. <!USEMAP  #EMPTY >
```

(153) map specification (152.4):

```
            (153.1)
------ map name ... (151)
    |       (153.2)
    --- RNI (reserved name indicator) ... "#"
        | (153.3)
        "EMPTY"
```

```
1. MyMapSp
2. #EMPTY
```

```
<!-- my comment --  -- my other comment -->
```

(154–170) *link feature (not covered)*

(171) SGML declaration (002.2):

```
            (171.1)
----- MDO (markup declaration open) ... "<!"
        |    (171.2)
        "SGML"
        |    (171.3)
        ps + (parameter separator) ... (065)
        |    (171.4)
        minimum literal ... ("ISO 8879:1986" or later version)
        |    (171.5)
        document character set ... (172)
        |    (171.6)
        ps + (parameter separator) ... (065)
        |    (171.7)
        capacity set ... (180)
        |    (171.8)
        ps + (parameter separator) ... (065)
        |    (171.9)
        concrete syntax scope ... (181)
        |    (171.10)
        ps + (parameter separator) ... (065)
        |    (171.11)
        concrete syntax ... (182)
        |    (171.12)
        ps + (parameter separator) ... (065)
        |    (171.13)
        feature use ... (195)
        |    (171.14)
        ps + (parameter separator) ... (065)
        |    (171.15)
        application-specific information ... (199)
        |    (171.16)
        ps * (parameter separator) ... (065)
        |    (171.17)
        MDC (markup declaration close) ... ">"
```

```
<!SGML ISO 8879:1986.......
        CHARSET .....
        CAPACITY .....
        SCOPE .....
        SYNTAX .....
        FEATURES .....
        APPINFO .....>
```

(172) document character set (171.5):

```
            (172.1)
----- "CHARSET"
        | (172.2)
        ps + (parameter separator) ... (065)
        | (172.3)
        character set descripton ... (173)
```

(173) character set description (172.3) (185.1):

```
            (173.1)
----- base character set ... (174)
        | (173.2)
        described character set portion ... (175)
        |
    (optional)
    (repeating)
        | (173.3)
        ps + (parameter separator) ... (065)
        | (173.4)
        base character set ... (174)
        | (173.5)
        ps + (parameter separator) ... (065)
        | (173.6)
        described character set portion ... (175)
```

(174) base character set (173.1 .4):

```
            (174.1)
----- "BASESET"
        | (174.2)
        ps + (parameter separator) ... (065)
        | (174.3)
        public identifier... (074)
```

```
BASESET "ISO 646:1983//CHARSET International Reference Version
(IRV)//ESC 2/5 4/0"
```

(175) described character set portion (173.2 .6):

```
            (175.1)
----- "DESCSET"
        |
    (repeatable)
        | (175.2)
        ps + (parameter separator) ... (065)
        | (175.3)
        character description... (176)
```

```
DESCSET 0 9 UNUSED
        9 2 9
```

(176) character description (175.3):

```
          (176.1)
----- described set character number ... (177)
       | (176.2)
      ps + (parameter separator) ... (065)
       | (176.3)
      number of characters... (179)
       | (176.4)
      ps + (parameter separator) ... (065)
       |       (176.5)
       ----- base set character number ... (178)
          |      (176.6)
          --- minimum literal ... (076)
          |      (176.7)
          --- "UNUSED"
```

```
1. 0 9 UNUSED
2. 9 2 9
```

(177) described set character number (176.1):

```
          (177.1)
----- character number ... (064)
```

```
9
```

(178) base set character number (176.5):

```
          (178.1)
----- character number ... (064)
```

```
9
```

(179) number of characters (176.3):

```
          (179.1)
----- number ... (056)
```

```
2
```

(180) capacity set (171.7):

```
              (180.1)
----- "CAPACITY"
       |    (180.2)
      ps + (parameter separator) ... (065)
       |          (180.3)
      ----- "PUBLIC"
       |      |  (180.4)
       |     ps + (parameter separator) ... (065)
       |      |  (180.5)
       |     public identifier ... (074)
       |          (180.6)
      ----- "SGMLREF"
                 |
           (repeatable)
              |    (180.7)
             ps + (parameter separator) ... (065)
              |    (180.8)
             name (reference capacity set) ... (055)
              |    (180.9)
             ps + (parameter separator) ... (065)
              |    (180.10)
             number ... (056)

CAPACITY
    SGMLREF
    ELEMENTS 64000
```

(181) concrete syntax scope (171.9):

```
               (181.1)
----- "SCOPE"
       |    (181.2)
      ps + (parameter separator) ... (065)
       |    (181.3)
      --- "DOCUMENT"
       |    (181.4)
      --- "INSTANCE"

SCOPE
    INSTANCE
```

(182) concrete syntax (171.11):

```
                (182.1)
---  "SYNTAX"
        |       (182.2)
      ps + (parameter separator) ... (065)
        |       (182.3)
     --- public concrete syntax ... (183)
        |       (182.4)
     --- shunned character number identification ... (184)
             |  (182.5)
             ps + (parameter separator) ... (065)
             |  (182.6)
             syntax-reference character set ... (185)
             |  (182.7)
             ps + (parameter separator) ... (065)
             |  (182.8)
             function character identification ... (186)
             |  (182.9)
             ps + (parameter separator) ... (065)
             |  (182.10)
             naming rules ... (189)
             |  (182.11)
             ps + (parameter separator) ... (065)
             |  (182.12)
             delimiter set ... (190)
             |  (182.13)
             ps + (parameter separator) ... (065)
             |  (182.14)
             reserved name use ... (193)
             |  (182.15)
             ps + (parameter separator) ... (065)
             |  (182.16)
             quantity set ... (194)
```

(183) public concrete syntax (182.3):

```
                (183.1)
-----  "PUBLIC"
          | (183.2)
       ps + (parameter separator) ... (065)
          | (183.3)
       public identifier ... (074)
          | (183.4)
          |-- ps + (parameter separator) ... (065)
          |     | (183.5)
          |   "SWITCHES"
          |     |
          -----
               |
       (repeatable)
               | (183.6)
             ps + (parameter separator) ... (065)
               | (183.7)
             character number ... (064)
               | (183.8)
             ps + (parameter separator) ... (065)
               | (183.9)
             character number ... (064)
```

PUBLIC "ISO 8879:1986//SYNTAX Reference//EN"

(184) shunned character number identification (182.4):

```
             (184.1)
----- "SHUNCHAR"
        |  (184.2)
       ps + (parameter separator) ... (065)
        |
        |-----
        |    | (184.3)
        |    "NONE"
        |
        |----------
        |  (184.4) |  (184.5)
      "CONTROLS"    character number ... (064)
        |            |
      ----------|
              (optional)
              (repeatable)
                    |  (184.6)
                   ps + (parameter separator) ... (065)
                    |  (184.7)
                   character number ... (064)
```

1. *SHUNCHAR NONE*
2. *SHUNCHAR 12 14 16*
3. *SHUNCHAR CONTROLS 12 14 16*

(185) syntax-reference character set (182.6):

```
             (185.1)
----- character set description ... (173)
```

BASESET "ISO 646-1983//CHARSET International Reference Version
(IRV)//ESC 2/5 4/0" .
DESCSET 0 128 0

(186) function character identification (182.8):

```
          (186.1)
----- "FUNCTION"
        | (186.2)
       ps + (parameter separator) ... (065)
        | (186.3)
      "RE"
        | (186.4)
       ps + (parameter separator) ... (065)
        | (186.5)
       character number ... (064)
        | (186.6)
       ps + (parameter separator) ... (065)
        | (186.7)
      "RS"
        | (186.8)
       ps + (parameter separator) ... (065)
        | (186.9)
       character number ... (064)
        | (186.10)
       ps + (parameter separator) ... (065)
        | (186.11)
      "SPACE"
        | (186.12)
       ps + (parameter separator) ... (065)
        | (186.13)
       character number ... (064)
        |
     (optional)
     (repeatable)
        | (186.14)
       ps + (parameter separator) ... (065)
        | (186.15)
       added function ... (187)
        | (186.16)
       ps + (parameter separator) ... (065)
        | (186.17)
       function class ... (188)
        | (186.18)
       ps + (parameter separator) ... (065)
        | (186.19)
       character number ... (064)

 FUNCTION RE 10
          RS 12
          SPACE 32
          TAB SEPCHAR 9
```

(187) added function (186.15):

```
          (187.1)
----- name ... (055)

 TAB
```

(188) function class (186.17):

```
         (188.1)
----- "FUNCHAR" (functional character)
  |      (188.2)
  --- "MSICHAR" (markup scan-in character)
  |      (188.3)
  --- "MSOCHAR" (markup scan-out character)
  |      (188.4)
  --- "MSSCHAR" (markup scan suppress character)
  |      (188.5)
  --- "SEPCHAR" (separator character)

   SEPCHAR
```

(189) naming rules (182.10):

```
        (189.1)
---  "NAMING"
     | (189.2)
     ps + (parameter separator)  ...  (065)
     | (189.3)
     "LCNMSTRT"
     |
     ---
     |
  (repeatable)
     | (189.4)
     ps + (parameter separator)  ...  (065)
     | (189.5)
     parameter literal  ...  (066)
     |
     ---
        | (189.6)
        ps + (parameter separator)  ...  (065)
        | (189.7)
        "UCNMSTRT"
        |
        ---
        |
     (repeatable)
        | (189.8)
        ps + (parameter separator)  ...  (065)
        | (189.9)
        parameter literal  ...  (066)
        |
        ---
           | (189.10)
           ps + (parameter separator)  ...  (065)
           | (189.11)
           "LCNMCHAR"
           |
           ---
           |
        (repeatable)
           | (189.12)
           ps + (parameter separator)  ...  (065)
           | (189.13)
           parameter literal  ...  (066)
           |
           ---
              | (189.14)
              ps + (parameter separator)  ...  (065)
              | (189.15)
              "UCNMCHAR"
              |
              ---
              |
           (repeatable)
              | (189.16)
              ps + (parameter separator)  ...  (065)
              | (189.17)
              parameter literal  ...  (066)
              |
              ---
```

```
                          |  (189.18)
                        "NAMECASE"
                          |  (189.19)
                         ps + ... (065)
                          |  (189.20)
                        "GENERAL"
                          |  (189.21)
                         ps + ... (065)
                          |
                         |----------|
                          | (189.22) | (189.23)
                        "NO"        "YES"
                          |          |
                          ----------|
                                     |  (189.24)
                                    ps + ... (065)
                                     |  (189.25)
                                   "ENTITY"
                                     |  (189.26)
                                    ps + ... (065)
                                     |
                                    |----------|
                                     | (189.27) | (189.28)
                                   "NO"        "YES"
```

```
NAMING LCNMSTRT ""
       UCNMSTRT ""
       LCNMCHAR "-."
       UCNMCHAR "-."
       NAMECASE GENERAL YES
                ENTITY  NO
```

(190) delimiter set (182.12):

```
            (190.1)
----- "DELIM"
        |  (190.2)
       ps + (parameter separator) ... (065)
        |  (190.3)
       general delimiters ... (191)
        |  (190.4)
       ps + (parameter separator) ... (065)
        |  (190.5)
       short reference delimiters ... (192)
```

```
DELIM GENERAL  SGMLREF
      SHORTREF SGMLREF
```

(191) general delimiters (190.3):

```
          (191.1)
----- "GENERAL"
       | (191.2)
      ps + (parameter separator)... (065)
       | (191.3)
      "SGMLREF"
       |
   (optional)
   (repeatable)
       | (191.4)
      ps + (parameter separator) ... (065)
       | (191.5)
      name ... (055)
       | (191.6)
      ps + (parameter separator) ... (065)
       | (191.7)
      parameter literal ... (066)
1. GENERAL   SGMLREF
2. SHORTREF SGMLREF
```

(192) short reference delimiters (190.5):

```
          (192.1)
----- "SHORTREF"
       | (192.2)
      ps + (parameter separator) ... (065)
       | (192.3)
       |----------|
       | (192.4)  | (192.5)
      "NONE"      "SGMLREF"
       |          |
       |----------|
                  |
              (optional)
              (repeatable)
                  | (192.6)
                ps + (parameter separator) ... (065)
                  | (192.7)
                parameter literal ... (066)
1. SHORTREF NONE "#"
2. SHORTREF SGMLREF "#"
```

(193) reserved name use (182.14):

```
          (193.1)
----- "NAMES"
       | (193.2)
      ps + (parameter separator) ... (065)
       | (193.3)
      "SGMLREF"
       |
    (optional)
    (repeatable)
       | (193.4)
      ps + (parameter separator) ... (065)
       | (193.5)
      name (keyword) ... (055)
       | (193.6)
      ps + (parameter separator) ... (065)
       | (193.7)
      parameter literal (new keyword) ... (066)

NAMES SGMLREF
      ELEMENT "MYELEM"
```

(194) quantity set (182.16):

```
          (194.1)
----- "QUANTITY"
       | (194.2)
      ps + (parameter separator) ... (065)
       | (194.3)
      "SGMLREF"
       |
    (optional)
    (repeatable)
       | (194.4)
      ps + (parameter separator) ... (065)
       | (194.5)
      name (keyword) ... (055)
       | (194.6)
      ps + (parameter separator) ... (065)
       | (191.7)
      number (keyword value) ... (056)

1. QUANTITY  SGMLREF
2. QUANTITY SGMLREF LITLEN 2000 NAMELEN 32
```

(195) feature use (171.13):

```
        (195.1)
----- "FEATURES"
      |  (195.2
      ps + (parameter separator) ... (065)
      |  (195.3)
      markup minimization features ... (196)
      |  (195.4)
      ps + (parameter separator) ... (065)
      |  (195.5)
      link type features
      |  (195.6)
      ps + (parameter separator) ... (065)
      |  (195.7)
      other features ... (198)
```

(196) markup minimization features (195.3):

```
         (196.1)
----- "MINIMIZE"
      | (196.2)
      ps + (parameter separator) ... (065)
      | (196.3)
      "DATATAG"
      | (196.4)
      ps + (parameter separator) ... (065)
      |
      -----------
      | (196.5) | (196.6)
      "NO"      "YES"
      |         |
      ----------|
                | (196.7)
                ps + (parameter separator) ... (065)
                | (196.8)
                "OMITTAG"
                | (196.9)
                ps + (parameter separator) ... (065)
                |
                -----------
                | (196.10)| (196.11)
                "NO"       "YES"
                |          |
                ----------|
                           | (196.12)
                           ps + ... (065)
                           | (196.13)
                           "RANK"
                           | (196.14)
                           ps + ... (065)
                           |
                           -----------
                           | (196.15)| (196.16)
                           "NO"       "YES"
                           |          |
                           ----------|
                                      | (196.17)
                                      ps + ... (065)
                                      | (196.18)
                                      "SHORTTAG"
                                      | (196.19)
                                      ps + ... (065)
                                      |
                                      -----------
                                      | (196.20)| (196.21)
                                      "NO"       "YES"
```

MINIMIZE DATATAG NO OMITTAG YES RANK NO SHORTTAG NO

(197) *link type features (not covered)*

(198) other features (195.7):

```
        (198.1)
----- "OTHER"
      | (198.2)
      ps + (parameter separator) ... (065)
      | (198.3)
      "CONCUR"
      | (198.4)
      ps + (parameter separator) ... (065)
      |
      -----------
      | (198.5) | (198.6)
    "NO"      "YES"
      |          | (198.7)
      |          ps + (parameter separator) ... (065)
      |          | (198.8)
      |          number ... (056)
      |          |
      ----------|
                 | (198.9)
                 ps + (parameter separator) ... (065)
                 | (198.10)
                 "SUBDOC"
                 | (198.11)
                 ps + (parameter separator) ... (065)
                 |
                 -----------
                 | (198.12)| (198.13)
               "NO"      "YES"
                 |          | (198.14)
                 |          ps + ... (065)
                 |          | (198.15)
                 |          number ... (056)
                 |          |
                 ----------|
                            | (198.16)
                            ps + ... (065)
                            | (198.17)
                            "FORMAL"
                            | (198.18)
                            ps + ... (065)
                            |
                            -----------
                            | (198.19)| (198.20)
                          "NO"      "YES"
```

OTHER CONCUR NO SUBDOC YES 15 FORMAL NO

(199) application-specific information (171.15):

```
                (199.1)
----- "APPINFO"
      |     (199.2)
      ps + (parameter separator) ... (065)
      |     (199.3)
      --- "NONE"
      |     (199.4)
      --- minimum literal ... (076)

APPINFO
   NONE
```

Glossary

The glossary contains a list of terms related to SGML and to the additional topics covered in this book. It includes:

- SGML delimiter characters
- SGML keywords
- SGML production charts
- related ISO and *de facto* standards
- CALS tables, ISO 9573 math, HTML, HyTime and ICADD related terminology, element names and attribute names
- typesetting concepts
- popular image formats

Entity names for extended characters, such as 'eacute' ('é'), do not appear. For these names see Chapter 14.

All text before the dash, '—', is used to sort the entries, even when not highlighted. For example, '**Frame** attribute — ...' appears before '**Frame** element —...'.

When a term has more than one definition, each definition is preceded by a number in square brackets, starting at '*[1]*'. As an exception to this rule, element and attribute names are separated from other entries, and are distinguished by using a capital first letter. For example, there are separate entries for 'superscript' (raised character) and 'Superscript' (the element name). But two elements with the name 'Superscript' would be numbered as described above.

A reference to another entry is highlighted in bold typeface. In some cases, a term is not referenced from the main text at all, only from other entries in the glossary. Note that in this case the term does not appear in the index, because the index does not cover the glossary.

As in the main text, a highlighted word or phrase followed by a superscript number is actually a syntactic variable, and the number may be used to locate the relevant chart in the *Road Map* section.

Symbols and digits

" — Literal delimiter, `attrib="value"`. See **LIT**.

— *[1]* Reserved name indicator delimiter, `#INCLUDE`. See **RNI**. *[2]* Character separating a URL for an Internet based document from a subdocument location, `http:www.myserver.com/mydoc#chapter2`.

% — Parameter entity reference open delimiter, `%entity;`. See **PERO**.

& — *[1]* And connector, `(a & b & c)`. See **AND**. *[2]* Entity reference open delimiter, `&entity;`. See **ERO**.

&# — Character reference open delimiter, `&#123;` or `&#TAB;`. See **CRO**.

' — Literal alternative delimiter, `attrib='value'`. See **LITA**.

(— Group open delimiter, `((a & b) | c)`. See **GRPO**.

) — Group close delimiter, `((a & b) | c)`. See **GRPC**.

* — Optional and repeatable indicator, `(a*,b,c+)`. See **REP**.

+ — *[1]* Required and repeatable indicator, `(a*,b,c+)`. See **PLUS**. *[2]* Inclusion indicator, `(a,b,c) +(d,e)`. See **PLUS**.

, — Sequence connector, `(a,b,c)`. See **SEQ**.

- — *[1]* Exclusion, `(a,b,c) -(d,e)`. See **MINUS**. *[2]* Omit-tag switch. The **start-tag**[014] or **end-tag**[019] may not be omitted, `<!ELEMENT MyElem - - ....>`. See **MINUS**.

-- — Comment delimiter (both open comment and close comment), `-- comment --`. See **COM**.

/ — Null end-tag, `H<sub/2/O is water`. See **NET**.

; — Reference close delimiter, `&entity;`. See **REFC**.

< — Start-tag open delimiter, `<element>`. See **STAGO**.

<! — Markup declaration open delimiter, `<!ELEMENT ..>`. See **MDO**.

</ — End-tag open delimiter, `</element>`. See **ETAGO**.

<? — Processing instruction open delimiter, `<? pagebreak>`. See **PIO**.

= — Value indicator, `attrib=value`. See **VI**.

> — *[1]* Markup declaration close delimiter, `<!ELEMENT ..>`. See **MDC**. *[2]* Processing instruction close delimiter, `<? pagebreak>`. See **PIC**. *[3]* Tag close delimiter, `</element>`. See **TAGC**.

? — Optional occurrence indicator, `(a?, b, c?)`. See **OPT**.

[— Declaration subset open delimiter, `<!DOCTYPE [...]>`. See **DSO**.

] — Declaration subset close delimiter. `<!DOCTYPE [...]>`. See **DSC**.

]] — Marked section close delimiter. `<[INCLUDE[...]]>`. See **MSC**.

| — Or connector. `(a|b|c)`. See **OR**.

16-bit — Character set that uses 16 binary digits, which allows 65 536 values for representing characters. See **Unicode** and **7-bit**.

32-bit — Character set that uses 32 binary digits, which allows 4 294 967 296 values for representing characters. A forthcoming 32-bit character set is **ISO/IEC 10646**. See **ASCII**, **7-bit** and **8-bit**.

7-bit — Character set or image format that uses 7 binary digits (**bits**), which allows only 128 values for representing characters. See **ASCII**, **ISO/IEC 646:1991** and **8-bit**.

8-bit — Character set or image format that uses 8 binary digits (**bits**), which allows 256 values for representing characters. See **ASCII** or **7-bit** for original limited character sets. 8-bit sets are sometimes known as 'extended' character sets. See **ISO/IEC 8859/1**.

9573 math — The **ISO/IEC TR 9573** DTD fragment concerned with math formulae – a convenient abbreviation coined for use in this glossary.

A

A element — An **HTML** element that locates the source or target of an **anchor**.

AAP *(American Association of Publishers)* — Organization of publishers that have defined various standard **DTDs**, which have been used as the basis for the latest **ISO** DTDs. See **ISO 12083**.

Above element — A **9573 math** element used in the **Pile** and **Matrix** elements to contain one row of the matrix. Directly contained within a **Cols** element. See **Above1** element.

Above1 element — A **9573 math** element used in **Piles** and **Matrix** elements to contain the first row of the matrix. Directly contained within a **Cols** element. See **Above** element.

abstract syntax — The inherent **syntax** rules for **SGML**, as shown in the charts in the *Road Map* chapter of this book. Keywords are used to define a **concrete syntax**[182] from the abstract syntax (though there is also an implied default concrete syntax). For example, the abstract concept of a markup declaration open delimiter defines a keyword of MDO, which may be used to fix the concrete syntax for this object as '<!'. If a concrete syntax is not made explicit in the **SGML declaration**[171], then the **reference concrete syntax** defaults are used.

accent — A diacritical mark near or through a letter. For example, 'é'. The **ISOlat1** set of **entities** defines references for common European accented characters. For example, '`&eacute;`'.

Action attribute — Used in the **Form** element to specify a script to process the form.

Action Link — See **Alink** element.

added function[187] — The **name**[055] of a special function, such as 'SPACE' or 'TAB'.

Address element — An **HTML** element used to store the name and location of the author of the **page**.

Align attribute — *[1]* Part of several **CALS table** elements, used to horizontally justify text. Legal values 'left', 'right', 'center', 'justify' and 'char'. *[2]* Used in several **9573 math** elements; to horizontally justify formula (in the **Df** element), numerator to denominator (in the **Frac** element) and rows of the **Pile** element. *[3]* Part of several **HTML** elements, used to horizontally justify an object.

Alink attribute — Used in the **Body** element to specify the color of an active **hypertext link**.

ambiguous mixed content — A **model group**[127] containing **mixed content**[025] employing any **sequence connector** operator other than OR, which may confuse the parser and cause errors relating to line end character significance.

American Standard Code for Information Interchange — See **ASCII**.

ancestor — A concept derived from the family tree describing an **element**[013] that encloses the subject element, either directly as a **parent**, or indirectly as part of a larger **hierarchy** of elements. For example, a Book element would be the ancestor of a Paragraph, and also of the Chapter containing the Paragraph. See **child** and **sibling**.

anchor — A **tag** embedded in the text that serves as the **target** for a **hypertext link**. The link is 'anchored' because it stays with the relevant text if it is moved due to insertions or deletions earlier in the document. Sometimes used to describe an element that serves as both the target and **source** ends of a link.

Anchor — See **A** element.

AND — The **reserved name** for the keyword used to specify the character that indicates lack of ordering constraints in a **group**. The default character is '&'. See **and connector**, SEQ and OR, and the *Road Map* chart (131.1).

and connector — The character that indicates that two surrounding items in a **group** are allowed in any order. The default character is '&'. The example '(a & b)' indicates that 'b' may either follow or precede 'a'. See AND, **or connector** and **sequence connector**.

ANY — The **reserved name** for the keyword used in a **content model**[126] to indicate that the **element**[013] may contain all other elements (including itself). May be changed to another name in a **variant concrete syntax**. See EMPTY and the *Road Map* chart (126.4).

APPINFO — The **reserved name** for the keyword which identifies and precedes **application-specific information**[199]. See the *Road Map* chart (199.1).

applet — A semi-compiled **Java** program accessed by a **Web browser** for activation on the local system. Source code has an extent of '.java'. Semi-compiled code, or 'bytecode', has an extent of '.class'. Machine specific compilers are available from 'http://java.sun.com/download.html'. See **Applet** element.

Applet element — An **HTML** element used to reference a Java program, or **applet**, via a **URL**. For example, '<applet code="http://mycorp.com/java/code/myprog.class" ...>'.

application-specific information[199] — Information to be passed to an application, usually concerning an added layer of information in the document structure. In such cases, **element**[013] names, **attribute** names or attribute values have significance to specific applications. See **HyTime** and **ICADD**.

architectural form — The use of **SGML** constructs to add a further layer of meaning. A syntax that rests upon SGML, just as SGML rests upon **ASCII** or another text format. Only specialist software applications make use of the additional information. Typically, a processing instruction format, element name, or attribute name and value provides the extra information. See **ICADD** and **HyTime** for example applications.

Area element — An **HTML** element used in the **Map** element to assign a **URL** to a specified area of an image. Part of the 'client-sided' **image map** scheme.

ASCII *(American Standard Code for Information Interchange)* — The most popular scheme for representing common characters (Latin alphabet, Arabic digits and typewriter symbols) in computer memory. Defined by ANSI *(American National Standards Institute)*. A unique **7-bit** value is assigned to each character, including '65' for 'A' and '49' for the digit '1' (the value of a character should not be confused with a digit character, such as '1'). The only relevant alternative is **EBCDIC**, used on IBM mainframe systems. See **ISO/IEC 646:1991, ISO/IEC 8859/1** and **Unicode**.

associated element type[072] — A reference to an **element**[013], or **group** of elements in an **attribute definition list declaration**[141] or **short reference mapping**[150]. Attaches the attributes to one or more elements.

associated notation name[149a] — The name of a declared notation to be associated with a **data attribute**.

ATTCAP — The **reserved name** for the keyword that assigns **capacity point** maximum values to the storage of an entity name plus the NAMELEN value for each associated notation.

ATTCHCAP — The **reserved name** for the keyword that assigns **capacity point** maximum values to characters in an attribute.

ATTCNT — The **reserved name** for the keyword that defines the maximum number of **attribute** values in an **attribute definition list**[142], by default '40'. The 'attribute count' keyword. See ATTLIST.

ATTLIST — The **reserved name** for the keyword that indicates that a **markup declaration** defines a list of attributes. May be changed to another name in a **variant concrete syntax**. See **attribute definition list declaration**[141]. Determines allowed or required **attributes** in an **element**[013] or **group** of elements, including any default values. See ATTCNT for maximum number of **attribute definition**[143] constructs in the list, and the *Road Map* chart (141.2).

attribute — An **element**[013] parameter that modifies or refines the meaning of the element, and consists of a name and a value. The attribute is named to distinguish it from other attributes and values in the same element. Defined in the **DTD** using an **attribute definition list**[142].

attribute definition[143] — Method of defining a single **attribute**. For example, `'MyAttr CDATA #REQUIRED'`, which defines Myattr to contain text, which must be entered.

attribute definition list[142] — Method of defining **attributes** within a **declaration**.

attribute definition list declaration[141] — Method of defining **attributes** and attaching them to a given **element** or **group** of elements, using a **declaration**.

attribute name[144] — Method of defining a name for a single **attribute**. For example, `'MyAttr'`.

attribute specification[032] — A single attribute embedded in a **start-tag**[014] or **entity declaration**[101], ideally consisting of both a name and associated value, though either part may be omitted in some circumstances using **minimization** techniques.

attribute specification list[031] — The **attribute** names and current values as they appear in a **start-tag**[014], for example '`<myelem    myatt1="red" myatt2=654>`'.

attribute type — Classification of an **attribute** value such as NAME or NUMBER that affects the characters that may be entered, and may also add significance (such as ID and IDREF, which indicate **hypertext link**s). The full list of types are shown in Chapter 14.

attribute value[035] — The current value assigned to the **attribute**. The value may obey one of several restrictions. An attribute of type NUMBER, for example, could not contain letters. See **attribute type**.

attribute value literal[034] — An **attribute** value enclosed by double or single quotes. The choice is left to the document author, but must match (if a single quote starts the literal, a single quote must also end it). The choice may be dictated by the content – if the value contains a double quote, it may be included as a character (rather than a **character reference**[062]) by delimiting with single quotes: '`'a "quoted" value'`'.

attribute value specification[033] — A value associated with a single attribute, depending on the type of value may be enclosed by quotes, '`"my   value"`', '`MyVal`'.

ATTSPLEN — The **reserved name** for the keyword used to define the length of allowed character data in an **attribute specification list**[031], by default '960' characters. The 'attribute specification length' keyword. The maximum length of a **start-tag**[014] will normally be defined by the sum of NAMELEN and ATTSPLEN.

AVGRCAP — The **reserved name** for the keyword that assigns **capacity point** maximum values to tokens defined in an attribute **name group**[069] or **name token group**[068].

AVI *(Audio Video Interleave)* — Full motion video format developed by Microsoft.

B

B element — An element containing bold style text in the **HTML** model.

Background attribute — Used in the **Body** element in **HTML** to fill the **page** background pattern from a picture.

Background Color — See **Bgcolor** attribute.

base character set[174] — A reference to a defined character set, such as **ISO/IEC 646:1991**. A 'base' which can be modified in a **described character set portion**[175]. Included for human reference only. See BASESET.

base document element[011] — The outermost **element**[013] of the document instance, or base document. When only one document structure exists, this is the same thing as the **document element**[012]. For example, an element called Book may be the document element for a book.

base document type declaration[009] — The main document structure (usually the only document structure), enclosing the **declaration**s that make up the **DTD**.

base set character number[178] — The character number, or numbers in the **base character set**[174] to which a character or series of characters are to be mapped. A number of '32' in the sequence '160 5 32' maps the active characters 160–164 to the base characters 32–26, so that character 160 is treated as character 32 (a space).

Basefont element — An **HTML** element that uses a **Size** attribute to set the default font size.

BASESET — The **reserved name** for the keyword that references a standard **character set** in the **SGML declaration**[171]. For example, the **ISO/IEC 646:1991** standard. See **base character set**[174] and the *Road Map* chart (174.1).

basic SGML document — One of the conformance testing **SGML declaration**[171] configurations, involving the **reference concrete syntax** and **reference capacity set** and the inclusion of SHORTTAG and OMITTAG. See **minimal SGML document**.

Bgcolor attribute — Used in the **Body** element in **HTML** to set the **page** background color. See **Text** attribute.

Big element — An **HTML** element that specifies a larger font. See **Small** element.

bit — A 'binary digit'. The smallest unit of information on a computer, taking a value of '0' or '1' (or 'on' or 'off'). Collections of bits make larger units, with values that can be calculated using binary arithmetic ('00' = 0, '01' = 1, '10' = 2, '11' = 3). For example, 8 bits combine to form a **byte**, and a **7-bit** character set uses 7 bits to store unique character values, allowing only 128 possibilities.

Body element — An **HTML** element that encloses the actual document, following the **Head** element that contains information *about* the document.

bold — A heavy variation of a normal typeface. Cross-referenced terms in this glossary appear in bold typeface.

Bold — See **B** element.

Border attribute — Used in the **HTML** elements **Img** and **Table** to determine the thickness (or presence) of border lines.

Box element — A **9573 math** element used to encase part of a formula in a box.

bracketed text[107] — The content of the **entity** is **markup**. Markup delimiters are supplied by the **parser** from further information in the declaration. Possible types are 'STARTTAG' (**start-tag**[014]), 'ENDTAG' (**end-tag**[019]), 'MS' (**marked section**[069]) and 'MD' (**markup declaration**). For example, a bracketed text entity of type 'STARTTAG' may have a content of 'mytag', which, depending on the **concrete syntax**[182] in use, may become '<mytag>' when replacing a reference.

Break element — A **9573 math** element for splitting multiple line formula.

Browser — An application designed to read and display tagged text, allowing **hypertext links** to be followed. See **HTML Browser**.

BSEQLEN — The **reserved name** for the keyword that specifies the length of a blank sequence in a **short reference** string, by default '960' characters. The 'blank sequence length' keyword. Part of the **quantity set**[194] clause.

By element — A **9573 math** element used in the **Diff** element. The container for the denominator value. Used with the **Diffof** element, which contains the numerator.

byte — A unit of memory composed of 8 **bit**s (short for 'by eight'). Using binary arithmetic, a byte can store values between '00000000' and '11111111' (or '0' to '255' in decimal). Currently, most **character set**s use one byte to represent one character, giving 256 combinations for an **8-bit** character set. When one bit is ignored, or used for parity checking, this leaves only 128 character values available in a **7-bit** set, such as **ASCII**. Proposed character sets use two or four bytes for each character, vastly expanding the range of available characters. Some image formats use byte values to represent pixels.

C

C — *[1]* An **ESIS** command indicating that the **SGML** input was valid. See **SGMLS**. *[2]* Control Character Set, as in **C0**.

C0 — Control Character Set Zero. The first 32 **ASCII** characters. See **ESC 2/1 4/0**.

CALS *(Continuous Acquisition and Lifecycle Support)* — Set of standards (before 1994 standing for *Computer-aided Acquisition and Logistics Support*), including **DTD**s, **CCITT Group IV**, **CGM** and **IGES**, and an electronic delivery standard for transfer of documentation between defense contractors and the US Department of Defense. Notable for **CALS table**s and the **CALS declaration**. Contact 'http://www.acq.osd.mil/cals/'.

CALS declaration — Variant of the **SGML declaration**[171] defined for the **CALS** standard. Notable for extended **NAMELEN** maximum to a value of '32' characters, allowing much longer element names and attribute names and values (which can be particularly useful for complex and extensive **ID** values).

CALS table — An **SGML** table model defined in the **DTD**s developed in the **CALS** initiative, now used in many other applications due to widespread software support, including **WYSIWYG** editing. Defined in 'MIL SPEC 28001-B Appendix A-50', and refined by the **SGML Open** committee in 1995. See Chapter 10 for details.

CAPACITY — The **reserved name** for a keyword that has three related roles. It identifies an **external entity** as containing **capacity set**[180] override values. It also directly identifies override values in the **SGML declaration**[171]. Finally, it specifies whether exceeding stated (or implied) capacity limits will generate errors. See the *Road Map* chart (131.1).

capacity point — An abstract value that is mapped to a real value representing one or more bytes. Used to calculate memory requirements from usage of objects with pre-defined **capacity set**[180] values.

capacity set[180] — Set of definitions for the maximum quantity of various objects, intended to help a **parser** prepare memory for storage of the document components. For example, the **reference capacity set** allows up to 35 000 **IDREF** values in a document. Many applications ignore these values, and simply use the available memory.

CAPS *(Computer Aided Publishing System)* — Combined database and pagination system, possibly used for on-demand printing, and possibly involving the use of **SGML**.

catalog — A file containing mappings between an **entity name**[102] or **public identifier**[074] and their **system identifier**[075] counterparts. For example, `MyEnt` may be mapped to `C:\ENTS\MYENT.SGM` and `-//MyCorp//DTD My DTD// EN` may be mapped to `C:\ENTS\MYDTD.DTD`. Used by an **entity manager**. See **SGML Open** for a standard catalog format.

CCITT Group IV — Compression scheme for bi-level (on/off pixels, not suited for representing gray scales or colors) bit-mapped (**raster**) image data, optimized for images containing lines of text. Adopted as an **ODA** format (along with CCITT Group III). Adopted as one of the **CALS** standards. May be stored in a **TIFF** file 'wrapper'.

CDATA — The **reserved name** for the keyword that specifies **character data** content for an **element**[013] or **entity**. May be changed to another name in a **variant concrete syntax**. Identifies element or **entity** content that contains text characters but not **tag**s, so '<' will not be seen as significant. See RCDATA and the *Road Map* charts (100.1), (106.1), (109.2), (125.1) and (145.1).

Cellpadding attribute — Used by the **Table** element in **HTML** to adjust the space between the cell content and its borders. See **Cellspacing** attribute.

Cellspacing attribute — Used by the **Table** element in **HTML** to adjust the space between cells. See **Cellpadding** attribute.

Center element — An **HTML** element used to center all enclosed structures. See **Div** element.

CGI *(Common Gateway Interface)* — A standard method for software to dynamically create customized **HTML** pages, facilitating a two-way exchange of information between the **Web server** and the user of a **Web browser**. A CGI script can be written in any language (though the most popular is Perl), and can therefore access various sources of information, such as an SQL database. One use of a CGI script is to process **form**s that are filled in by the user, and another is to create and return customized HTML pages based on information gathered from such a form. Contact 'comp.infosystems.www.authoring.cgi' newsgroup and 'http://hoohoo.ncsa.uiuc.edu/cgi/interface.html'.

CGM *(Computer Graphics Metafile)* — An **ISO** standard (ISO 8632) for representing two-dimensional object based, **vector** images. Adopted as part of the **CALS** standard (MIL-D-28003). Also adopted as part of the **ODA** standard. Contact 'http://www.agocg.ac.uk:8080/agocg/CGM.html'.

Char attribute — Character-based alignment in the **CALS table** structure. Defines the character to align a column of entries on. An implied CDATA type. Typical value of full-point, '.', for decimal alignment. Used with **Charoff** attribute, which positions the significant character. Appears in the **Tgroup, Colspec, Spanspec** and **Entry** elements.

character — A letter, digit or symbol, represented within a computer by a numeric code. Generally grouped into **character set**s.

character[049] — A character not restricted by the **SGML** standard, which can be included in a **non-SGML data entity**[006]. The term 'character' can be misleading in this respect, as the lack of restrictions allows each **byte** to hold any value, and so be used for any purpose, such as to store compressed image data.

character data[047] — Data consisting of normal text characters, no markup recognition to be attempted. Defined using the CDATA keyword. See **system data**[045].

character data entity[005a] — An non-system specific character-based object that should transfer between systems without requiring editing, unlike a **specific character data entity**[005b]. See CDATA.

character description[176] — The mapping of the active character set on to a 'base' character set, usually using a combination of three values – the first giving a character number, the second giving a range (starting at the first value), and the third giving the base number on to which this range is mapped. A definition of '128 32 0' would map character 128–160 to the first 32 characters in the base set.

character number[064] — A decimal value that represents a character. For an **8-bit** character set, the number will be in the range 0–255. As the letter 'A' has a value of 65 in **ASCII**, its character number would be '65'.

Character Offset — See **Charoff** attribute.

character reference[062] — A reference that has a replacement value of a single **character**. Requires a preceding '#' symbol. For example, '{' or '&#TAB;'. The first example includes a **character number**[064].

character reference open — The character(s) that identify a **character reference**[062], by default '&#'. See CRO.

character set — An ordered set of **character** definitions. A value is assigned to each character shape (or '**glyph**'). The number of characters held in a set is determined by the number of **bits** assigned to each character. Currently, most character sets are **8-bit** sets, holding 256 characters. See **ASCII**, **EBCDIC**, **ISO/IEC 646:1991** and **ISO/IEC 10646**.

character set description[173] — The definition of the character set used on the local system, including a 'base' set, which is probably a publicly defined set (such as **ISO/IEC 646:1991**), and possible modifications to this set.

Charoff attribute — Specifies horizontal location of character used to vertically align entry content in a **CALS table** column, in combination with the **Char** attribute. Indicates percentage of entry width. For example, a value of '33' places the significant character one third of the entry width from the left edge of the cell.

CHARSET — The **reserved name** for the keyword that identifies an **external entity** containing a **character set** definition or a direct specification in the **SGML declaration**[171]. See the *Road Map* chart (172.1).

Checked attribute — An **HTML** attribute to the **Input** element. Used to pre-select a check-box option.

child — A concept derived from family trees that describes an **element** that is enclosed by another element (as part of a **hierarchy** of elements). One element is the child of another, and an element may have several children. For example, a Chapter element may be the child of a Book element, and itslef may contain several Section children. See **parent** and **sibling**.

Citation — See **Cite** element.

Cite element — An **HTML** element used to contain a citation (reference or quotation).

Clear attribute — An **HTML 3.2** attribute to the **Br** element that forces following text to clear 'all' floating images (the default), or just the floating images on the 'left' or 'right' sides.

Close attribute — A **9573 math** attribute used in the **Fence** element. Holds the character used to close the fence.

Code element — An **HTML** element used to contain examples of computer code, typically displayed in a mono-spaced font.

Col element — A **9573 math** element used in the **Matrix** element to determine the number of columns in the matrix.

Colname attribute — A **CALS table** attribute that assigns a name to a numbered column, so that the column can be referred to sensibly, and in such a way that the deletion or insertion of another column will not affect such references.

Cols attribute — *[1]* Determines the number of columns in the **CALS table** structure. It is a required **NUMBER** type, appearing in the **Tgroup** and **Entrytbl** elements. *[2]* An **HTML** attribute to the **Textarea** and **Frameset** elements.

Colsep attribute — Column separation specification in the **CALS table** structure. It is an implied **NUMBER** type, controlling the appearance of a vertical line to the right of the column. Appearing in the **Colspec**, **Spanspec** and **Entry** elements. A value of '0' = no line, '1' = line. Greater than '1' also indicates a line (though non-standard extensions vary line style with higher values).

Colspan attribute — An **HTML 3.2** attribute to the **Td** and **Th** elements, used to span a table cell over subsequent columns. See **Rowspan**.

Colspec element — Column specification in **CALS table** structure. Specifies column name (for easy reference), column width, alignment of contents and border lines. Example: `'<colspec    colname="colors"    colwidth="3*" align="center" colsep="1">'`.

Column Separator — See **Colsep** attribute.

Column Specification — See **Colspec** element.

Column Width — See **Colwidth** attribute.

Colwidth attribute — Column width specification in the **CALS table** structure. Specifies the width of the current column, possibly in relation to the width of other columns. Appearing in the **Colspec** element. An implied **CDATA** value. A numeric value is assumed to be a number of points. A prefix of 'PT' is the same. Other measurement options are 'CM' (centimeters), 'MM' (millimeters), 'PI' (picas) and 'IN' (inches). Also, proportional to other columns using '*'. If no value is given, a value of '1*' is assumed.

COM — The **reserved name** for the keyword that defines characters used as comment start and comment end delimiters, by default '--'. For example '-- `this is a comment` --'.

comment[(092)] — Part of a **markup declaration** that exists only to describe the purpose of the declaration. Similar to comments in program source code. Comments have no effect on processing and do not appear in published documents. A comment may be inserted by a **DTD** author or by a document author (in a **comment declaration**[(091)]). It is delimited by '--' characters, as in '`-- this is a comment --`'.

comment declaration[(091)] — A **markup declaration** that exists only to hold at least one **comment**[(092)]. To define the declaration type, the first comment must immediately follow the declaration delimiters, MDO, giving '<!--'.

comment delimiter — Character(s) that identify the start or end of a comment. By default '--'. See COM.

Common Gateway Interface — See **CGI**.

Compact attribute — An **HTML** attribute to all list types, used to reduce the space between items.

compose — The process of converting **tag**ged data into formatted output, including hyphenation and justification of the text.

compound document — A document containing more than just text, for example images.

concrete syntax[(182)] — The settings for **character set**s, **delimiter**s, and delimiter role values. The explicit **syntax** rules for **SGML**, defined using the keywords provided by the **abstract syntax**. For example, the abstract concept of a markup declaration open delimiter has a keyword MDO, which may be used to define the concrete syntax for this object as '<!'. If a concrete syntax is not made explicit in an **SGML declaration**[(171)], then the **reference concrete syntax** defaults are used.

concrete syntax scope[(181)] — This definition specifies whether the **concrete syntax**[(182)] applies to the **prolog**[(007)] and the **document instance set**[(010)] or just to the document instance set (the prolog uses the **reference concrete syntax** instead).

connector[(131)] — A symbol that connects tokens and describes the relationship between them. The OR connector, '|', indicates a choice of tokens; 'a | b' provides a choice between A and B. The AND connector, '&', indicates optional ordering; 'a & b' specifies that A and B must appear but in any order. The SEQ connector, ',', indicates a sequence; 'a , b' specifies that A precedes B.

CONREF — The **reserved name** for the keyword that identifies an **attribute** whose content will dictate the content of the **element**[(013)] (if a value is entered). See **content reference**. May be changed to another name in a **variant concrete syntax**. See the *Road Map* chart (147.8).

content[(024)] — The content of an element, delimited by a **start-tag**[(014)] and **end-tag**[(019)]. An **empty element** has no content.

Content attribute — An **HTML** attribute to the **Meta** element that provides a value associated with meta data (identified by the **Name** attribute).

content model[(126)] — The definition of the content of an **element**[(013)], including **child** elements, text, and possible **exceptions**[(138)].

content reference — An **attribute** type with the special property that, if a value is specified, it renders the content of the element empty, and the application is expected to use the attribute value to provide new content.

content token[128] — Part of a **model group**[127], defining the use of text, or an **element**[013] or **group** of elements.

control character — A non-visible character that is used by the system to perform special tasks, such as end a line of text.

CONTROLS — The **reserved name** for the keyword that represents all **control characters** in a **character set**. Used to aid specification of **shunned characters**. See the *Road Map* chart (184.4).

Coords attribute — An **HTML** attribute to the **Area** element, used to define the coordinates of an active area of an image.

core concrete syntax — Most basic part of an **SGML declaration**[171] that conforming systems must be able to support, or must instead support the **reference concrete syntax**, which is identical except that the core concrete syntax does not support the **short reference** feature. Specified using the **public identifier**[074] 'ISO 8879:1986//SYNTAX Core//EN'.

CR *(Carriage Return)* — A control character used to terminate lines, alone or in combination with **LF** *(Line Feed)*, by many operating systems. The RE *(Record End)* is assigned to this character by the **reference concrete syntax**.

CRO — The **reserved name** for the keyword that specifies which character(s) indicate the start of a **character reference**[082], by default '&#'. See the *Road Map* chart (062.1).

CURRENT — The **reserved name** for the keyword that makes an attribute take a previous value if no value is entered. See **current attribute**. May be changed to another name in a **variant concrete syntax**. See the *Road Map* chart (147.7).

current attribute — An attribute requirement option of CURRENT, indicating that the attribute value, if not stated, is the same as a previously declared value. For example, if the Section element for section one had a Status value of 'secret', and the Section element for section two had no value, its Status attribute would inherit the value of 'secret'.

D

data attribute — An **attribute** that contains a value to be sent to an application able to process the data referred to in the **external entity**. See **data attribute specification**[149b].

data attribute specification[149b] — A collection of **data attribute**s. The attribute values are to be processed by an external application, requiring more information about the data format it supports. For example, to successfully render an image format the application may need to know the resolution or compression scheme used.

data character[048] — A **character** in the legal **SGML** set that may be used as data in all **entity** types.

data content — The element can only contain data, not **child** elements. See **element content**[026] and **mixed content**[025].

data entity — Non-parsable, non-SGML data. See **parser** and **SGML Entity**.

data stream — Term used to describe the processing of a data file, character by character, with the first character in the file heading the stream of input to the application. Some data formats are designed to assist processing in a single direction, including **SGML**, which is why the **SGML declaration**[171] must precede the **prolog**[007], which in turn must precede the **document instance set**[010] (at no point should a **parser** need to 'rewind' to an earlier point in the file).

data text[106] — An **entity** containing text, either system dependent or system independent.

DATACHAR — The character class that groups together all characters *not* assigned **delimiter** roles. See the *Road Map* chart (050.2).

Dd element — An **HTML** element describing a definition entry, following a definition term, **Dt** element, and containing any number of other text structures. Enclosed by a **Dl** element.

declaration — A **tag** that is used to help specify the document structure (**element declaration**[116] or **attribute** declaration), manage the document (**entity declaration**[101] or **marked section declaration**[093]), or add comments (**comment declaration**[091]). By default, identified by the characters '<!' and '>' (see **MDO** and **MDC**).

declaration subset — A mechanism by which some **declaration**s can contain other declarations, by default enclosed in square brackets, '[' and ']'. For example, the declarations that form the **DTD** are enclosed in the **document type declaration**[110].

declaration subset open — The character(s) that identify the start of a **declaration subset**. See **DSO**.

declared content[125] — The definition of an element that is an **empty element**, or contains only text, which may or may not allow **entity reference**s. See **CDATA**, **RCDATA** and **EMPTY**.

declared value[145] — The type of value that an **attribute** may take. Some types, such as NAME and NUMBER, only restrict the characters that may appear; others, such as ID and IDREF, provide a special meaning to the attribute value.

DEFAULT — The **reserved name** for the keyword that makes a particular (and only one) **entity** definition applicable to all unmatched **entity reference**s. May be changed to another name in a **variant concrete syntax**. See **default entity** and the *Road Map* chart (103.3).

default entity — An entity that provides a replacement value for all references to non-existent entities. Possibly used to prevent error messages, or replace references to unknown entities with a message, such as 'SOMETHING MISSING HERE'. An **entity declaration**[101] containing the keyword **DEFAULT**. For example, '<!ENTITY #DEFAULT "ITS MISSING!">'. There can only be one default entity in a **DTD**.

default value[147] — The value of an **attribute** when no value is entered by the document author during insertion of the **element**[013] containing that attribute. Alternatively, the value can be pre-defined (FIXED), be REQUIRED or optional (IMPLIED), or take the same value as the previous occurrence of the attribute (CURRENT).

Definition Entry — See **Dd** element.

Definition List — See **Dl** element.

Definition Term — See **Dt** element.

Degree element — A **9573 math** element used in the **Root** and **Power** elements to hold the degree of root or power. When the degree is '2', the alternative **Sqrt** and **Square** elements are used, and they do not require a degree value.

DELIM — The **reserved name** for the keyword that specifies and precedes any override values to the **reference concrete syntax** default **delimiter role**s. See the *Road Map* chart (190.1).

delimiter — Characters used to separate **SGML** markup **tag**s from raw text. In the **reference concrete syntax** they include '<', '</', '>', '<!' and '<?'. See STAGO, ETAGO, TAGC, MDO and PIO respectively.

delimiter role — A character or series of characters that identify **markup** embedded within the text have a delimiter role. By default, the '<' character has a delimiter role, sometimes in conjunction with other characters, such as '<!' and '<?'. See **delimiter set**[190].

delimiter set[190] — The default or modified set of physical representations of each **delimiter role**. By default, for example, the **start-tag**[014] delimiters are '<' and '>'. Using the STAGO keyword in this clause it can be changed, perhaps to '!', so that a start-tag appears as '!mytag>'.

DELMCHAR — A **concrete syntax** character class that groups all characters used as a **delimiter**. See the *Road Map* chart (051.3).

described character set number[177] — Part of the scheme for mapping parts of an extended character set to portions of the 'base' character set. Describes the start character number of the extended or modified set. This number is followed by another number stating the range from this number. For example, '128 32' specifies characters 128–160. See DESCSET.

described character set portion[175] — The scheme for mapping parts of an extended character set to portions of the 'base' character set. See DESCSET.

descriptive markup — A **markup** scheme that describes the significance of each part of a document, without referring to how the document should appear when published, which is the task of **procedural markup**. **SGML** facilitates descriptive markup (but does not enforce it). A descriptive document can easily be translated into procedural markup, but the opposite is not true.

DESCSET — The **reserved name** for the keyword that precedes any changes to the BASESET standard **character set**. See **described character set portion**[175] and the *Road Map* chart (175.1).

DeskTop Publishing — See **DTP**.

Df element — Definition of a display formula in the **ISO 9573 math** model. One of the outermost **element**s in the **DTD** fragment.

Dfg element — Definition of a display formula group in the **9573 math** model. An outermost element in the **DTD** fragment.

Dfref element — Definition of a reference to a display formula in the **ISO 9573** math model. An outermost element in the **DTD** fragment.

Diff element — A **9573 math** element that encloses the numerator of a differential. It contains a **Type** attribute to specify a normal or partial differential.

Diffof element — A **9573 math** element contained in the **Diff** element which specifies the numerator of the differential. See **By** element.

digit — The **abstract syntax** character class that groups the characters used to describe a number ('0'–'9'). See the *Road Map* chart (052.2).

Dir element — An **HTML** element used to produce multi-column directory listings (or similar construct). See **Menu** element and **Ul** element.

Directory List — See **Dir** element.

DIS *(Draft International Standard)* — A standard in progress to becoming an **IS**. See **ISO**.

Display Formula — See **Df** element.

Display Formula Group — See **Dfg** element.

Display Formula Reference — See **Dfref** element.

Div element — An **HTML 3.2** element that groups other structures that are aligned in the same way, using an **Align** attribute. See **Center** element.

Division — See **Div** element.

Dl element — An **HTML** element describing a definition list, containing at least one pair of **Dt** and **Dd** elements. Commonly used for glossary lists.

DNS *(Domain Name Server)* — A server that stores the relationships between **domain names** and **IP address**es (e.g. 'pindar.co.uk' is the domain name for IP address '194.193.96.10').

Docorsub attribute — A **HyTime** attribute to the **Nmlist** element that identifies an entity. The entity provides the location and name of a remote document that contains a referenced object.

DOCTYPE — The **reserved name** for the keyword that identifies a **markup declaration** as a **document type declaration**[110]. May be changed to another name in a **variant concrete syntax**. See the *Road Map* chart (110.2).

DOCUMENT — The **reserved name** for the keyword that specifies that a declared **concrete syntax** is applied to both the **prolog**[007] and **document instance set**[010]. The keyword **INSTANCE** describes the alternative possibility. See the *Road Map* chart (181.3).

document character set[172] — The character set used by the local system, and by documents stored on the local system. For human reference only.

document element[012] — The outermost **element**[013] in the document **hierarchy**. The ultimate **ancestor** of all elements in the document. The element declared in the **document type declaration**[010], which must be in the **DTD**, but need not be the outermost element described there.

document instance set[010] — The 'real' document, following system and document defining rules. Defines the content of the document, including **markup** and data.

Document Style Semantics and Specification Language — See **DSSSL**.

document type declaration[110] — The name and definition of a document type. Contains the **DTD**. See DOCTYPE.

document type declaration subset[112] — The container for the **declaration**s that comprise the **DTD**, employing a **declaration subset**.

Document Type Definition — See **DTD**.

document type name[111] — The name of the outermost **element**[013] in the following document. For example '<!DOCTYPE **myelem** .....>'.

document type specification[028] — An indicator of which **DTD** the **element**[013] belongs to (assuming more than one DTD can be used concurrently).

domain name — The natural language equivalent of an **IP address**. For example, 'bradley.co.uk' is the domain name for IP address '194.193.96.10'. The IANA (*Internet Assigned Numbers Authority*) is responsible for coordinating and managing the assignment of domain names, which must be unique (there cannot be two 'bradley.co.uk' names). Part of the name denotes the type of organization ('.org' = organisation, '.com' = commercial, '.co' = commercial, '.edu' = education, '.gov' = governmental). The final part of the name denotes the country (omitted for the United States).

down-convert — Term used to describe the process of converting data from an information rich format, such as **SGML**, to a less rich, or display-oriented format, such as **RTF**. Generally categorized as a **low energy** conversion process. See **up-convert**.

DP *(Draft Proposal)* — See **ISO**.

ds[071] — A declaration separator. It may be just a space character, but may also include some **markup** (for example, a **comment**[092]).

DSC — The **reserved name** for the keyword that identifies the character(s) that ends a declaration subset, by default ']'. See DSO and the *Road Map* charts (110.10) and (149b.5).

DSO — The **reserved name** for the keyword that identifies the character(s) that starts a declaration subset, by default '['. See DSC and the *Road Map* charts (093.3), (094.2), (110.8) and (149b.2).

DSSSL *(Document Style Semantics and Specification Language)* — An **ISO** standard (ISO/IEC 10179:1995) used to specify transformation and format information relating to **SGML** structured documents, replacing the more limited **FOSI** approach. Released in April 1996. Contact 'http://occam.sjf.novell.com:8080/dsssl/dsssl96'. See **DSSSL Online**.

DSSSL Lite— Previous name for **DSSSL Online**.

DSSSL Online — Previously called 'DSSSL Lite', this is a subset of the full **DSSSL** standard aimed at adding remote formatting instructions to **SGML** documents. The online version is used to **compose** SGML documents on-screen. This approach potentially offers a more powerful alternative to the current use of

HTML on the **Web**, as no prior conversion is needed to a generic **DTD**, and the information provider controls the appearance of the information when it is rendered on the user's system. Contact 'http://occam.sjf.novell.com:8080/docs/dsssl-o/do951212.htm'.

Dt element — An **HTML** element describing a definition term, preceding a definition entry, **Dd** element, and containing text that describes the following definition. Enclosed by a **Dl** element.

DTD — The **reserved name** for the keyword that identifies an **external entity** identified by a **formal public identifier**[079] as an **entity** that contains at least part of a **DTD**.

DTD *(Document Type Definition)* — The instructions that codify rules for a particular type of document. Used by a **parser** to check that a **tag**ged document conforms to the pre-defined document structure rules. Built using a number of **element declaration**[116] and **attribute** declaration codes in the **prolog**[007].

DTP *(DeskTop Publishing)* — An application designed to **compose** and **paginate** documents, and operate on desktop computers, usually employing a **WYSI-WYG** interface.

DTR *(Draft Technical Report)* — See **ISO**.

dual-role public text — An **external identifier**[073] consisting of both a **public identifier**[074] and a **system identifier**[075], in which the public identifier takes the role of locating a data file describing a data format, and the system identifier takes the role of locating a program that can process an instance of that data.

E

EBCDIC *(Extended Binary Coded Decimal Interchange Code)* — An equivalent to **ASCII** used on IBM mainframe systems. Similar characters are represented, but are assigned different values (in fact there are several variants of EBCDIC). A text file copied from an EBCDIC-based computer to an ASCII-based computer should be translated, or the result will be unintelligible.

EE *(Entity End)* — System signal (not necessarily a character) signifying the end of an entity (may be the end-of-file character).

ELEMCAP — The **reserved name** for the keyword that assigns **capacity point** maximum values to the number of elements in a document.

element[013] — An identified component of a document, usually consisting of a **start-tag**[014], content and an **end-tag**[019] (though an **empty element** consists only of a start-tag). The terms 'element' and '**tag**' are sometimes used interchangeably, but this is an inaccurate comparison – an element is composed of one or more tags, and also of the text between start and end tags.

ELEMENT — The **reserved name** for the keyword that identifies an **element declaration**[116]. May be changed to another name in a **variant concrete syntax**. See the *Road Map* chart (116.2).

element content[026] — The element cannot directly include text, as opposed to an element with **mixed content**[025], which can. The element encloses at **subele-**

ments (**child** elements). All line-feed characters in element content are ignored (not treated as spaces).

element declaration[(116)] — Definition of an **element**[(013)] in the **DTD** using a **markup declaration**. The element is given a **name**[(055)] and a definition of its content.

element set[(114)] — A group of **element**[(013)] declarations within the **document type declaration**[(110)]. May be held in an **external entity** (see ELEMENTS).

Element Structure Information Set — See **ESIS**.

element token[(130)] — The smallest unit of information in a **model group**[(127)], consisting of either an element name (**generic identifier**[(030)]), such as 'mytag', or an **occurrence indicator**[(132)], such as '&'.

element type[(117)] — The name of the **element**[(013)] or **group** of elements being defined in an **element declaration**[(116)].

ELEMENTS — The **reserved name** for the keyword that identifies an **external entity** described by a **public identifier**[(074)] as containing only a group of **element declaration**[(116)] tags.

Em element — An **HTML** element that encloses text to be emphasized. No particular style is dictated.

Emphasis — See **Em** element.

EMPTY — The **reserved name** for the keyword that specifies an **element**[(013)] with no content. There is no **end-tag**[(019)]; the **start-tag**[(014)] acts as a marker in the text. May be changed to another name in a **variant concrete syntax**. See **empty element** and the *Road Map* charts (125.3) and (153.3).

empty element — Element with no content. Typically a place holder for an image or cross-reference. For example, 'this picture<pic id="X123"> is in the text'. See EMPTY keyword.

empty end-tag[(021)] — An **end-tag**[(019)] that has no content, '</>', and inherits its description from the most recently opened **start-tag**[(014)].

empty start-tag[(016)] — A **start-tag**[(014)] with no content, '<>', which inherits its description from the previous start-tag in the **data stream**.

end-tag[(019)] — Closing unit of an **element**[(013)], when it is not an **empty element**. A **tag** that locates the end of a logical unit of information in the text. By default identified by the characters '</' and '>' (see ETAGO and TAGC). Always accompanied by a preceding **start-tag**[(014)].

end-tag minimization[(124)] — The part of an element definition that specifies whether the **end-tag**[(019)] may be omitted without generating an error (though an error will still be generated if an end-tag is omitted in illegal circumstances). The character 'O' indicates the possibility of omission. The character '-' forbids omission.

ENDTAG — The **reserved name** for the keyword that states the content of an **entity** is an **end-tag**[(019)]. If the entity contains 'mytag', by default this would become '</mytag>' in the text. May be changed to another name in a **variant concrete syntax**. See the *Road Map* chart (107.2).

ENTCAP — The **reserved name** for the keyword that assigns **capacity point** maximum values to storage of defined entities.

ENTCHCAP — The **reserved name** for the keyword that assigns **capacity point** maximum values to characters of entity text.

ENTITIES — The **reserved name** for the keyword that specifies that the **attribute** value consists of one or more **entity reference**s, 'myattr="myent1 myent2"'. May be changed to another name in a **variant concrete syntax**. See the *Road Map* chart (145.3).

entity — A named object that can be referred to. In **SGML**, a data fragment usually stored in a separate file or delimited by quotes, referred to by an **entity declaration**[101].

ENTITY — The **reserved name** for the keyword that identifies an **entity declaration**[101]. Also used in an **attribute** to specify that the attribute value is an **entity reference**. May be changed to another name in a **variant concrete syntax**. See the *Road Map* charts (101.2), (145.2) and (189.25).

entity declaration[101] — The **markup declaration** that defines an **entity** name and associated content (either directly or by reference.) See ENTITY.

entity end — See EE.

entity level — The content of an **entity** may include an **entity reference**. Entities may therefore be embedded within other entities, like Russian dolls. The ENTLVL keyword may be used to specify the maximum number of embedded levels.

entity manager — Software designed to locate and access data held in an **entity**. An essential component of a **parser**. Uses a **catalog** file to match entity names to system files.

entity name[102] — The name of an **entity**, for use in references to the entity.

entity reference — Special character sequence identifying an external object (an **entity**) to be inserted at the current point in the data. The reference includes the name of the entity. A typical entity reference representing a special character would be 'é'.

entity reference close — The character that separates the end of an entity name from following text in an **entity reference**, by default ';'. This character is not required if the name is followed by a space or other blank character (for example, 'the caf&eacute is open'). See ERC.

entity set[113] — A group of **entity** declarations within the **document type declaration**[110]. May be held in an **external entity**, where they are typically used to represent extended characters, such as the **ISOlat1** set. See ENTITY.

entity text[105] — The content of an **entity**, either enclosed in quotes within the declaration, or referenced from the declaration using a **public identifier**[074] or **system identifier**[075].

entity type[109] — The type of an **entity**, identifying its content as a subdocument, character data, system specific data or non-SGML data with associated notation name.

ENTLVL —The **reserved name** for the keyword that specifies the number of allowed nested **entity level**s, by default '16'.

Entry element — Table cell **element**[013] in the **CALS table** structure. One of several in a **Row** element, defining columns within the row.

Entry Table — See **Entrytbl** element.

Entrytbl element — An alternative to the **Entry** element in the **CALS table** model, allowing the cell to contain an embedded table. Not widely used due to lack of software support.

ERO — The **reserved name** for the keyword that specifies which character starts an **entity reference**, by default '&'. See the *Road Map* chart (059.1).

ESC — The name of a control character that usually preceded one or more special instruction characters. Combined, these characters are known as an 'escape sequence'. In **ISO 2022**, a **7-bit** or **8-bit character set** is enlarged by the use of escape sequences that swap-in alternative groups of characters. There are two control groups, called C0 and C1 (each consisting of 32 characters), and four normal, or 'graphical' groups, called G0, G1, G2 and G3 (each consisting of 94 or 96 characters). The default groups are C0 and G0, which together define 128 characters, but an 8-bit character set can simultaneously employ both control sets and two of the graphical sets (**ISO/IEC 8859/1** defines both G0 and G1). The value of the characters following ESC are sometimes presented in the form 'X/Y', for example '2/1' (which is the hexadecimal representation '21' – decimal '33'). Pre-defined character sets are identified by an escape sequence. The first character defines the graphical set, the second defines the control set.

ESC 2/1 4/0 — The **C0** set of **ISO/IEC 646:1991** International Reference Version (**IRV**) character set (32 characters). See **ESC**.

ESC 2/5 4/0 — Full **ISO/IEC 646:1991** International Reference Version (**IRV**) character set (196 characters). See **ESC**.

ESC 2/8 4/0 — See **ISO/IEC 646:1991** International Reference Version (**IRV**) character set (196 characters). See **ESC**.

ESC 2/8 4/2 — See **ASCII** (196 characters). See **ESC**.

ESIS *(Element Structure Information Set)* — The **ISO** standard (**ISO/IEC 13673:1995**) that describes the content and structure of a document. Used for conformance testing. A parser should be able to produce ESIS output from an SGML document (See Chapter 13).

ETAGO — The **reserved name** for the keyword that specifies which character(s) begin an **end-tag**[019], by default '<?'. See TAGC and the *Road Map* charts (021.1) and (022.1).

exceptions[138] — The elements that may override the strict document structure **hierarchy** below the **element**[013] being defined. **Inclusions**[139] are elements that can be used anywhere in the hierarchy below the defined element. **Exclusions**[140] are elements that cannot be used anywhere in the hierarchy below the defined element, usually overriding inclusions made at a higher level. For example, a Book element may 'include' a Figure element, to be used anywhere in the book's structure, but an embedded Footnote element may then 'exclude' the Figure because it would be unwise to allow a figure in a footnote.

exclusion indicator — Symbol that identifies a **group** of **exclusions**[140], by default '-'. See MINUS and **inclusion indicator**.

exclusions[140] — Elements not valid within the defined **element** structure. Usually used to override **inclusions**[139] defined at a higher level in the hierarchy. Default indicator '-' (MINUS). See **exceptions**[138].

EXGRPCAP — The **reserved name** for the keyword that assigns **capacity point** maximum values to **exceptions**[138].

EXNMCAP — The **reserved name** for the keyword that assigns **capacity point** maximum values to names that appear in **exceptions**[138].

external entity — An **entity** stored outside the main **SGML** document, usually in a separate file, and located by a **public identifier**[074] or **system identifier**[075].

external entity specification[108] — The unique identifier used to locate an **external entity**.

external identifier[073] — The unique identifier of an **entity** whose content is not stored in the **entity declaration**[101]. The identifier can be a **public identifier**[074] or a **system identifier**[075].

external link — A **hypertext link** to another document, or to part of another document, which is not supported by the ID and IDREF linking scheme, but is supported by the **HyTime** standard and by **Web browser**s working with **HTML** documents. See **internal link**.

F

F element — An inline formula in the **9573 math** model. An outermost element in the **DTD** fragment.

family — A group of related **font**s. Perhaps a **roman** typeface, *italic* typeface and **bold** typeface, all based on the same character shape designs.

feature use[195] — The optional **minimization** and **formal public identifier**[079] features of **SGML** are enabled/disabled within this clause.

FEATURES — The **reserved name** for the keyword that identifies and precedes information regarding which **minimization** features are allowed in the document. See the *Road Map* chart (195.1).

Fence element — A **9573 math** element that fences a formula, containing a **Type** attribute that specifies the type of fence, and **Open** and **Close** attributes if the open fence differs from the close fence. An enclosed **Middle** element can define another fence between the open and close fences.

firewall — Software or hardware that protects an internal network from unauthorized external access. A firewall may be needed to separate private **Intranet** pages from public **Internet** pages.

FIXED — The **reserved name** for the keyword that makes an **attribute** value permanent (not changeable by the document author). See **fixed attribute** and the *Road Map* chart (147.2).

fixed attribute — An **attribute** containing a pre-defined value that cannot be changed by a document author. Mainly used to map a user-defined **element**[013] or attribute to a defined role in an **architectural form** scheme such as **HyTime** or **SDA**. See FIXED.

floating image — An **HTML** concept introduced in **HTML 3.2** that allows images to be placed in the left or right margin of the document. They are 'floating' because text within the document is not broken by the presence of the images. However, the **Br** element may optionally place following text below the images. See **Img** element.

Fname attribute — A **9573 math** attribute contained in the **Mfn** element that specifies a non-standard function name (standard names are specified using the **Type1** and **Type2** attributes in the Mfn element).

font — A set of **characters**, including at least the standard alphabet, conforming to a consistent design, traditionally of a fixed size and style, and tailored for a particular output device (though this is no longer typical). Also called 'fount'. Several related fonts may form a **family**.

Font element — An **HTML 3.2** element that uses a **Size** attribute to set the **font** size.

form — An **HTML** feature that allows a **Web browser** to send user input back to the **Web server**. Introduced in **HTML 2.0**. See **Form** element.

Form element — An **HTML** element introduced in **HTML 2.0** that identifies a section of the document that can be filled in by the user for transmission back to the **Web server**. Includes elements that specify buttons, radio buttons, check boxes, text fields and menus. See **Input** and **Select** elements.

FORMAL — The **reserved name** for the keyword that specifies each **public identifier**[074] should be a **formal public identifier**[079], and may therefore be checked for legal syntax. See the *Road Map* chart (198.17).

formal public identifier[079] — An organized and strictly formatted version of a **public identifier**[074]. Each required part of the name is separated from other parts by two solidus characters '//'.

Formatting Output Specification Instance — See **FOSI**.

Formula Number — See **Num** attribute.

FOSI *(Formatting Output Specification Instance)* — A **CALS** defined (MIL-STD-28001 Appendix B) vendor independent format for specifying publishing formats and styles for each tagged object in an **SGML** document. Currently supported by several applications that are designed to work with technical manuals. A precursor to the **DSSSL** standard. A FOSI is in fact an SGML document that conforms to the FOSI 'outspec' **DTD**. The elements and attributes defined in this DTD are used to describe the formats and styles to be applied to elements defined in the the user's own DTD. Contact 'http://www.neuro.sfc.keio.ac.jp/~ayako/CALS/CALS2/MIL-M-28001.app-b10-'. In the example below, the 'e-i-c' element (element-in-context) specifies settings for an element called 'Sub', when it appears within an element called 'Para'. The Charlist element (characteristics list) specifies that the 'Sub' element inherits all style information from the current settings, but then the Font element overrides the point size and baseline positioning to create the effect of subscript text:

```
<e-i-c gi="sub" context="para">
  <charlist inherit="1">
  <font size="6pt" offset="-1pt">
</e-i-c>
```

Frac element — A **9573 math** element that encloses a fraction, containing an **Align** attribute that aligns the numerator to the denominator.

frame — An unofficial **HTML** feature supported by some **Web browser**s. A single window is split into frames, each frame holding a different document which can be scrolled independently. Particularly useful for holding a table of contents or banner. See **Frame** element.

Frame attribute — Specification of border lines around a **CALS table**. An implied attribute. By default no border lines appear. Options are 'all' (box the table), 'sides' (vertical lines left and right), 'topbot' (horizontal lines above and below), 'top', 'bottom' and 'none' (the default). Must be used to draw a line to the right of the last column, or below the last row, as the **Colsep** attribute and **Rowsep** attribute definitions do not apply for these locations.

Frame element — An unofficial **HTML** element that specifies and encloses a **frame**.

Frameset element — An **HTML** element used in **frame**s that specifies an area divided into columns and rows using the **Cols** and **Rows** attributes.

From element — A **9573 math** element contained in the **Plex** element.

FTP *(File Transfer Protocol)* — A standard method for computers to access files on other, remote computers. Used by **Anchor** elements in **HTML** to locate and access documents on servers that supports FTP anywhere on the **Web**. Specified in a **URL** using 'ftp://.....'. See alternative **HTTP** connection method.

FUNCHAR — The **reserved name** for the keyword that identifies an 'inert' **function character**[054]. A function that is ignored by the **parser**. See the *Road Map* charts (054.8), (186.1) and (188.1).

FUNCTION — The **reserved name** for the keyword that identifies and precedes the assignment of characters to **function character**[054] roles.

function character[054] — A category of **markup character**[051] that identifies characters which perform a useful function role, such as RS and MSICHAR.

function character identification[186] — Definition of names and character values for special characters. For example, 'SPACE' can be defined and given a value of '32', and may then be explicitly referred to using '&#SPACE;'. They are most commonly used to aid creation of **short reference** definitions.

function class[188] — The type of function being defined, which can be ignored by the parser (inert FUNCHAR), a separator character (SEPCHAR), a markup detection 'switch-off' character (MSOCHAR), a markup detection 'switch-on' character (MSICHAR) or a markup suppress (for next character only) character (MSSCHAR).

function name[063] — The name of a special character, such as 'RE', as used in a **character reference**[062]. Such a reference is used when the function indicated should be acted upon. For example, '&#TAB;' should shift following text to the next tab position, whereas '	' (a **character number**[064] representing the Tab **character** in **ASCII**) would merely insert a Tab character into the data.

G

G — Graphical Character Set, as in **G0**. Part of a **character set** fragment that does not contain control codes. See **ESC**.

G0 — Graphical Character Set Zero. Part of **ISO 2022**. See **G**.

G4MIL-R-28002 — The **CALS** standard for a bit-mapped image format and compression scheme (actually **CCITT group IV**).

GCA *(Graphic Communications Association)* — A non-profit association formed in 1986 to apply computer technology to printing and publishing. A promoter of **SGML** and other standards through training and development committees and the organization of conferences, including 'SGML 9*x* Europe' and 'SGML 9*x* (USA)' (at which **SGML Open** holds its committee meetings). Contact 'http://gca.sgml.com'. See **SGML Users' Group**.

GENERAL — The **reserved name** for a keyword that has two roles. It specifies whether or not the case of a **name**[055] (other than an entity name) is significant, by interpreting the following keyword, which is either 'YES' or 'NO'. It also identifies and precedes any overrides to the **reference delimiter set** defaults. See the *Road Map* charts (189.20) and (191.1).

general delimiters[191] — Major part of the mechanism that translates the **abstract syntax** into the **concrete syntax**[182] by defining physical characters for delimiter roles (such as '<' for STAGO), though default settings exist which need not be explicitly included, and are referred to using the keyword 'SGMLREF'.

general entity — An **entity** that may be referenced from the general text, as opposed to a **parameter entity**, which can only be used within **markup**. By default, a reference to a general entity is preceded by an ampersand character, such as '&myent;'. See **general entity reference**[059].

general entity name[103] — The name of the **general entity**, or the default name '#DEFAULT'.

general entity name list[035a] — An **attribute** value consisting of **entity** names, acting as references to the entities.

general entity reference[059] — An **entity reference** that can be placed in the text, but not in **markup**. To be used by document authors.

generalized — Not specific to a particular application or typesetting specification.

generalized markup — Document markup that uses **generic coding** techniques, and also defines the document structure to aid automated processing. See **SGML**.

generic — Not designed for a specific purpose. A generic **tag** would describe an important word as an emphasized word instead of an italic word, so allowing a different choice of style to be applied depending on the needs of particular media (for example, italic for paper output, red for screen output). See **generic coding**.

generic coding — Document markup that does not specify format and style explicitly, but refers to general names, such as 'title'. The name identifies a **macro** or style-sheet name which contains the explicit format or style information. This is a significant step toward **generalized markup**.

generic identifier[(030)] — The name of an **element**[(013)], which must conform to restrictions of length (see NAMELEN) and character usage (see NAME).

generic identifier specification[(029)] — The full name of the **element**[(013)], which may include a rank stem if the **rank** feature is in use.

geometric graphics — See **vector**.

GI *(Generic Identifier)* — See **generic identifier**[(030)].

GIF *(Graphic Interchange Format)* — The *de facto* **raster** 8-bit image format used with **HTML** on the **Web**. Originally GIF 87, transparent backgrounds were added with **GIF 89**. Up to 256 colors are available, and are chosen from the image content, so a picture of a sunset could contain 256 shades of red. Used in preference to **JPEG** on the Web for graphical logos, button images and rules, but not for natural color images. See **X-Bitmap** and **X-Pixelmap**.

GIF 87 — See **GIF**.

GIF 89 — Latest version of **GIF** that adds transparent backgrounds. Also provides multiple pass decompression, slowly improving image quality whilst allowing the download to be cancelled at any time.

glyph — A graphic symbol, as it appears on paper or screen. Every **character** is realized as a glyph from a specified **font**.

GML *(Generalized Markup Language)* — Precursor to **SGML**, developed in 1969 by IBM.

granularity — The degree to which an element is divided into **child** elements. A complex **hierarchy** denotes a 'fine' granularity. Simple structures with few levels indicate a 'coarse' granularity.

Graphic Communications Association — See **GCA**.

group — A collection of names, typically **element**[(013)] names, possibly organized in a strict fashion using the **connector**[(131)] symbols, '&', '|' and ',', and possibly quantified using the **occurrence indicator**[(132)] symbols '*', '+' and '?'. By default, a group is bounded by brackets, '(' and ')'. The three subtly different types of group are the **model group**[(127)] (used only to build a document **hierarchy**), the **name group**[(069)] and **name token group**[(068)] (used for many purposes).

GRPC — The **reserved name** for the keyword that specifies the character(s) used to identify the end of a **name group**[(069)], **name token group**[(068)] and **model group**[(127)], by default ')'. For example '(a, b)'. See the *Road Map* charts (068.9), (069.9) and (127.9).

GRPCAP — The **reserved name** for the keyword that assigns **capacity point** maximum values to the number of **content token**[(128)] objects allowed in a document. The 'group capacity' keyword.

GRPCNT — The **reserved name** for the keyword that specifies the maximum number of tokens in a **name group**[(069)] or **name token group**[(068)], by default '32' tokens. The 'group count' keyword.

GRPGTCNT — The **reserved name** for the keyword that defines the maximum number of tokens in all the **group**s in a **content model**[(126)], by default '96' tokens. The 'group grant total count' keyword.

GRPLVL — The **reserved name** for the keyword that specifies the maximum number of **group** nesting levels, by default '16' levels. The 'group level' part of the **quantity set**[194] clause.

GRPO — The **reserved name** for the keyword that specifies the character to be used to open a **group**, by default '('. The 'group open' keyword. For example, '(a, b)'. See the *Road Map* charts (068.1), (069.1) and (127.1).

H

H1 element — An **HTML** element that encloses a major heading, usually the title of the document. The most important of 6 levels of heading, with the smallest having the name **H6**.

H2 element — An **HTML** element that encloses an important heading. Less important than **H1**, more important than **H3**.

H3 element — An **HTML** element that encloses a heading. Less important than **H2**, more important than **H4**.

H4 element — An **HTML** element that encloses a heading. Less important than **H3**, more important than **H5**.

H5 element — An **HTML** element that encloses a heading. Less important than **H4**, more important than **H6**.

H6 element — An **HTML** element that encloses a minor heading. Less important than all other headers, and should only be used when a sixth level of heading is required.

head — Start-point of a **hypertext link**. Equivalent to the **source** of a link. Points to the **tail**. In **HTML** the head is an **Anchor** element containing an **Href** attribute.

Head element — An **HTML** element that encloses information about the document, including the document **Title** element, as opposed to the **Body** element which encloses the document content.

Height attribute — An **HTML 3.2** attribute to the **Img** and **Applet** elements, used to specify the height of the image or **applet** working area.

Href attribute — In the **HTML** standard an attribute of the **Anchor** element that contains the **URI** location of a document, or a specific location within the remote or current document. The '#' symbol separates a **URL** for a document from the subdocument named location.

hierarchy — A concept derived from family trees that describes **element**[013] relationships. The elements Book/Chapter/Section/Paragraph would form a hierarchy, with each layer viewed as one branch of a **tree**, from which smaller branches diverge to create the next level.

high energy — A complex task involving human intervention, which is therefore costly. A term typically used to describe the process of **up-convert**ing data to **SGML** format. See **low energy**.

home page — The initial 'welcome' **Web page** that contains links to other pages on an **Internet** site. Usually named 'index.html' (which is assumed by the **Web browser** if no file name appears in the **URL**).

Horizontal space — See **Hspace** attribute.

hot spot — An area of a graphical image that acts as a link to associated information when selected.

Href attribute — An **HTML** attribute to the **A** and **Area** elements.

Hspace attribute — An **HTML 3.2** attribute to the **Img** element, used to determin the horizontal space to make available for the image.

HTML *(HyperText Markup Language)* — A non-application-specific **DTD** developed for delivery and presentation of documents over the **Web**, to be **compose**d using an **HTML browser**. Contact 'alt.html' and 'comp.infosystems.www.html' newsgroups. See **HTML Level One**, **HTML Level Two** and **HTML Level Three**.

HTML 1.0 — See **HTML Level One**.

HTML 2.0 — See **HTML Level Two**.

HTML 3.0 — See **HTML Level Three**.

HTML 3.2 — See **HTML Level Three**.

HTML browser — A **browser** application that understands and **compose**s from HTML markup. Recognizes and activates **Anchor** element links.

Html element — An **HTML** element that encloses the entire document (or **page**), including the **Head** element and **Body** element.

HTML Level One — First and universally supported version of **HTML**. Loosely related to **SGML** (a **DTD** was later retro-fitted). No support for **form**s, tables or **frame**s. Superseded by **HTML Level Two**.

HTML Level Three — Latest version of **HTML**. At the time of writing, **HTML 3.2** (released June 1996, the first official release since HTML 2.0. It can be downloaded from the Internet via 'http://www.w3.org/pub/WWW/MarkUp/Wilbur/HTML3.2.dtd'). An **SGML** application, including a **DTD**. Includes support for tables and **frame**s.

HTML Level Two — Second and well supported version of **HTML**. Closely related to **SGML**, including a **DTD**. Includes support for **form**s. Superseded by **HTML Level Three**.

HTTP *(HyperText Transfer Protocol)* — The commonest means of communication between a **Web server** and **Web browser**, using a **URL**. Used by **Anchor** elements in **HTML** to locate and access documents on servers that supports HTTP anywhere on the Web, 'http://www. ...'. Contact 'ftp://info.cern.ch/pub/www/doc/http-spec.txt.Z'. See **FTP**.

Http-equiv attribute — An **HTML** attribute to the **Meta** element, used to place information in a **HTTP** header field.

hyperlink — See **hypertext link**.

hypermedia — The same concept as **hypertext**, with the addition of allowing a mix of information types, including audio and visual media. See **HyTime** and **multimedia**.

Hypermedia/Time-based Document Representation Language — See **HyTime**.

hypertext — Text that does not follow a single narrative flow. A **hypertext link** allows the reader to follow an alternative path through a document. In electronic versions of traditional documents, this may mean simply activating references to other parts of the text. Sometimes, the 'text' part of the name is taken to mean any part of a document, including images, and the term is then used interchangeably with **hypermedia**.

hypertext link — A link between a **source** reference and a **target** object. Sometimes called a 'hyperlink'. Such links enable the creation of **hypertext** documents. See ID, IDREF and **Hytime**.

HyperText Markup Language — See **HTML**.

Hypertext Reference — See **Href** attribute.

HyTime *(Hypermedia/Time-based Document Representation Language)* — Standard mechanism for use of **SGML** to represent time-based data such as music, animation or film. Released in 1992, and defined as **ISO/IEC 10744**. See **HyTime application**. Several techniques allow **hypertext** linking between SGML documents and between SGML and other format documents, including methods that identify target objects by their location in the file (see Chapter 9 for a demonstration of its use to provide inter-document ID-based hypertext linking). Contact 'http://www.sgmlopen.org/sgml/docs/library/archform.html' and 'http://www.techno.com/TechnoTeacher/HyTime.html'.

HyTime application — A **HyTime** compliant **DTD**, including **HyTime elements** that conform to a **HyTime architectural form**.

HyTime architectural form — An **architectural form** defined in the **HyTime** standard. Specific attribute names and value are recognized by a HyTime-aware application.

HyTime element — An **SGML** defined **element**[013] that includes **attributes** and attribute values recognizable to a **HyTime** application. An attribute called 'HyTime' takes a value that identifies the **HyTime architectural form** – for example 'hytime NAME #FIXED 'clink''.

I

I element — An **HTML** element that contains text to be displayed in *italic* typeface.

ICADD *(International Committee for Accessible Document Design)* — A committee formed in 1992 to promote access to documents by print-impaired readers. An ICADD compliant **DTD** uses **fixed attributes** to map complex structures to a simpler pre-defined document structure. The DTD effectively carries information on how to convert a **document instance set**[010] to another document conforming to the ICADD DTD. Once converted, existing software can represent the contained information in various forms suitable for the print-impaired, including Grade 2 Braille, large print and voice synthesis. Included in **ISO 12083**. See **SDA**. Contact 'icadd@asuvm.inre.asu.edu' and 'http://www.sil.org/sgml/ICADDiso.html'.

ID — The **reserved name** for the keyword that defines an **attribute** to be the **target** of an **internal link**. The 'identifier' keyword. May be changed to another name in a **variant concrete syntax**. See the *Road Map* chart (145.4).

Id attribute — *[1]* A **CALS table** attribute that is used to uniquely identify a table. *[2]* A **9573** math attribute that is used in and uniquely identifies a specific instance of a **Df**, **Dfg** or **Mark** element.

id reference list[037] — An **attribute** value consisting of a list of references to ID (**target**) attributes.

id reference value[038] — An **attribute** value that forms the **source** of a **hypertext link**. See **IDREF**.

id value[036] — An **attribute** value that forms the **target** of a **hypertext link**. See **ID**.

IDCAP — The **reserved name** for the keyword that assigns **capacity point** maximum values to the number of ID attributes. The 'identifier capacity' keyword.

IDREF — The **reserved name** for the keyword that identifies an **attribute** as the **source** of an **internal link**. May be changed to another name in a **variant concrete syntax**. See the *Road Map* chart (145.5).

IDREFCAP — The **reserved name** for the keyword which assigns **capacity point** maximum values to the number of **IDREF** attributes. The 'identifier reference capacity' keyword.

IDREFS — The **reserved name** for the keyword that identifies a group of **IDREF** type **attributes**, separated by spaces. For example, 'myref="ref1 ref7 ref9"'. May be changed to another name in a **variant concrete syntax**. The 'identifier references' keyword. See the *Road Map* chart (145.6).

IEC *(International Electrotechnical Commission)* — Organization working on standards, sometimes in partnership with the **ISO**. The next version of **SGML** will be labeled 'ISO/IEC 8879'. Contact 'http://www.hike.te.chiba-u.ac.jp/ikeda/IEC/'.

IETF *(Internet Engineering Task Force)* — The international community (comprising network designers, operators, researchers and vendors) concerned with the smooth operation and future of the **Internet** architecture. Contact 'http://www.ietf.org/'. See **W³C**.

IGES *(Initial Graphics Exchange Specification)* — A three-dimensional **vector** CAD drawing data format. Used as part of the **CALS** standard (MIL-D-28000).

IGNORE — The **reserved name** for the keyword that identifies a **marked section**[096] with content that should not be passed to an application by a **parser** (to be omitted when the document is published). May be changed to another name in a **variant concrete syntax**. See the *Road Map* chart (100.2).

Image — See **Img** element.

image map — An **Internet** concept. Areas within an image, such as a circle or rectangle, can be identified and made active. When the mouse is clicked on an image associated with a map, the coordinates of the cursor are transmitted to the

Web server, which uses the map coordinates to determine whether an active area has been selected, and an appropriate script is activated. This is termed a 'server-sided' image map. Some **Web browser**s can link areas directly to **URL**s specified in the **HTML** page. This, more direct method, is called 'client-sided'. Typically, an image map is used to provide an attractive menu screen that accesses other **pages**. See the **Ismap** attribute.

Img element — An **HTML** element that references an image data file using the **Src** attribute. An **Ismap** attribute is used to help create an **image map**.

IMPLIED — The **reserved name** for the keyword that specifies an **attribute** value is optional, and need not be entered by the document author. When a value is not entered, the application may assume a default value. May be changed to another name in a **variant concrete syntax**. See the *Road Map* chart (147.9).

INCLUDE — The **reserved name** for the keyword that identifies a **marked section**[096] with content that must be included in **parser** output (in other words, it has no effect, but may be easily changed to IGNORE and back as required). May be changed to another name in a **variant concrete syntax**. See the *Road Map* chart (100.3).

inclusion indicator — Symbol that identifies a **group** of **inclusions**[139]. See PLUS and **exclusions indicator**.

inclusions[139] — An element valid within the defined **element**[013] structure, and within other enclosed elements (without having to also include it in their definitions). May be overridden at a lower level in the **hierarchy** using **exclusions**[140]. For example, a Reference element may be defined as an inclusion in a Book definition, and excluded within the Reference element definition (indicating that it may be used anywhere except within itself). See **inclusion indicator**.

inert function — A function defined in the **SGML declaration**[171] that is ignored by the **parser**. Rarely used, an inert function would have some role deemed significant to the application.

inferior — See **subscript**.

Inline Formula —See **F** element.

Input element — An **HTML** element used in the **Form** element to provide user input objects. One must have a **Type** attribute value of 'submit', creating a button that, when selected, sends all current values back to the **Web server**.

INSTANCE — The **reserved name** for the keyword that specifies the defined **concrete syntax** applies only to the **document instance set**[010], not to the **prolog**[007], which uses the **reference concrete syntax** defaults. See the *Road Map* chart (181.4).

Integral element — A **9573 math** element that defines an integral limit.

internal entity — An **entity** that exists within the main **SGML** document, and is named and stored within an **entity declaration**[101]. The content is delimited by quote characters. See **external entity**.

internal link — A **hypertext link** that has a **source** point and a **target** point in the same document. See ID, IDREF and **external link**.

internal reference — See **internal link**.

International Committee on Accessible Document Design — See **ICADD**.

International Electrotechnical Commission — See **IEC**.

International Organization for Standardization — See **ISO**.

International Standards Organization — See **ISO** (which, despite appearances, is not actually an abbreviation of this name, and in any case is properly called the 'International Organization for Standardization').

Internet — Scheme for connecting computer systems using the **TCP/IP** network protocols, originating in US defense, gaining popularity within universities, then business, and latterly as a general platform for the **Web** and electronic mail. Overseen by the **IETF**.

Internet Engineering Task Force — See **IETF** .

Intranet — A local 'closed' version of the **Internet**, for access by a local community (typically by company employees) using tools developed for the Internet, including **Web browsers**.

IP address — Unique **Internet** server identifier number, for example '145.123.252.231'. For ease of use they are associated with easier to remember **domain name**s, such as 'bradley.co.uk', on a **DNS**.

IRV *(International Reference Version)* — Standard version of **ISO/IEC 646:1991**, using the currency symbol, '¤', in place of the dollar character, '$', found in **ASCII**.

IS *(International Standard)* — A standard released by the **ISO**.

Ismap attribute — An **HTML** attribute to the **Img** element that indicates an **image map** is associated with the image.

Isindex element — An **HTML** element that accepts a user input value that is passed back to the **Web server** for processing. See **form** for a better, more flexible approach.

ISO *(International Organization for Standardization)* — The organization responsible for release of the **SGML** standard under the designation 'ISO 8879' and various other standards. Most of the related standards discussed in this book are released by the working group **WG8**. An 'IS' is an International Standard. A DTR is a 'Draft Technical Report'. Located at 'ISO Central Secretariat/1, rue de Varembe/CH-1211 Geneva 20/Switzerland'. The name 'ISO' is not an abbreviation, but is intended to describe equality, just as it is used in a name such as '*iso*sceles' (a triangle with two *equal* sides).

ISO 10179 — See **DSSSL**.

ISO 10180 — See **SPDL**.

ISO 10744 — See **HyTime**.

ISO 12083 — Ratified versions of the **AAP DTDs**. Devised for general publishing needs.

ISO 2022 — A standard for extending the range of a character set by the use of the **ESC** 'escape sequence' codes, which switch-in and switch-out alternative blocks of characters.

ISO 639 — Definition of codes specifying the language of an **entity**. 'EN' for English. See Chapter 14.

ISO 8613 (MP) — Information Processing -- Text and Office Systems -- Office Document Architecture (**ODA**) and Interchange Format (now replaced 'Office' with 'Open').

ISO 8632 — See **CGM**.

ISO 8879 — See **SGML**.

ISO 8879:1986 — See **SGML**. '1986' is the year of issue.

ISO 9069 — See **SDIF**.

ISO 9070 — Official scheme for determining an **owner identifier**[080] in a **formal entity declaration**[079].

ISO owner identifier[081] — An **external entity** that has been defined by the **ISO**, and has owner details consisting of the ISO publication number. For example 'ISO 8879:1986'. The first part of a **formal public identifier**[079] referring to an ISO owned entity.

ISO text description[087a] — The formal text description of an **ISO** defined **entity** within a **formal public identifier**[079]. For example, the text description for one of the character entity sets is 'Added Latin 1'.

ISO/IEC 10179 — See **DSSSL**.

ISO/IEC 10646 — An **ISO** defined **32-bit** coded **character** set for information interchange. See **ASCII** and **ISO/IEC 646:1991**. It defines a unique computer value for 4294967296 characters. The lower 7 bits correspond to the **ASCII** (US) **7-bit** character set, the lower 8 bits correspond to **ISO/IEC 8859/1** (Latin-1), and the lower 16 bits correspond to the **Unicode** character set.

ISO/IEC 10744:1991 — See **HyTime**.

ISO/IEC 13673:1995 — See **RAST**.

ISO/IEC 646:1991 — The **ISO** defined **7-bit** coded **character set** for information interchange. Almost identical to **ASCII**, from which it is derived. See the first 128 entries of the **ISO/IEC 8859/1** character set in Chapter 14. Also see **ISO/IEC 10646**.

ISO/IEC 8859/1 — A **character set** based on **ASCII**, but adding symbols and European accented characters (see **ISOlat1**) by employing an **8-bit** character set. Used in **HTML**, Microsoft Windows and some UNIX systems. See also **ISO/IEC 646:1991**, of which it is a superset, and both **Unicode** and **ISO/IEC 10646**, of which it is a subset.

ISO/IEC 8879 — Official designation of forthcoming update of the **SGML** standard.

ISO/IEC TR 9573 — Technical report complementing **ISO 8879**, which includes techniques for encoding general text, tables, mathematical formula and Japanese text. The mathematical structures are widely supported by software, but tables are commonly coded using the **CALS table** model.

ISOlat1 *(ISO Latin 1)* — An **entity set**[113] that describes a **character set** grouped under **formal public identifier**[079] 'ISO 8879:1986//ENTITIES Added Latin 1//EN', consisting mostly of European accented letters.

italic — Characters that are slanted and cursive (script-like), as in '*italic*'. See **roman**.

Italic — See **I** element.

Italic element — A **9573 math** element that is used to present text in **italic** style when it would normally appear in **roman** style. See **Roman** element.

J

Java — A multi-platform object-oriented programming language developed by Sun. Originally developed in 1992, it was intended to be embedded in consumer devices. In 1995 it was enhanced, and aimed at **Internet** applications. Semi-compiled Java code modules, or **applet**s, are accessed by a **Web browser**, interpreted or compiled (just-in-time compilation), then executed on the local machine. Platform independence includes machine and operating system neutral interfaces, including a graphical user interface. Contact 'http://Java.sun.com' and 'comp.lang.java' newsgroup.

JPEG — Popular 24-bit **raster** image format devised by the Joint Photographic Experts Group. An efficient compression scheme, but at the cost of accuracy as it does not faithfully reproduce the original image, and is therefore described as a 'lossy' format. May be stored within a **TIFF** file 'wrapper'. Used on the **Web** and **Internet** in general, in preference to **GIF** for natural color images, but not for button images, rules or logos.

K

Kbd element — An **HTML** element that encloses text representing keyboard input, usually displayed in a mono-spaced font.

Keyboard — See **Kbd** element.

keyword — A word appearing in the **data stream** that is significant to an SGML **parser**. For example, PUBLIC is a keyword that precedes a **public identifier**[074] for an **entity**. In some cases used to create a **concrete syntax** for the document. For example, STAGO is a keyword used to define the character that indicates the presence of a **start-tag**[014].

L

language — *[1]* Defined **markup** scheme. See **meta-language**. *[2]* Part of a **public identifier**[074] that indicates the human language used in the data contained in the **entity**. English text contains the identifier 'EN'.

L^{A}T$_E$X — Popular **macro**-based extension to the T$_E$X typesetting language, facilitating **descriptive markup**.

LC letter — A group of characters recognized as lower-case letters ('a'–'z').

LCNMCHAR — The **reserved name** for the keyword that identifies and precedes a list of additional characters to be allowed within a **name**[(055)], beyond the default set (of a–z, A–Z and 0–9). The **reference concrete syntax** adds characters '-' and '.'. See UCNMCHAR, LCNMSTRT, and the *Road Map* charts (052.3) and (189.11).

LCNMSTRT — The **reserved name** for the keyword that identifies and precedes a list of additional characters to be allowed as the first character of a **name**[(055)], beyond the default set (of a–z and A–Z). Note that any additions here are automatically included as legal characters for the rest of the name. See UCNMSTRT, LCN-MCHAR, and the *Road Map* charts (053.3) and (189.3).

LF *(Line Feed)* — Special character used (sometimes in combination with **CR**) to end a line in **ASCII** and **ISO/IEC 646:1991**. Also used in SGML as an RS (record start).

Li element — An **HTML** element that is used within the **Ol** and **Ul** elements to identify a single item in a list.

Link attribute — An **HTML 3.2** attribute to the **Body** element that specifies a new color for **hypertext** reference text contained in the **A** element. The color for a link not yet visited. See **Alink** and **Vlink**.

List Item — See **Li** element.

LIT — The **reserved name** for the keyword used to define the character(s) that enclose an **attribute** value that may contain spaces, by default, a quotation mark ' " '. The 'literal delimiter' keyword. For example, `val="the value"`. See LITA for the alternative form, and the *Road Map* charts (034.1 .3), (066.1 .3), (075.1 .3) and (076.1 .3).

LITA — The **reserved name** for the keyword used to define the character(s) that enclose an **attribute** value that may contain spaces, by default, an apostrophe ' ' '. The 'literal alternative delimiter' keyword. See the *Road Map* charts (034.4 .6), (066.4 .6), (075.4 .6) and (076.4 .6).

literal alternative — A character assigned the role of delimiting a text string. An 'alternative' to the **literal delimiter**. For example, `val='the value'`. Equivalent and alternative to **literal delimiter**. If either a quotation mark or an apostrophe appears within the value, the alternative character should be chosen as a delimiter to avoid confusing the **parser**. For example, `val='a "quoted" word'`. See LITA.

literal delimiter — A character assigned the role of delimiting a text string. See LIT and **literal alternative**.

LITLEN — The **reserved name** for the keyword that defines the maximum number of characters in an **attribute** value (among others), default value '240'. The 'literal length' keyword.

low energy — A process that is fully or highly automated, relatively effortless to perform (once the necessary software filters are written), and therefore cost efficient. Often used to describe conversions from **SGML** format to other formats (known as a **down-convert**ing process). See **high energy**.

lower case — Small letters. The lower case equivalent of the **upper case** letter 'A' is 'a'. The name is derived from the fact that these **character**s were found in the lower part of the printer's type case. See **LC Letter**, LCNMSTRT and LCNMCHAR.

M

macro — A group of typesetting instructions that may be activated by reference to a name. One instruction replaces many, and may take a meaningful name. A feature of **generic coding** schemes. For example, a **macro call** named 'Title' will activate a **macro definition** of the same name (it may contain instructions to center the following text, and compose it in 18pt Helvetica typeface). An equivalent feature, termed 'style-sheets', is found in some modern word processors and DTP systems.

macro call — A named reference to a **macro definition**. See **macro**.

macro definition — A collection of one or more **markup** tags given a name for use by a **macro call** in the **data stream**. See **macro**.

Map element — An **HTML** element that defines active areas for an associated image, using **Area** elements. The **Name** attribute value links the map to a specific **Img** element.

map name[151] — The **name**[055] of a declaration that maps at least one **short reference** to an **entity**.

map specification[153] — The name of a specification for using **short reference** mappings in a specific context. May be 'EMPTY', in which case no mappings are in use within the given context.

MAPCAP — The **reserved name** for the keyword which assigns **capacity point** maximum values to **short reference** mapping and delimiters. The 'mapping capacity' keyword.

Marginheight attribute — An **HTML** attribute to the **Frame** element, specifying the space between the top and bottom margins of a frame and its enclosed text.

Marginwidth attribute — An **HTML** attribute to the **Frame** element, specifying the space between the left and right margins of a frame and its enclosed text.

Mark element — A **9573 math** element that contains an **Id** attribute and is used to set the point in the first formula beneath which remaining formulae will be aligned. Typically, all formulae are aligned on an equals symbol. Remaining formulae contain a **Markref** element with a matching **Refid** attribute value.

marked section[096] — A segment of the document marked for special processing. This text may be ignored or not checked for embedded **markup** during the **parse** process.

marked section close — See MSC and **marked section end**[095].

marked section declaration[093] — A **markup declaration** containing a **marked section**[096].

marked section end[095] — The end of a segment of the document or **DTD** marked for special processing, by default ']]>'. See MDC.

marked section start[094] — The beginning of a segment of the document or **DTD** marked for special processing, by default '<!['. See MDO.

Markref element — A **9573 math** element that contains a **Refid** attribute and is used to set the point in the current formula that should be aligned with an equivalent point in the first formula, indicated using a **Mark** element. Typically, formulae are aligned on an equals sign.

markup — A **tag** added to electronic data to specify style (**descriptive markup**) or add structure (**procedural markup** or **generalized** markup) to the data. In **SGML**, an object is identified by an **element**[013], and consists of an **empty element**, or a combination of a **start-tag**[014] and **end-tag**[019] surrounding the affected text.

markup character[051] — A character class that groups characters used to identify **markup**.

markup declaration — A special tag that is *not* used to mark-up a document, but is used for many other purposes, such as to build the document structure rules (the **DTD**), identify and locate each **entity** or define alternative document segments. By default it is delimited by '<!' and '>' characters (see MDO and MDC).

markup declaration close — The character(s) that indicate the end of a **declaration**. See MDC.

markup declaration open — The character(s) that indicate the start of a **declaration**. See MDO.

markup delimiter — A character or characters that signify the start or end of **markup** embedded in the text. In **SGML**, some default markup delimiters are '<', '</', '>', '<?', '<!', '&', '%' and ';'. If these characters are required as data, they are represented by an **entity reference** such as '<' (less than, '<'). They may be changed in a **variant concrete syntax**.

markup minimization — One or more techniques that allow **markup** tags to be shortened providing the effect is not ambiguous. Techniques may be enabled or disabled, including DATATAG (normal characters serving simultaneously as markup characters), OMITTAG (tags may be omitted) and SHORTTAG (parts of a tag may be omitted).

markup minimization features[196] — Selects optional **minimization** features, including data tag, **omit tag**, rank and **short tag** features.

markup-scan-in character — A character that re-starts **markup** recognition after being switched-off using a **markup-scan-out character**. Together, these characters surround text not to be checked for markup, and have an effect much like a **marked section**[096] of type CDATA. See **markup-scan-suppress character**.

markup-scan-out character — A character defined to switch-off **markup** recognition, which can be re-started later using a **markup-scan-in character**. Together, these characters have an effect much like a marked section of type CDATA. See **markup-scan-suppress character**.

markup-scan-suppress character — A character defined to switch-off markup recognition for the next character only. May be used to switch **character sets**. See **markup-scan-in character** and **markup-scan-out character**.

Matrix element — A **9573 math** element that encloses a matrix (table), consisting of **Cols** elements to identify each column, each in turn containing an **Above** element, and one or more **Above1** elements to identify each row in the column.

Maxlength attribute — An **HTML** attribute to the **Input** element, specifying the maximum number of characters that may be entered in a text field.

MD — The **reserved name** for the keyword used in an **entity declaration**[101] to specify the content of the **entity** should become a **markup declaration** when inserted into the document (by default, it will be surrounded by the symbols '<!' and '>'). See the *Road Map* chart (107.4).

MDC — The **reserved name** for the keyword that defines the character(s) used to indicate the end of a **markup declaration** in the **data stream**, by default '>'. The 'markup declaration close' keyword. See the *Road Map* charts (091.5), (095.2), (101.8), (110.12), (116.10 .13), (141.8 .13), (148.8), (150.10), (152.8) and (171.17).

MDO — The **reserved name** for the keyword that defines the character(s) used to indicate the start of a **markup declaration** in the **data stream**, by default '<!'. The 'markup declaration open' keyword. See the *Road Map* charts (091.1), (094.1), (101.1), (110.1), (116.1), (141.1), (148.1), (150.1), (152.1) and (171.1).

Menu element — An **HTML** element containing a list of short items, ideally a list of menu options from a program.

Meta element — An **HTML** element containing information intended to be read and interpreted by the browser.

meta-language — A language for defining another **language**. **SGML** is an example, using a **DTD** to define a bespoke **markup** language.

Mfn element — A **9573 math** element used to define a function.

Middle element — A **9573 math** element that produces a vertical line within a **Fence** element. A **Style** attribute is used to specify the style of the fence, and may be 'single', 'double', 'triple', 'dash', 'dots' or 'bold'. A **Type** attribute specifies the type of fence, such as 'bar' or 'bracket'.

MIL-D-28000 — The **CALS** standard for encoding two-dimensional CAD (computer-aided design) drawings. See **IGES**.

MIL-M-28001 — The **CALS** standard for encoding textual data. A number of **SGML** Document Type Definitions (or **DTDs**).

MIL-D-28003 — The **CALS** image format standard for representation of two-dimensional objects. See **CGM**.

MILS-STD-1840A — The 'Automated Interchange of Technical Information' Standard for combining and delivering data in the various formats defined as part of the **CALS** standard. Including **IGES** (MIL-D-28000), **SGML** (MIL-M-28001), **CCITT Group IV** (G4MIL-R-28002) and **CGM** (MIL-D-28003).

MIME *(Multi-purpose Independent Mail Extensions)* — A standard for identifying the formats in a mixed media mail message, including pictures and text. **HTML** is a MIME format, as specified by the header line 'Content-Type: text/html'. **JPEG** is another, identified by 'content-Type: image/jpeg'. MIME is used by the **Web** to send information on the file content type. Contact `comp.mail.mime` newsgroup.

minimal SGML document — An **SGML** document conforming to the **core concrete syntax** and the **reference capacity set**, employing none of the optional features.

minimization — Techniques for abbreviating or omitting **element**[013] tags to simplify and improve the efficiency of keying **SGML** documents. As most **markup** is now generated automatically by **SGML-aware** word processors, most of these techniques are rarely used.

minimized — A **tag** that has been abbreviated, without affecting its purpose or meaning. See **minimization**.

MINIMIZE — The **reserved name** for the keyword that identifies and precedes instructions to select optional **SGML** features. See the *Road Map* chart (196.1).

minimized end-tag[020] — An **end-tag**[019] that is physically incomplete, using one or more of several available **minimization** techniques.

minimized start-tag[015] — A **start-tag**[014] that is physically incomplete, using one or more of several available **minimization** techniques.

minimum data[077] — Text in a **minimized literal**[076].

minimum data character[078] — A character that conforms to one of the restricted classes of character likely to be accessible on any system. Such characters make up the content of a **minimum literal**[076].

minimum literal[076] — A string of characters, delimited by single or double quotes, which must be from a controlled subset of available characters likely to be available on all possible systems. When read by a **parser**, leading and trailing spaces are removed, and line-ending characters are removed or converted into spaces to create a 'normalized' string suitable for comparison. For example, a **public identifier**[074] is a minimized literal that may be compared with an entry in a **catalog** file.

MINUS — The **reserved name** for the keyword that defines the character used to state that omitting of a **start-tag**[014] or **end-tag**[019] is not allowed, by default the hyphen symbol, '-'. Also used to precede a **group** that contains at least one **element**[013] to be excluded. See the *Road Map* charts (123.2), (124.2) and (140.1).

mixed content[025] — The content of the **element**[013] may consist of both text and **markup**. Line-ending characters are significant, becoming spaces in most cases, which can cause a problem known as **ambiguous mixed content** in certain circumstances.

model group[127] — A scheme for grouping **element**[013] references, and describing how they may be ordered within a document. Each **group** may contain more groups, each using different ordering techniques. Used in the **DTD** to define the document **hierarchy**. Very similar to a **name group**[069], which cannot embed other groups. Delimited by the MGO and MGC characters, by default '(' and ')'.

Morerows attribute — Defines the number of rows over which a **CALS table** model **Entry** element spans. An implied attribute with a default value of '0', meaning no span. Larger values identify the number of extra rows to occupy beneath the current row.

MS — The **reserved name** for the keyword used within an **entity declaration** to specify that the content of the **entity** represents a **marked section**[096], and should be delimited by appropriate characters (by default '<![' and ']]>') when inserted into the document. The 'marked section' keyword. May be changed to another name in a **variant concrete syntax**. See the *Road Map* chart (107.3).

MSC — The **reserved name** for the keyword that defines the character(s) used to indicate the end of a **marked section**[096], by default ']]'. The 'marked section close' keyword. See the *Road Map* chart (095.1).

MSICHAR — The **reserved name** for the keyword that defines a **markup-scan-in character**. The 'markup-scan-in character' keyword. See the *Road Map* charts (054.6) and (188.2).

MSOCHAR — The **reserved name** for the keyword that defines a **markup-scan-out character**. The 'markup-scan-out character' keyword. See the *Road Map* charts (054.5) and (188.3).

MSSCHAR — The **reserved name** for the keyword that defines a **markup-scan-suppress character**. The 'markup-scan-suppress character' keyword. See the *Road Map* charts (054.7) and (188.4).

multimedia — The same as **hypermedia**, except that differing information types may be synchronized – for example, music accompanying a video clip, described by a scrolling caption. See **HyTime**.

Multi-purpose Independent Mail Extensions — See **MIME**.

N

name[055] — A word containing characters that conform to the rules for a name. The first letter of the name has more restrictions than subsequent letters (see **name start character**[053] and **name character**[052]). Objects that must conform to the character restrictions of a name include an **element**[013] name, an **attribute** name, and also some attribute values. See NAMELEN for length of name restrictions, and LCNMSTRT, UCNMSTRT, LCNMCHAR and UCNMCHAR for additional characters that may be included in a name.

NAME — The **reserved name** for the keyword that specifies an **attribute** value is restricted to a single word conforming to the character restrictions of a **name**[055]. May be changed to another name in a **variant concrete syntax**. See the *Road Map* chart (145.7).

Name attribute — An **HTML** attribute to the **A** element, where it is used to identify the **target** object of the link; in the **Meta** element, where it is used to name a unit of information; in the **Input** element, where it is used to group buttons for selection purposes; in the **Applet** element, where it is used to identify an **applet** for communication with other active applets; in the **Param** element, where it is used to identify a parameter valuse; in the **Frame** element, where it is used to identify the frame for use as a target.

name character[052] — A **character** that conforms to the rules for characters allowed in a **name**[055]. The characters allowed include all those allowed in the **name start character**[053], plus additional characters, by default, '-' and '.'.

Name End — See **Nameend** attribute.

name group[069] — A **group** of **name**[055] specifications. For example, '(value | another | third-val)'.

Name Length — Maximum number of characters in an **element**[013] name (among others). Value defined by the NAMELEN keyword (default value '8' characters). See **CALS declaration** for popular change of value to '32'.

name list[039] — An **attribute** value consisting of a list of names, such as 'John x-y-z train'.

Name List — See **Nmlist** element.

Name Location — See **Nameloc** element.

Name Start — See **Namestart** attribute.

name start character[053] — A **character** that conforms to the rules for characters allowed at the start of a **name**[055], by default '-' and '.'. The rest of the name may include the same characters, plus some others not allowed as the first character.

name token[057] — The same as a **name**[055], except that there are no special restrictions on the first character.

name token group[068] — A group of **name token**[057] specifications. For example, '(-value | -another | third-val)'.

name token list[040] — An **attribute** value consisting of at least one **name token**[056].

NAMECASE — The **reserved name** for the keyword that identifies and precedes instructions that dictate whether general names and **entity** names are deemed to be case-sensitive. See **upper case** and **lower case**, and the *Road Map* charts (145.8) and (189.18).

Nameend attribute — The name end value for a span range defined in the **CALS table** model. Both name start (**Namest**) and name end values are derived from column names defined by the **Colname** attribute of the **Colspec** element, and ultimately resolve back to a column number. These attributes appear in the **Spanspec** element and are used to define a new name for a span using the **Spanname** attribute. For example, '<spanspec namestart="third" nameend="fifth" spanname="threefive">'.

NAMELEN — The **reserved name** for the keyword used to define the maximum number of characters in a **name**[055] (default value '8' characters). The 'name length' keyword. See **CALS declaration** for popular change of value to '32'.

Nameloc element — The suggested name for an **element**[013] that contains attributes significant to a **HyTime**-aware application, though any legal name may be used as the element is actually identified by the presence of an attribute called **Hytime** holding a value of 'nameloc'.

NAMES — The **reserved name** for the keyword used to specify that an attribute value is restricted to a series of **name**[055] values. For example, 'myattr="name1 name2"'. May be changed to another name in a **variant concrete syntax**. See the *Road Map* charts (145.8) and (193.1).

Namest attribute — The name start value for a span range defined in the **CALS table** model. See **Nameend** attribute for a full description.

Nametype attribute — The name of a **HyTime** attribute to the **Nmlist** element that specifies whether the element content is an entity name or an ID value in the remote document. Legal values are 'entity' (the default) and 'element'.

NAMING — The **reserved name** for the keyword that identifies and precedes instructions that define the characters that may be used in a **name**[055], and determine whether the name is case-sensitive (is matched only with a reference using exactly the same combination of **upper case** and **lower case** letters). See the *Road Map* chart (189.1).

naming rules[189] — The definition of characters that may appear in a **name**[055], including restrictions on the first character. By default the characters '-' and '.' may be used in the rest of the name, but not for the first character. Also specifies whether case is deemed significant in general, or in **entity** names specifically. See LCNMSTRT, UCNMSTRT, LCNMCHAR and UCNMCHAR.

NDATA — The **reserved name** for the keyword that indicates the content of an **external entity** is composed of non-SGML data (for example, an image format). The 'non-SGML data' keyword. A name follows the keyword, identifying the format to match declarations to references. May be changed to another name in a **variant concrete syntax**. See the *Road Map* chart (109.3).

nested element — An **element**[013] that may contain itself, directly, or indirectly via another element, thus allowing potentially endless recursion (though note the practical limit set by TAGLVL).

NET — The **reserved name** for the keyword defining the **net enabled** delimiter character, default value '/'. The 'null end-tag' keyword. May be changed to another name in a **variant concrete syntax**. See the *Road Map* charts (018.5) and (023.1).

net enabled — Single character delimiter option for brief elements. Set to solidus, '/', in the **reference concrete syntax**. For example, 'Water is H<sub/2/O' is short-hand for 'Water is ₂O'. See **net-enabling start-tag**[018] and **null end-tag**[023].

net-enabling start-tag[018] — A **start-tag**[014] that ends with a special character, which is used again in place of the normal **end-tag**[019]. For example, 'H<sub/2/O' is the same as 'H₂O'. See NET.

Nmlist element — The suggested name for an **element**[013] that contains attributes significant to a **HyTime**-aware application, though any legal name may be used as the element is identified by the presence of an attribute called **Hytime** holding a value of 'nmlist'. Contained with a **Nameloc** element, it provides the target ID value or entity name in the remote document.

NMTOKEN — The **reserved name** for the keyword that restricts an **attribute value**[035] to the characters defined as legal within a **name token**[057]. The 'name token' keyword. May be changed to another name in a **variant concrete syntax**. See NMTOKENS and the *Road Map* chart (145.9).

NMTOKENS — The **reserved name** for the keyword that restricts an **attribute value**[035] to a series of words containing characters defined as legal within a **name token**[057]. The 'name tokens' keyword. May be changed to another name in a **variant concrete syntax**. See NMTOKENS and the *Road Map* chart (145.10).

NO — The **reserved name** for the keyword that specifies that one of the features of **SGML** is inactive. See the *Road Map* charts (189.22 .27), (196.5 .10 .15 .20) and (198.5 .12 .19).

No Break — See **Nobr** element.

Nobr element — An **HTML 3.2** element used to contain text which should not be wrapped over multiple lines. The 'no break' element. The **Wbr** element can override this rule at specific points in the text.

Noframes element — An **HTML** element used in a **frame** to contain text which should be displayed if the browser has no frame capability. See **Frame** element.

non-SGML data entity[006] — An **entity** that may contain anything, so is not restricted to legal SGML characters. Many image formats would be stored in such entities.

NONE — The **reserved name** for the keyword that specifies no content in one of several definitions. See the *Road Map* charts (184.3), (192.4) and (199.3).

NONSGML — The **reserved name** for the keyword that represents all characters not included as legal **SGML** characters. See the *Road Map* chart (049.2).

Noresize attribute — An **HTML** attribute to the **Frame** element to specify that the frame cannot be re-sized by the user.

normalize — The process of converting a **minimized** element into a fully tagged element. The normalized form of '`<em>emphasis</>`' is '`<em>emphasis</em>`'.

NORMSEP — The **reserved name** for the keyword that defines the number of characters each **markup** separator uses in a **normalize**d structure, by default '2'. The 'normalized separator' keyword.

Noshade attribute — An **HTML 3.2** attribute to the **Hr** element, used to specify no shading of the horizontal rule.

notation — Representation of natural phenomena by signs. Speech is represented by a written notation (involving letters, punctuation and left-to-right or right-to-left ordering), and also by a braille notation. In computing this term is used interchangeably with 'data format', such as **ASCII**, **CGM** and **SGML**.

notation[146] — An **attribute** type that identifies the value as the name of a **notation**, previously defined using a **notation declaration**[148].

NOTATION — The **reserved name** for the keyword that restricts the value of an **attribute** to the name of a previously declared **notation** type. May be changed to another name in a **variant concrete syntax**. See the *Road Map* charts (146.1), (148.2) and (149a.2).

notation declaration[148] — A **declaration** that assigns a unique name to a non-SGML format, and may identify a document describing the format, and/or a program capable of processing the format.

notation identifier[149] — The part of a **notation declaration**[148] that identifies a document describing the alien format, and/or a program that is able to process the format (for example, an image viewer).

notation name[041] — An **attribute** value consisting of the name of a **notation** that describes the format of the data contained by the element.

NOTCAP — The **reserved name** for the keyword that assigns **capacity point** maximum values to defined **data content** notation names. The 'notational capacity' keyword.

NOTCHCAP — The **reserved name** for the keyword that assigns **capacity point** maximum values to characters in a **notation identifier**[149]. The 'notational character capacity' keyword.

Nowrap attribute — An **HTML 3.2** attribute to the **Th** and **Td** elements, used to specify that the content of the table cell should not be wrapped over multiple lines.

NSGMLS — The 'New SGML Structured' parser that replaces **SGMLS**. A freely available command-line based parser. See Chapter 13. Contact 'jjc@jclark.com'.

null end-tag[023] — An **end-tag**[019] that consists of a single special character, which is used again at the end of the **start-tag**[014]. For example, 'H<sub/2/O' is the same as 'H₂O'. See **NET**.

Num attribute — The number of a formula or formula group in the **9573 math** model. An implied CDATA attribute used in the **Df** and **Dfg** elements.

number[056] — A word containing characters that conform to the rules for a number. Used for some **attribute** values and other objects. Only digits are allowed, as in '345'.

NUMBER — The **reserved name** for the keyword that restricts an **attribute** value to a numeric value. May be changed to another name in a **variant concrete syntax**. See the *Road Map* chart (145.11).

number list[042] — An **attribute** value consisting of a list of **number**[056] values, such as '12345 9876 3 27856'.

number of characters[179] — A **number**[056] that describes how many characters are to be mapped from part of an extended character set to part of the 'base' character set.

number token[058] — A word containing characters that conform to the rules for a **name**[055], except for the first character, which conforms to the rules for a **number**[056]. For example, '345' or '3XY'. See **NUTOKEN**.

number token list[043] — An **attribute** value consisting of a list of **number token**[058] values, such as '123X 456y 987'. See **NUTOKENS**.

NUMBERS — The **reserved name** for the keyword that restricts an **attribute** value to a series of numeric values. May be changed to another name in a **variant concrete syntax**. See the *Road Map* chart (145.12).

Numer element — A **9573 math** element used in a **Frac** element to enclose the numerator of the fraction.

numeric character reference — A **character reference** containing a numeric value representing a character. For example, 'A' represents 'A' in **ASCII**.

NUTOKEN — The **reserved name** for the keyword that restricts an **attribute** value to a **number token**[058] value. The 'number token' keyword. May be changed to another name in a **variant concrete syntax**. See the *Road Map* chart (145.13).

NUTOKENS — The **reserved name** for the keyword that restricts an **attribute** value to a series of **number token**[058] values. The 'number tokens' keyword. May be changed to another name in a **variant concrete syntax**. See **number token list**[043] and the *Road Map* chart (145.14).

O

o — The **reserved name** for the keyword that indicates that a **start-tag**[014] or **end-tag**[019] may be omitted from the document. The 'omit' keyword. May be changed to another name in a **variant concrete syntax**. See the *Road Map* charts (123.1) and (124.1).

occurrence indicator[132] — Describes how many times an **element**[013] or **group** of elements may occur at a specific legal place within a document. An indicator of '?' (**OPT**), specifies zero or one occurrences. An indicator of '*' (**REP**), specifies any number of occurrences (including zero). An indicator of '+' (**PLUS**), specifies one or more occurrences.

ODA *(Open Document Architecture)* — Until 1990 known as 'Office Document Architecture'. A standard (ISO 8613) for defining document components for interchange between differing word processors and desktop publishing systems. An attempt to classify the features of such systems. It combines a structure view of the document (in similar fashion to **SGML**), with a layout view that specifies where on the page, and possibly on *which* page, an object appears. Contact 'http://sil.org/sgml/odanov10.html'.

Of attribute — A **9573 math** attribute used in the **Mfn** element when a non-standard function is being defined. Holds the value of the function, and used in conjunction with the **Fname** attribute.

Of element — A **9573 math** element used in the **Plex**, **Root** and **Square** elements. Contains the operand value.

Office Document Architecture — Old name for 'Open Document Architecture'. See **ODA**.

Ol element — An **HTML** element containing an ordered list, consisting of **Li** elements.

OMITTAG — The **reserved name** for the keyword that determines the possibility of omitting a **start-tag**[014] or **end-tag**[019], where applicable. Set to either 'YES' or 'NO'. See the *Road Map* chart (196.8).

omitted tag minimization[122] — Determines whether the **start-tag**[014] or **end-tag**[019] of a declared **element**[013] may be absent in the document. Assumes the use of the 'OMITTAG' feature.

Open attribute — A **9573 math** attribute describing the **Fence** element left fence character when it differs from the right fence character.

Open Document Architecture — See **ODA**.

Operator element — A **9573 math** element that encloses the operator to be used in a **Plex** element limit.

OPT — The **reserved name** for the keyword that defines the character used to represent a choice of tokens in a **group**, default value '?'. The 'optional occurrence' keyword. See the *Road Map* chart (132.1).

Option element — An **HTML** element used within the **Select** element to identify a single item in a menu list. The **Selected** attribute to this element pre-selects one item in the list.

optional feature — A features of the **SGML** language that is optional, switched on or off within the **SGML declaration**[171] using **reserved name**s (SHORTREF, CONCUR, DATATAG, OMITTAG, RANK, SHORTTAG, SUBDOC, FORMAL, IMPLICIT and EXPLICIT).

OR — The **reserved name** for the keyword that defines the character to be used as an **or connector**. See the *Road Map* chart (131.2).

or connector — Character that indicates a choice of item from a **group** (default character '|'). The example '(a | b)' indicates that 'a' may be present or 'b' may be present, but not both. See **sequence connector** and **and connector**. See OR.

Ordered List — See **Ol** element.

Orient attribute — A **CALS table** attribute to the **Table** element that is used to specify the orientation of the table, which can be 'port' (portrait) or 'land' (landscape).

OTHER — The **reserved name** for the keyword that identifies and precedes instructions regarding miscellaneous features of **SGML**, including the optional concurrency and subdocument options, and the use of **formal public identifier**[079] restrictions. See the *Road Map* chart (198.1).

other content[027] — Miscellaneous **markup** and **entity reference**s.

other features[198] — Allows less common features of **SGML** to be activated, including concurrent documents, subdocuments and formal documents. Not generally activated, and not further discussed in this book.

other prolog[008] — Allows concurrent document structures (**DTD**s).

Over element — A **9573 math** element used in the **Frac** element to hold the fraction denominator. Used in conjunction with the **Numer** element.

owner identifier[080] — The part of a **formal public identifier**[079] that identifies the owner of the specified **external entity**.

P

P element — An **HTML** element used to contain a paragraph.

page — Common term for an **HTML** document. See **Web page**.

Page Description Language — See **PDL**.

Page Wide — See **Pgwide** attribute.

pagination — The process of placing **compose**d text and other parts of a document, such as images, onto at least one page, or as an intermediate step into a **PDL** (*Page Description Language*) such as **PostScript**.

Paragraph — See **P** element.

Param element — An **HTML** element used within the **Applet** element to specify a parameter value to be sent to the **Java** program. Includes the paired **Name** and **Value** attributes to identify and set the parameter valu.

parameter — Feature of a **tag** that can contain modifying variables. A parameter value may have a meaning associated with its location in the tag (for example, name followed by size, '`*FONT times 18:`') or indicated by a parameter name (for example, 'name' and 'size', '`<font size=18 name="times">`'). An **attribute** is an **SGML** parameter, and each attribute has a name and value (so the order of parameter appearance is not significant).

parameter entity — An **entity** that may be referred to only within **markup**. Used mostly to aid construction of a **DTD**, but may also be used by document authors within a **marked section**[096]. A parameter entity may share the same name as a **general entity** without confusion, as it is distinguished by the **PERO** character in both the declaration and reference.

parameter entity name[104] — The **name**[055] of a **parameter entity**, including the required prefix of '%' (**PERO**) to distinguish the name from an identically named **general entity**.

parameter entity reference[060] — An **entity reference** that can be entered only within **markup**, so is mostly the province of the **DTD** author rather than the document author. See **general entity reference**[059].

parameter entity reference open delimiter — The character used to indicate a **parameter entity**, by default a percent symbol, '%'. For example, '%myent;'. See **PERO**.

parameter literal[066] — Text enclosed by quotes within **markup** that may also contain **entity reference**s. Either double or single quotes may be used, though not mixed, and the choice may depend on the existence of one of these characters appearing in the text. For example, '`'double "quotes" in the text'`'.

parent — A concept derived from family trees that describes an **element**[013] that encloses another element as part of a **hierarchy** of elements. For example, a Book element may be the parent of several Chapter elements. See **child** and **sibling**.

parse — Decoding and understanding, using the rules of a grammar. In **SGML**, the process of checking the legal use of **markup**, as performed by a **parser**.

parser — Software designed to **parse** the content of an **SGML document**[001]. May be built in to more specific application software, such as a word processor to aid and control the authoring or editing process. As an example, see **SGMLS** and **NSGMLS** and Chapter 13.

PCDATA — The **reserved name** for the **keyword** that represents normal character data. The 'parsable character data' keyword. Preceded by the **RNI** character, '#', to avoid confusion with an identical **element**[013] name, when used within a

model group[127] (for example, '(PCDATA | #PCDATA) *'). May be changed to another name in a **variant concrete syntax**. See the *Road Map* chart (129.2).

PDF *(Portable Document Format)* — The **PDL** used by Adobe Acrobat, derived from **PostScript** for on-screen page display. Contact 'comp.text.pdf' newsgroup.

PDL *(Page Description Language)* — Data format for describing the content of a page of information. Includes commands for positioning each line of text on the page, drawing lines and painting graphics. **PostScript** is a popular PDL.

PERO — The **reserved name** for the keyword that identifies and specifies the character that is used to identify a **parameter entity reference**[060], by default '%'. The 'parameter entity reference open' keyword. See the *Road Map* charts (060.1) and (104.1).

Pgwide attribute — A **CALS table** attribute to the **Table** element that specifies whether the table is contained within a single text column ('0') or spans across all columns ('1'). The 'page wide' attribute.

PI — The **reserved name** for the keyword that identifies **entity** content as a **processing instruction**[044]. The 'processing instruction' keyword. May be changed to another name in a **variant concrete syntax**. See the *Road Map* chart (106.3).

PIC — The **reserved name** for the keyword that identifies the character(s) assigned significant to identifying the end of a **processing instruction**[044], by default '>'. The 'processing instruction close' keyword. See the *Road Map* chart (044.3).

PICT — A Macintosh-based **vector** (but also **raster**) image format. See **WMF** for PC variant and **CGM** for widely used standard.

Pile element — A **9573 math** element that encloses a pile, using an embedded **Above1** element and **Above** elements. Default 'center' alignment can be changed to 'left' or 'right' using the **Align** attribute.

PILEN — The **reserved name** for the keyword that defines the maximum number of characters in a **processing instruction** (default value '240'). The 'processing instruction length' keyword.

PIO — The **reserved name** for the keyword that defines the character(s) assigned significant to identifying the start of a **processing instruction**[044], by default '<?'. The 'processing instruction open' keyword. See the *Road Map* chart (044.1).

Plex element — A **9573 math** element that defines a non-standard limit, using an embedded **Operator**, **From** and **To** elements, and the **Of** element.

PLUS — *[1]* The **reserved name** for the keyword that defines the character used to indicate required and repeatable occurrence restrictions on an **element**[013], default value '+'. See the *Road Map* chart (132.2). *[2]* The **reserved name** for the keyword that defines the symbol used to indicate inclusions, by default '+'. See the *Road Map* chart (139.1).

Portable Document Format — See **PDF**.

Pos attribute — A **9573 math** attribute that positions a character in the **Sub**, **Sup** and **Over** elements.

Posf attribute — A **9573 math** attribute that specifies the position of the first character in the **Tensor** element.

PostScript — The widely used **PDL** developed by Adobe. See **PDF**.

primitive content token[129] — Part of a **model group**[127] that does not consist of further nested model groups, but of a single item, such as an **element**[013] name or text identifier ('`#PCDATA`').

procedural markup — A **markup** scheme that describes how a document should look, possibly including **font** descriptions, and character styles such as **roman** and **italic**. See **descriptive markup**.

processing instruction[044] — Application specific text (to be processed by an application). See PIO and PIC. To be used only when absolutely necessary. A PI entity or SDATA entity should be used in preference.

processing instruction close — The character(s) that indicate the end of a **processing instruction**[044]. See PIC.

processing instruction open — The character(s) that indicate the start of a **processing instruction**[044]. See PIO.

Product element — A **9573 math** element used in the **Plex** element.

prolog[007] — The document structure rules (essentially the **DTD**).

ps[065] — A character or string within **markup** that takes the role of separating each **parameter**. The most obvious candidate is the space character.

PUBLIC — The **reserved name** for the keyword that precedes a **public identifier**[074] containing non-system-specific information locating the **entity**. May be changed to another name in a **variant concrete syntax**. See the *Road Map* charts (073.4), (180.3) and (183.1).

public concrete syntax[183] — A **public identifier**[074] for a **concrete syntax**, optionally followed by character substitutions relating to the character set clause.

public identifier[074] — An **external entity**[073] identifier that is not system specific (in terms of identifying either format or **entity** location). This identifier is expected to be compared with an entry in a **catalog** file, which provides the location and name of the system file. The public identifier may be a **formal public identifier**[079], in which case it has a rigid format that describes the owner, registered status and language of the entity.

public text class[086] — The part of a **formal public identifier**[079] that describes the content of an **external entity**. Various class options include DTD and ENTITIES. In the latter case, the entity may only contain more entities.

public text description[087] — The part of a **formal public identifier**[079] that describes the information contained in the **external entity**. Enlarges on information provided by the **public text class**[086].

public text display version[090] — The part of a **formal public identifier**[079] that distinguishes between versions of public text stored in an entity.

public text language[088] — The part of a **formal public identifier**[079] that identifies the language used in the **external entity**. A two character **ISO 639** defined code, such as '`EN`' for English.

Q

QUANTITY — The **reserved name** for the keyword that identifies and precedes instructions on **quantity set**[194] override values. See the *Road Map* chart (194.1).

quantity set[194] — Definition of quantity limits on various objects and structures. Default values are provided by the **reference quantity set** using the SGMLREF keyword. Override values are set using **reserved name** keywords. Similar but not to be confused with **capacity set**[180] details. See QUANTITY.

R

rank — An optional and rarely used **SGML** feature that adds a level indicator to the **generic identifier**[030]. For example, 'header.3'. The suffix is implied if absent from subsequent elements, allowing elements to be easily grouped, and later distinguished from elements contained within another rank level (perhaps to be composed differently).

raster — Method of representing images electronically using computer memory to create a grid, with one or more bits representing a pixel (1 bit allows black and white pictures, 4 bits allow 16 colors, or shades of grey, and 16 bits allow over 65000 colors). The resolution (pixels per inch) is determined at the time of creation, and the resulting picture is not usually amenable to scaling or rendering at a different resolution. Compression schemes include **JPEG** and **CCITT Group IV**. The alternative representation scheme, designed to overcome some of the limitations of the raster technique is the **vector** scheme.

RCDATA — The **reserved name** for the keyword that specifies that the content of an **element**[013] or **marked section** may be composed of characters and **entity references**. The 'replaceable character data' keyword. May be changed to another name in a **variant concrete syntax**. See CDATA and the *Road Map* charts (100.4) and (125.2).

RE — The **reserved name** for the keyword that identifies the character acting as a 'record end' delimiter, default value '13'. May be changed to another name in a **variant concrete syntax**. See the *Road Map* charts (005.1), (054.1), (061.2), (063.1), (078.2) and (186.3).

record — A document may be divided into manageable chunks, called 'records'. A record is comparable to a line of text. Whereas ASCII would *end* a line with characters such as **CR** or **LF** (or both), a record is delimited by characters that identify the record start (RS) and record end (RE). When a document is **composed**, a record boundary is either ignored or replaced by a space, depending on the context.

record end delimiter — The character(s) that indicates the end of a **record**. See RE.

record start delimiter — The character(s) that indicates the start of a **record**. See RS.

REFC — The **reserved name** for the keyword that identifies the character used to indicate the end of an **entity reference**, default value ';'. The 'reference close' keyword. Used in both the **general entity reference**[059] and **parameter entity reference**[060]. See the *Road Map* chart (061.1).

reference capacity set — The default **capacity set**[180] values that determine the maximum number of various objects, and apply if no override values are supplied. All default values are '35000', multiplied by a given **capacity point** value. For example, the storage required to hold ID values is given as $35000 \times$ NAMELEN. If NAMELEN is set to '8' characters, this gives '280000' capacity points of storage, and if each capacity point is equivalent to 1 **byte**, this gives the same number of bytes.

reference concrete syntax — A number of implied default settings that define quantity limits and the SGML language syntax. For example, TAGLEN has the implied value of '960' and STAGO has the implied value of '<'. Values may be overridden within the **SGML declaration**[171] (see **CALS declaration**). See SGMLREF.

reference delimiter set — The default characters assigned to recognizing **markup** in text. For example, a **start-tag**[014] by default begins with an open chevron, '<', and ends with a close chevron, '>'. Overriding values are assigned using the **delimiter set**[190] clause.

reference end[061] — The character that completes the **entity reference**, by default a semi-colon ';'.

Reference identifier — See **RefId** attribute.

reference quantity set — The default settings for a number of limits on various objects. For example, the reference value for the length of a name is 8 characters. See **quantity set**[194] and SGMLREF.

Refid attribute — The identifier of a referenced formula or formula group in **9573 math**. A required attribute of type IDREF. Appearing in the **Dfref** and **Markref** elements.

registered — A **public identifier**[074] for an **external entity** that is registered to ensure that it is unique, so that it can be referred to without ambiguity. See **registered owner identifier**[082]

registered owner identifier[082] — A **public identifier**[074] registered with the ISO, and therefore guaranteed unique. The public identifier begins with '+//', followed by the name of the owner. When an entity is owned by the ISO it has a different format, consisting of the publication number. See **ISO owner identifier**[081].

REP — The **reserved name** for the keyword that identifies the character used to indicate that an **element**[013] or **group** may repeat any number of times, or be absent, by default '*'. One of several **occurence indicator**[132] types used to define limits on the number of times an element may appear. See the *Road Map* chart (132.3).

replaceable character data[046] — Text that may contain an **entity reference**. Any references will be replaced by the entity content. See RCDATA.

replaceable parameter data[067] — The actual text of a **parameter literal**[066].

REQUIRED — The **reserved name** for the keyword that dictates an **attribute** value must be entered. May be changed to another name in a **variant concrete syntax**. See the *Road Map* chart (147.6).

required attribute — An **attribute** that must have a value entered by the document author as the **element**[013] is created. In the **element declaration**[067] this is indicated with the '**REQUIRED**' keyword. Typically, an **SGML-aware** word processor automatically presents a dialog box for entry of a required attribute value when such an element is inserted into the document.

reserved name — The default name for a keyword, used to help create a **concrete syntax**[182] from the **abstract syntax** of the **SGML** language. For example, the reserved name for the keyword that allows characters to be assigned to the role of indicating the beginning of a **start-tag**[014] is 'STAGO', and a definition of 'STAGO !' assigns '!' to this role (replacing the default value of '<').

reserved name use[193] — The mechanism by which a keyword can be changed to another word (while retaining its meaning). The **reserved name** keyword precedes its replacement value (keywords used in the **SGML declaration**[171] cannot be changed). For example, 'ELEMENT "MYELEM"' replaces the keyword 'ELEMENT' with the new keyword 'MYELEM'.

Rich Text Format — See **RTF**.

RNI — The **reserved name** for the keyword that defines the character to use as a 'reserved name indicator'. This character identifies a **reserved name** when it is used in a context where a user-defined name (such as an **element**[013] name) may also appear. Typical examples of use are '#PCDATA' and '#IGNORE'. See the *Road Map* charts (103.2), (129.1), (147.1 .5), (153.2) and (149a.1).

roman — A character style. The characters are printed or displayed normally, as these words are. See **italic**.

Roman element — A **9573 math** element that specifies **roman** text style where text would normally be displayed in **italic** style. See **Italic** element.

Root element — A **9573 math** element used to describe any root value other than a square root, containing a **Degree** element and **Of** element.

Row element — Table row in the **CALS table** structure. Contains one or more table cell (**Entry**) elements, within the table head element, **Thead**, table body element, **Tbody**, and table footer element, **Tfoot**.

Rows attribute — An **HTML** attribute to the **Textarea** element and **Frameset** element (a Netscape extension) to specify how many rows of text can appear.

Rowspan attribute — An **HTML** attribute to the **Th** element and **Td** element to specify how many table rows the cell spans over. See **Colspan** attribute.

RS — The **reserved name** for the keyword that defines the character to be used in the role of a 'record start' (by default character '10' decimal). May be changed to another name in a **variant concrete syntax**. See the *Road Map* charts (005.2), (054.2), (063.2), (078.1) and (186.7).

RTF *(Rich Text Format)* — A proprietary format developed by Microsoft that describes the format and style of a text-based document using **tags**. Particularly suited to exchange of documents between computer platforms. For the specification, contact 'ftp://ftp.primate.wisc.edu/pub/RTF'.

S

s[005] — A blank 'space', such as a space character or record end, used to separate parameters in **markup**. The space is ignored during publishing, because it is never used to separate normal text words.

Samp element — An **HTML** element that contains text identified as sample data. To be displayed in a distinctive fashion.

Sample — See **Samp** element.

SCOPE — The **reserved name** for the keyword that specifies whether the **concrete syntax**[182] applies only to the document instance or to the **prolog**[007] as well. See the *Road Map* chart (181.1).

Scrolling attribute — An **HTML** attribute to the **Frame** element that controls the presence of scroll-bars to view content larger than the **frame** area.

SDA *(SGML Document Access)* — A specification for an **architectural form**, specifically using **fixed attribute**s to support the **ICADD** initiative. Attribute names are significant; they specify how the following fixed value should be used in the SDA **DTD**. This DTD defines the following elements: Anchor (mark spot on page); Au (author); B (bold); Book (document element); Box (sidebar info); Fig (figure title); Fn (footnote); H1–H6 (headers); Ipp (ink print page); It (italic); Lang (language); Lhead (list heading); List; Litem (list item); Note; Other (emphasis); Para (paragraph); Pp (print page number); Term (or keyword); Ti (book title) and Xref (cross reference). Allowable attribute names are **Sdaform**, **Sdarule**, **Sdabdy**, **Sdapref** and **Sdasuff**. See **ISO 12083** (Annex A.8) for more details. An example, mapping the Title element of a user-defined DTD to the ICADD element H1:

```
<!ATTLIST title SDAFORM  CDATA  #FIXED "h1"
```

Sdabdy attribute — Used to place an element in a wider context. Element mapping can be different for an element occurring in a body location as opposed to it occurring in a part location. See **Sdapart**.

Sdaform attribute — The name of an attribute that maps fixed attribute values to an element in the **SDA** defined **DTD** created by **ICADD**. The example below maps a Title element in the source DTD to the Ti element in the SDA DTD:

```
<!ATTLIST title SDAFORM   CDATA  #FIXED  "ti"
```

Sdapart attribute — Used to place an element in a wider context. Element mapping can be different for an element occurring in a part location as opposed to it occurring in a body location. See **Sdabdy**.

Sdapref attribute — The name of an attribute that maps fixed attribute values to prefix text that replaces an element during transformation to the **SDA** defined **DTD** created by **ICADD**. The example below maps an Abstract element in the source DTD to an obvious header in the SDA DTD. This may be usefully combined with the **Sdaform** attribute. See **Sdasuff** attribute.

```
<!ATTLIST abstract SDAPREF
              CDATA  #FIXED  '<h1>Abstract</h1>'
```

Sdarule attribute — The name of an attribute that maps fixed attribute values to an element in the **SDA** defined DTD created by **ICADD**. Much like **Sdaform**, but with contextual rules. The example below maps a Title element appearing in a Chapter element in the source DTD to a H2 element in the SDA DTD. The Title of a Section is converted into H3.

```
<!ATTLIST chap SDARULE  CDATA #FIXED  "title h2"
<!ATTLIST sect SDARULE  CDATA #FIXED  "title h3"
```

Sdasuff attribute — The name of an attribute that maps fixed attribute values to suffix text that replaces an element during transformation to the **SDA** defined **DTD** created by **ICADD**. The example below maps a Quote element in the source DTD to the quote character in the SDA DTD (as well as using **Sdapref** to prefix the content with another quote). This may be usefully combined with the **Sdaform** attribute.

```
<!ATTLIST quote SDASUFF   CDATA  #FIXED  '"'
                SDAPREF   CDATA  #FIXED  '"'>
```

SDATA — The **reserved name** for the keyword that identifies the content of an **entity** as system data. The 'system data' keyword. May be changed to another name in a **variant concrete syntax**. See the *Road Map* charts (106.2) and (109.4).

SDIF *(SGML Document Interchange Format)* — An **ISO** standard (ISO 9069) for combining related **entity** objects into a single file object, generally for transfer to another system. Not widely used.

Select element — An **HTML** element that encloses a menu from which a single item can be selected. Each option is defined using an **Option** element.

separator — One or more characters used within a defined context to separate objects, such as one markup **parameter** from another. See SEPCHAR.

separator character function — A specific character assigned the role of a **separator**.

SEPCHAR — The **reserved name** for the keyword that precedes information on additional 'separator characters'. Typically a space, tab, carriage return or line feed. RE = record end, RS = record start, SPACE = space and TAB = tab. May be used in a **character reference**[062], such as '&#TAB;'. See the *Road Map* charts (005.4), (054.4) and (188.5).

SEQ — The **reserved name** for the keyword that is used to determine ordering constraints on items in a **group**, default character is ','. The 'sequence connector' keyword. The example (a , b) indicates that 'b' must follow 'a'. See the *Road Map* chart (131.3).

sequence connector — The character that takes the role of specifying a choice of token, by default '|'. See SEQ.

SGML *(Standard Generalized Markup Language)* — The ISO 8879 standard developed in 1986 to assist electronic delivery and publication of text-based documents. Classified under 'Information processing – Text and office systems'. Developed and maintained by the ISO/IEC JTC1 SC18/**WG8** committee. A language is defined for creation of document structure rules in a **DTD**. Features of the language are either obligatory or optional (**shall** be implemented or **should** be implemented). An SGML document consists of three major parts: the **SGML**

declaration[171], the **prolog**[007] (containing the DTD) and the **document instance set**[010]. Contact 'comp.text.sgml' newsgroup. See **SGML Users' Group** and **SGML Open**.

SGML — The **reserved name** for the keyword that identifies a **markup declaration** as an **SGML declaration**[171]. See the *Road Map* chart (131.3).

SGML-aware — Application software designed to work with **SGML** documents (to include a **parser** and **entity manager**). An SGML-aware (sometimes termed 'SGML-sensitive') editor, for example, would use the **DTD** to control and guide the authoring process.

SGML-sensitive — See **SGML-aware**.

SGML character[050] — A character that may be legally entered in an **SGML** document. This generally includes all standard **ASCII** characters. Other characters may be represented by an **entity reference**, such as 'é', or a **character reference**[062], such as 'ë'.

SGML declaration[171] — First part of an **SGML document**[001], defining various system limits and default settings. May re-define both **reserved name** keywords and/or their values (for example, change the *name* 'ELEMENT' to 'MYELEM', or the *value* of 'TAGC' from '>' to ']').

SGML document[001] — Data file conforming to the **SGML** standard which may be validated using a **parser**. Includes an **SGML document entity**[002] (the bulk of the text document, or at least the document skeleton), and may also include some **external entity** objects, possibly in remote data files.

SGML Document Access — See **SDA**.

SGML document entity[002] — The essential core of an **SGML document**[001], including an **SGML declaration**[171], a **prolog**[007] and a **document instance set**[010]. This is the entire document, including system specific and document specific rules, apart from any **external entity** objects.

SGML entity — An **entity** containing **SGML** data, which can be **parsed**. See **data entity**.

SGML Open — A non-profit international consortium of suppliers supporting and promoting **SGML**. Responsible for setting or rationalizing standards that rest upon SGML. As examples, a standard **catalog** format has been agreed, and the **CALS table** model refined and harmonized. Contact 'http://www.sgmlopen.org/'. See **GCA** and **SGML Users' Group**. For **HTML** equivalents see **IETF** and **W3C**.

SGML subdocument[003] — Essentially a 'subroutine', sharing the system configuration, but defining its own document structure rules and document text. It cannot share structures and values with the main document, but could be used for document fragments conforming to a radically different structure to the main document.

SGML text entity[004] — A fragment of a document instance held separately, typically in another data file. An ideal mechanism for allowing common text to be shared by many documents, or for a large document to be split into manageable segments.

SGML Users' Group — A non-profit organization formed in 1984 to promote the use of **SGML** and the sharing of information. It has many regional and national chapters. Contact 'http://sil.org/sgml/sgmlug.html'. See **GCA** and **SGML Open**.

SGMLREF — The **reserved name** for the keyword used to state that default values exist and are active until overridden by replacement values. As this always applies in the context within which it is used, it is therefore redundant, and only appears to remind human readers of this mechanism. See the *Road Map* charts (180.6), (191.3), (192.5), (193.3) and (194.3).

SGMLS — A popular and freely available **parser**. See Chapter 13.

shall — A feature of **SGML** that must be supported by an SGML compliant application. See **should**.

Shape attribute — An **HTML** attribute to the **Area** element, that specifies the shape of an active area on the image. For example, a circle or a rectangle.

short reference — A **markup minimization** feature that allows pre-defined characters to 'stand-in' for **entity** references, which in turn are replaced by the entity content, including **markup** tags. For example, within a table a line-end character may be mapped to '`&row;`', which identifies an entity containing '`<row>`'.

short reference delimiters[192] — Additional **short reference** strings.

short reference mapping declaration[150] — Definition of a series of mappings between **short reference** strings and associated **entity** definitions. A particular mapping is activated by a **short reference use declaration**[152].

short reference set[115] — Types of **declaration** associated with the defining of **short reference**s. May be grouped in an **external entity** and referenced with a **public text class**[086] using the '`SHORTREF`' keyword.

short reference use declaration[152] — Method of activating a **short reference** map within a specific context, determined by the most recently opened **element**[013].

short tag — A tag that is minimized, perhaps by omitting the **generic identifier**, or tag **delimiter**s.

SHORTREF — The **reserved name** for the keyword used to identify **short reference mapping declaration**[150] instructions and define **short reference delimiters**[192]. May be changed to another name in a **variant concrete syntax**. See the *Road Map* charts (150.2) and (192.1).

SHORTTAG — The **reserved name** for the keyword that is used to declare whether it is possible to minimize a **start-tag**[014] or **end-tag**[019]. See the *Road Map* chart (196.18).

should — An optional feature of **SGML**. Although desired, a conforming system may omit such a feature. See **shall**.

SHUNCHAR — The **reserved name** for the keyword that identifies and precedes instructions that specify characters not allowed in an **SGML** document. The 'shunned characters' keyword. See the *Road Map* chart (184.1).

shunned character number identification[184] — Characters theoretically available in the 'base' character set, but undesirable due to their possible system specific roles. Control characters are typically shunned.

shunned characters — Characters that are available in an assigned **character set**, but would be dangerous to use as data characters. This would include **control characters**.

sibling — A concept derived from the family tree that describes an **element**[(013)] that is adjacent to other elements within a **hierarchy** of elements (much like brothers and sisters). It is at the same level, following and/or preceding other elements. For example, a Chapter element is likely to be a sibling to other Chapter elements. See also **parent** and **child**.

Size attribute — An **HTML 3.2** attribute to the **Hr** element, defining the thickness of the line, and the **Font** and **Basefont** elements, defining the size of the text.

Small element — An **HTML 3.2** element that encloses text to be displayed in a smaller point size. See **Big**.

SMDL *(Standard Music Description Language)* — Standard use of **SGML** to describe real-time music samples, related to (and precursor of) the **HyTime** concept. Contact 'http://www.techno.com/SMDL.html'.

source — The start-point for a **hypertext link**. The referencing text that points to a **target** object. For example, 'see Chapter 9<xref ref="CH9">'. See **IDREF**.

Source — See **Src** attribute.

SPACE — The **reserved name** for the keyword that represents a 'space' character, which has an important role in delimiting markup. May be changed to another name in a **variant concrete syntax**. See the *Road Map* charts (005.3), (016.1), (017.1), (018.1), (019.1), (039.2), (040.2), (042.2), (043.2), (054.3), (063.3), (078.3), (084.2) and (186.11).

Span Specification — See **Spanspec** element.

Spanname attribute — Provides a name for a range of columns in the **CALS table** model. A required NMTOKEN appearing in the **Spanspec** element. The assigned name refers to a range identified by the **Namest** and **Nameend** attributes.

Spanspec element — Table span specification **element**[(013)] in the **CALS table** structure. Optional feature that assigns a user-defined name to a range of columns, simplifying specification of all **Entry** elements that span the same column numbers.

SPDL *(Standard Page Description Language)* — An **ISO** standard (ISO 10180) that defines a language for representing text and graphics on a page. Released in December 1995. Equivalent and similar to the *de facto* **PostScript** language.

Special — The group name for the symbol characters ' '()+,-./:=? '. See the *Road Map* chart (078.7).

specific character data entity[(005b)] — An **entity** that contains system specific character sequences or **8-bit** values, which will probably need to be changed on transfer to another system.

Sqrt element — A **9573 math** element describing a square root.

Square element — A **9573 math** element that identifies part of a formula to be squared. See **Power** element for powers other than two.

Square Root — See **Sqrt** element.

Src attribute — An **HTML** attribute to the **Img** element, locating and identifying the image file, and to the **Frame** element, containing a **URL** locating an HTML file to display in the frame.

STAGO — The **reserved name** for the keyword that specifies character(s) used to identify the start of a **start-tag**[014], by default '<'. The 'start tag open' keyword. See the *Road Map* chart (014.1).

standard — An **ISO** or **IEC** publication defining a language or format.

Standard Generalized Markup Language — See **SGML**.

Standard Page Description Language — See **SPDL**.

Start attribute — An **HTML 3.2** attribute to the **Ol** element, specifying a start value for the first item in the list. The default value is '1'.

start-tag[014] — First part of an **element**[013]. When enclosing data, it is coupled with an **end-tag**[019]. Also the container of **attribute** values for the element.

start-tag minimization[123] — The method of defining whether a particular **start-tag**[014] in a particular location in the document structure can be implied rather than physically present. A value of 'o' allows omission, a value of '-' disallows omission.

start-tag open — The character(s) that identifies the start of a **start-tag**[014], by default '<'. See STAGO.

STARTTAG — The **reserved name** for the keyword that identifies the content of an entity as a **start-tag**[014]. The delimiters (by default '<' and '>') are inserted by the **parser** as the content replaces the **entity reference**. This name may be changed in a **variant concrete syntax**. See the *Road Map* chart (107.1).

status keyword[100] — The keyword that dictates how a marked section should be processed. The document segment may be ignored (omitted from **parser** output) using the keyword IGNORE, or be included but processed in other ways.

status keyword specification[097] — The mechanism that dictates how a **marked section**[096] of the document should be processed. The document segment may be marked as temporary, using the keyword TEMP, or be processed in other ways (see **status keyword**[100]).

Strike element — An **HTML 3.2** element that encloses text to be displayed with a line through it, indicating that the text has been 'removed'.

Strikethrough — See **Strike** element.

Strong element — An **HTML** element that encloses text to be highlighted, usually in a **bold** typeface.

Style attribute — A **9573 math** attribute to the **Fence** element that specifies the style of character used as the fence start and end.

Sub element — *[1]* A **9573 math** element containing **subscript** text. The **Pos** attribute allows subscript text to be re-positioned before or below the base character (instead of after it). *[2]* An **HTML 3.2** element containing **subscript** text.

SUBDOC — The **reserved name** for the keyword that activates the optional subdocument feature of **SGML**. May be changed to another name in a **variant concrete syntax**. See the *Road Map* chart (109.1).

subelement — An **element** that is directly contained within another element. Formal name for a **child** element.

subscript — Text positioned below the base line, as in 'H_2O'. Also known as 'inferior' text. See **superscript** and **Sub** element.

Subscript — See **Sub** element.

Suffix attribute — A **9573 math** attribute used in the **Tensor** element.

Sup element — *[1]* A **9573 math** element containing **superscript** text. The **Pos** attribute allows superscript text to be re-positioned before or above the base character (instead of after it). *[2]* An **HTML 3.2** element containing **superscript** text.

superior — See **superscript**.

superscript — Text positioned above the base line, as in 'W^3C'. Also known as 'superior' text. See **subscript** and **Sup** element.

Superscript — See **Sup** element.

SWITCHES — The **reserved name** for the keyword that identifies and precedes character re-mapping values, changing the **public concrete syntax**[183] definitions. See the *Road Map* chart (183.5).

syntactic literal — A **syntactic token** that consists of a special keyword, such as 'PUBLIC'.

syntactic production — The specification of one part of the SGML standard, including the identity (the **syntactic variable**) and one or more **syntactic token**s. Most of the syntactic productions are illustrated in the *Road Map* charts.

syntactic token — One element of an expression that comprises a **syntactic variable**. May consist of a **syntactic variable**, so building a **hierarchy** of structures, or of a syntactic literal, such as 'PUBLIC', a **delimiter role**, such as 'TAGC', or a **terminal variable** or **terminal constant**, such as 'EE' and 'RE'.

syntactic variable — The identity of a **syntactic production**, such as 'SGML declaration'.

syntax — All languages, including English, have defined rules of grammar. The **SGML** syntax defines how **tags** and **markup declarations** are stored and identified.

SYNTAX — The **reserved name** for the keyword that identifies and precedes instructions defining a **concrete syntax**[182]. See the *Road Map* chart (182.1).

syntax-reference character set[185] — The **character set** defined for use in a **document instance set**[010] (and possibly the **prolog**[007]). Often the same as the syntax defined for the **SGML declaration**[171] itself.

SYSTEM — The **reserved name** for the keyword that identifies a following string as a **system identifier**[075]. May be changed to another name in a **variant concrete syntax**. See the *Road Map* chart (073.1).

system data[045] — A quoted character string containing only characters suitable for use in a **processing instruction**[044] or **system identifier**[075].

system identifier[075] — System specific **external entity** identifier. Typically a file name and location. For example, 'C:\ENTS\MYBOOK.DTD'.

T

Table Body — See **Tbody** element.

Table Data — See **Td** element.

Table element — *[1]* Table enclosing **element**[013] in the **CALS table** structure. Contains a table using embedded **Tgroup** element grids, also specifying border lines and the width of the table. *[2]* Table enclosing **element**[013] in **HTML 3.2**.

Table Footer — See **Tfoot** element.

Table Group — See **Tgroup** element.

Table Header — See **Thead** element and **Th** element.

tag — A code embedded in the text, signifying the structure, format or style of the data. A tag is recognized from surrounding text by the use of **delimiter** characters. A common delimiter character for an **SGML** tag is the chevron, '<'.

tag close — The character(s) indicating the end of a tag. See TAGC.

TAGC — The **reserved name** for the keyword that specifies the character(s) used to identify the end of both a **start-tag**[014] and an **end-tag**[019], default value '>'. The 'tag close' keyword. See the *Road Map* charts (014.6), (016.2), (019.5) and (021.2).

TAGLEN — The **reserved name** for the keyword that specifies the maximum length in characters of a **start-tag**[014], including any **attribute** values (default value '960' characters). The 'tag length' keyword.

TAGLVL — The **reserved name** for the keyword that specifies the maximum number of open **element**[013] structures at any point in the document (default value '24'). The 'tag level' keyword. The value restricts the level to which **hierarchy** structures can be nested.

tail — The end-point of a **hypertext link**. Equivalent to the **target** of a link. A reference is traversed from the **head** to the tail. For example, a chapter Title element may be the tail of many references. In **HTML**, the tail is an **Anchor** element containing a **Name** attribute value.

target — The object of a **hypertext link**. It must be identified by a unique name or code, which can be used within a **source** object to form the link. See **Target attribute** and ID.

Target attribute — An **attribute** that holds a unique value suitable for reference by **source** elements. See ID.

Tbody element — Table body **element**[013] in the **CALS table** structure. Contains one or more table **Row** elements, for the main text of the table. See **Thead** and **Tfoot** elements.

TCP/IP *(Transmission Control Protocol/Internet Protocol)* — Data transport protocol for the **Internet**. Used by **HTTP** and **FTP** file transfer protocols. Contact 'comp.protocols.tcp-ip/newsgroup'.

Td element — An **HTML 3.2** element used in the **Table** element to hold the content of one normal cell. See **Th** element.

TEI *(Text Encoding Initiative)* — A group of representatives from learned societies in the humanities and social sciences, defining common **DTD**s for the coding and interchange of relevant documents. Contact 'http://mes01.di.uminho.pt/ Manuals/HTML/html-howto/tei.html' or 'http://www.uic.edu:80/orgs/tei/'.

Teletype — See **Tt** element.

TEMP — The **reserved name** for the keyword that identifies a **marked section**[(096)] as a temporary marked section. May be changed to another name in a **variant concrete syntax**. See the *Road Map* chart (197.4).

Tensor element — A **9573 math** element that defines tensors using the **Posf** and **Suffix** attributes.

terminal constant — A **syntactic token** that has no subcomponents, such as the **RE** (record end) signal/character. A constant value, but otherwise identical to a **terminal variable**.

terminal variable — A **syntactic token** that has no subcomponents, such as a character in the text. A variable in the sense that its value can be defined within the **SGML declaration**[(171)] value. For example, one terminal variable is **LC Letter**, but characters that may be included in the group of **lower case** letters can be re-defined. Otherwise identical to a **terminal constant**.

T$_E$X — Popular typesetting language. Particularly strong on mathematical formulae. It is sometimes found embedded in **SGML** documents. Contact 'http:// www.fi.muni.cz/TeXhelp/TeX-homepage.html' and 'comp.text.tex' newsgroup. See **L^{A}T$_E$X**.

TEXT — The **reserved name** for the keyword that identifies the content of an **entity** as text that conforms to legal **SGML** character usage. Used within a **formal public identifier**[(079)].

Text attribute — An **HTML 3.2** attribute to the **Body** element that specifies the color of the document text.

Text Encoding Initiative — See **TEI**.

text file — A data file containing textual characters, possibly conforming to the **ASCII** standard. Each character is represented by a unique value. There is no provision for styling the text, and little provision for formatting the text. A **markup** language assigns significance to sequences of ASCII characters, forming **tag**s. A text editor works directly with ASCII data, and most word processors can export and import text files.

text identifier[(084)] — The major part of a **formal public identifier**[(079)], describing the type, description and language of an **entity**.

Textarea element — An **HTML** element that uses **Cols** and **Rows** attributes to define a text box for entry of multi-line text input.

Tfoot element — Table footer **element**[(013)] in the **CALS table** structure. Contains one or more table **Row** elements, for footer text. Positioned before the table body (**Tbody** element) rows, to allow composing software to place text at the base of first page (of a large table) from which it is referenced (without performing two-pass pagination). See **Thead** element.

Tgroup element — Table group **element**[(013)] in the **CALS table** structure, enclosing a grid of cells. Specifies the number of columns in the grid. One **Table** element may contain several table groups to allow a change of column widths and number of columns. However, some applications limit use to a single table group.

Th element — An **HTML 3.2** element containing a table header cell.

Thead element — Table header **element**[013] in the **CALS table** structure. Contains one or more table **row** elements, for column headers. When the table is printed, the header rows may repeat after each page-break, and the enclosed text may also be highlighted. See **Tbody** element and **Tfoot** element.

TIFF *(Tagged Image File Format)* — An image-describing format devised by Microsoft and Aldus, now maintained by Adobe. The actual image data is held in one of several **raster** formats, depending on the compression requirements. Options include **CCITT Group IV** and **JPEG** compression. The current version is 6.0. Contact 'http://www.adobe.com/Support/TechNotes.html'.

Title element — *[1]* An **HTML** element that provides the title of the document, for display in the title bar of a document window. Part of the **Head** element content. *[2]* A **CALS table** element that provides the title of the table, for display above the table (or above each segment of a large table spread over several pages).

To element — A **9573 math** element used in the **Plex** element.

token — A unit of information in a **group**. Either a single object, such as the name of an **element**[013], or an entire embedded group which also contains tokens.

TOTALCAP — The **reserved name** for the keyword that assigns **capacity point** maximum values to the sum of all objects, by default '35 000'. Some **parser**s ignore this information.

Tr element — An **HTML 3.2** element containing a table row. Each row consists of **Th** and/or **Td** elements.

tree — A hierarchical structure which resembles a tree in that the structure can be viewed as branches. **SGML** elements form hierarchies, and are sometimes described using the family tree concept, including the use of names such as **ancestor**, **parent**, **child** and **sibling**.

ts[070] — A character or **entity reference** that separates one **token** from another in a **group**.

Tt element — An **HTML** element containing text representing teletype output, usually displayed in a mono-spaced font.

Type attribute — *[1]* A **9573 math** attribute to the **Break** element (to make it 'optional'); **Over** element ('dot', 'ring' etc.); **Diff** element (to set a 'partial' differential); and **Fence** element (type of fence, 'bracket', 'paren' etc.). *[2]* An **HTML** attribute to the **Input** element, specifying the type of input control, such as check-box, radio button and push button. Also in **HTML 3.2** to the **Ol**, **Ul** and **Li** elements, where it specifies the type of list item identifier, such as '1' or 'A'.

Type1 attribute — A **9573 math** attribute to the **Mfn** element (e.g. 'and', 'arc' etc.). See **Type2** attribute.

Type2 attribute — A **9573 math** attribute to the **Mfn** element, adding to function types made available via the **Type1** attribute (e.g. 'sec', 'tan' etc.). Only required due to the maximum number of **token** values in an attribute (in this case Type1) being '32'.

typesetting — The process of converting tagged data, possibly in **SGML** format, into completed pages. A combination of the **compose** and **paginate** operations.

U

U element — An **HTML** element that contains text to be underlined.

UC Letter — The name given to a group of characters described as **upper case** letters ('A'–'Z'). See **LC Letter**, **Digit** and **Special**.

UCNMCHAR — The **reserved name** for the keyword that specifies additional characters assigned to the classification of '**upper case** name characters', by default '-' and '.'. This class of characters also inherits **UCNMSTRT** definitions. See the *Road Map* charts (052.4) and (189.15).

UCNMSTRT — The **reserved name** for the keyword that specifies additional characters assigned to the classification of '**upper case** name start' characters. See **UCNMCHAR** and the *Road Map* charts (053.3) and (189.7).

Ul element — An **HTML** element that contains an unordered list, using **Li** elements.

unavailable text indicator[(085)] — An entity that is not available to the general public, perhaps only for use within an organization. Part of a **formal public identifier**[(079)], following the **public text class**[(086)] and consisting of the trailing characters '-//'. For example, '+//MyCorp//DTD MyDTD **-//** . . . . . . '.

unclosed end-tag[(022)] — An **end-tag**[(019)] that 'runs-in' to the next **start-tag**[(014)]. For example, '</mytag<another>...'.

unclosed start-tag[(017)] — A **start-tag**[(014)] that 'runs-in' to the next start-tag. For example, '<mytag<another>...'.

Underline — See **U element**.

Unicode — A **16-bit** character set devised by the Unicode Consortium (a group of largely American hardware and software suppliers). Several coding schemes are allowed, but in the canonical scheme every bit combination represents a distinct character. Using this scheme, Unicode can be viewed as a superset of **ASCII** (US) with '0000' to '00FF' (hexadecimal) being equivalent to ASCII '00' to 'FF'. Unicode has been adopted as a subset of **ISO/IEC 10646**, with '00000000' to '0000FFFF' being equivalent to the Unicode characters '0000' to 'FFFF'. Contact 'http://www.stonehand.com/unicode.html'.

Uniform Resource Locator — See **URL**.

Universal Resource Identifier — See **URI**.

Unordered List — See **Ul element**.

unregistered owner identifier[(083)] — A **formal public identifier**[(079)] for an entity that is not owned by the **ISO** and is not registered, so cannot be guaranteed to be unique. Such a public identifier begins with the characters '-//'.

UNUSED — The **reserved name** for the keyword that identifies characters not to be used from a **character set**. See the *Road Map* chart (176.7).

up-convert — Conversion of typeset data to **SGML** format. Usually a semi-manual, **high energy** task. The expense of up-converting to SGML is often cited as the main reason for not adopting SGML, though in some cases this cost is more than offset by the reduced cost of **down-convert**ing to various output formats.

upper case — Capital letters, such as 'THIS'. The upper case equivalent of the **lower case** letter 'a' is 'A'. The name is derived from the fact that these **characters** were found in the upper part of the printer's type case. See **UC Letter**, **UCNMSTRT** and **UCNMCHAR**.

URI *(Uniform Resource Identifier)* — The **Internet** addressing scheme. Includes the **URL** standard. Contact 'http://www.w3.org/pub/WWW/Addressing/ Addressing.html'.

URL *(Uniform Resource Locator)* — Subset of the **URI** protocol for addressing information on the **Web**. A typical URL would be 'http://www.bradley.co.uk/ index.html'. See **HTTP** and **FTP** for common server connection standards. Contact 'http://www.w3.org/pub/WWW/Addressing/Addressing.html' and 'ftp://ds.internic.net/rfc/rfc1630.txt'.

Usemap attribute — An **HTML 3.2** attribute to the **Img** element that indicates the image is associated with an **image map** of active areas.

V

Valign attribute — An **attribute** for defining the presence or absence of a vertical column separating line in a **CALS table**. Legal values 'top' (the default), 'bottom' and 'middle'.

Value attribute — An **HTML 3.2** attribute to the **Li** element that provides an overriding list item value (out of the normal sequence), and to the **Param** element, where it assigns a value to a parameter identified using a **Name** attribute.

value indicator — A symbol that represents an assignment, by default the equals sign '='. See **VI**.

Var element — An **HTML** element that contains text identified as a computer program variable, usually displayed in a mono-spaced font.

variant concrete syntax — A **concrete syntax**[182] designed for a specific use, modifying or replacing the **reference concrete syntax**.

Vec element — A **9573 math** element describing a vector.

vector — Method of representing images electronically using resolution and scale independent drawing commands, producing lines, points, arcs, filled areas and text. For example, 'DRAWTO 60 35; MOVETO 75 90; CIRCLE 50; ...'. Also known as 'geometric graphics'. Some formats use text-based commands as in the example, others use more compact machine readable schemes. **CGM** allows for both representations. The alternative representation is called a **raster** format (though a vector-based image must be converted into a raster-based image when rendered using an appropriate resolution). See also **IGES**, **PICT** and **WMF**.

Vertical Alignment — See **Valign** attribute.

Vertical Space — See **Vspace** attribute.

VI — The **reserved name** for the keyword that specifies the character assigned to take the role equating an **attribute** value to an attribute name, by default '='. The 'value indicator' keyword. See the *Road Map* chart (032.4).

Virtual Reality Modelling Language — See **VRML**.

Visited Link — See **Vlink** attribute.

Vlink attribute — An **HTML 3.2** attribute to the **Body** element that specifies the color of the **source** of a **hypertext link** that has already been traversed.

VRML *(Virtual Reality Modelling Language)* — A language that describes 3-dimensional objects. Used on the **Internet** to create 'virtual worlds'. Developed by Silicon Graphics, who also shaped VRML 2.0 (1996), which adds behaviours, sensors, sound and animation (from its 'Moving Worlds' specification). Contact 'http://vrml.sgi.com/moving-worlds'.

Vspace attribute — An **HTML 3.2** attribute to the **Img** element that specifies additional space above and below the image.

W

W³C *(World Wide Web Consortium)* — An industry consortium comprising over 120 organizations. Involved in the establishment of standards for the **Web**, including **DTD**s for versions of **HTML**. In agreement with major vendors, responsible for future versions of HTML, starting with **HTML 3.2** in June 1996. This organization has a close relationship with the **IETF** (see **SGML Open** for equivalent **SGML** monitoring organization). Contact 'http://www.w3.org/'.

Wbr element — An **HTML 3.2** element contained within a **Nobr** element to specify points in the text where a line break can be made (if necessary). The 'word break' element.

Web — Common abbreviation for the World Wide Web. An **Internet** service that uses the **HTTP** protocol and **HTML** format data files to provide an attractive document delivery service over standard telephone lines. Information is passed between a **Web server** and a **Web browser**. Various graphic formats are also supported, including **GIF** and **JPEG**. Created by researchers at CERN in Switzerland ('http://www.w3.org'). Not owned by any company, the Web is overseen by the **W³C** (and the Internet is overseen by the **IETF**).

Web browser — A computer application that receives **Web pages** from a **Web server** via the **Internet**, and **renders** them on-screen. See **Web**.

Web page — A data file containing **HTML** tagged text ready to be displayed by a **Web browser**. Although called a 'page', the file may be much longer than a physical page, and a closer analogy would be a scroll. However, Web page designers are encouraged to split long documents into smaller units, so as to keep network traffic to a minimum, and the name 'page' is a reminder of this philosophy.

Web server — A computer attached to the **Internet** that stores **Web pages** and delivers them to a **Web browser**. See **Web**.

WG8 *(ISO/IEC JTC1 SC18/WG8)* — The **ISO** working group responsible for a number of standards, starting with **SGML** in 1986, but recently including **HyTime** (1992), **SPDL** (1995) and **DSSSL** (1996). Contact 'http://www.ornl.gov/sgml/wg8/wg8home.htm'.

Width attribute — An **HTML 3.2** attribute to the **Hr** element that specifies the width of the line in comparison with the width of the window, and to the **Table** and **Applet** elements to define the width of the table or **applet** working area.

Windows MetaFile — See **WMF**.

WMF *(Windows MetaFile)* — A Microsoft Windows based **vector** image format. See **PICT** and **CGM**.

Word Break — See **Wbr** element.

World Wide Web — See **Web**.

World Wide Web Consortium — See **W³C** .

WWW *(World Wide Web)* — See **Web**.

WYSIWYG *(What You See Is What You Get)* — Acronym describing one approach to viewing data on-screen, where an attempt is made to replicate published output (What You See *on the screen* Is What You Get *on the page*). Text markup is hidden, and the text is composed using representative fonts and styles.

X

X-Bitmap — Simple 1-**bit** per pixel **raster** image format used on UNIX systems and also used by the **Web**. Pixels are set to black or transparent. Typical file extent is '.xbm'. Actually C language source code (an array) to be read by a compiler rather than a graphic viewer. See **JPEG**, **GIF** and **X-Pixelmap**.

X-Pixelmap — Simple 8-**bit**s per pixel **raster** image format used on UNIX systems (and X-Windows icons) and used by the **Web**. Pixels are set to one of 256 colors. Actually C language source code (an array) to be read by a compiler rather than a graphic viewer. Less memory efficient than **GIF**. Typical file extent is '.xpm'. See **JPEG** and **X-Bitmap**.

XBM — See **X-Bitmap**.

XPM — See **X-Pixelmap**.

Y

YES — The **reserved name** for the keyword that specifies usage of a given **SGML** feature. See the *Road Map* charts (189.23 .28), (196.6 .11 .16 .21) and (198.6 .13 .20).

Index

NOTES: The index identifies terms introduced in the main text (where they are displayed in bold). The glossary is not indexed, so a term in the glossary that is *only* referenced from other terms in the glossary will not appear in this index. All entries are shown in the present tense, singular form (except where the term is a syntactic token name or keyword, or where it is always used in another form), for example the 'hierarchy' entry also identifies usage of the word 'hierarchical.' Entries in capitals, such as 'ENTITY,' are SGML keywords. Entries with an initial capital letter, such as 'Table,' are DTD specific element or attribute names, and as they may be used in more than one DTD they are identified using bracketed qualifiers; for example there is an entry for 'Table (CALS)' and another entry for 'Table (HTML).'

Numerics

A

D

E

F

I

N

T

U